Essays and Studies 2013

Series Editor: Elaine Treharne

The English Association

The objects of the English Association are to promote the knowledge and appreciation of the English language and its literature, and to foster good practice in its teaching and learning at all levels.

The Association pursues these aims by creating opportunities of co-operation among all those interested in English; by furthering the recognition of English as essential in education; by discussing methods of English teaching; by holding lectures, conferences, and other meetings; by publishing journals, books, and leaflets; and by forming local branches.

Publications

The Year's Work in English Studies. An annual bibliography. Published by Blackwell.

The Year's Work in Critical and Cultural Theory. An annual bibliography. Published by Blackwell.

Essays and Studies. An annual volume of essays by various scholars assembled by the collector covering usually a wide range of subjects and authors from the medieval to the modern. Published by D.S. Brewer.

English. A journal of the Association, *English* is published three times a year by the Association.

The Use of English. A journal of the Association, *The Use of English* is published three times a year by the Association.

Newsletter. A *Newsletter* is published three times a year giving information about forthcoming publications, conferences, and other matters of interest.

Benefits of Membership

Institutional Membership

Full members receive copies of *The Year's Work in English Studies*, *Essays and Studies*, *English* (3 issues) and three *Newsletters*.

Ordinary Membership covers *English* (3 issues) and three *Newsletters*.

Schools Membership includes copies of each issue of *English* and *The Use of English*, one copy of *Essays and Studies*, three *Newsletters*, and preferential booking and rates for various conferences held by the Association.

Individual Membership

Individuals take out Basic Membership, which entitles them to buy all regular publications of the English Association at a discounted price, and attend Association gatherings.

For further details write to The Secretary, The English Association, The University of Leicester, University Road, Leicester, LE1 7RH.

Essays and Studies 2013

British Literature and Print Culture

**Edited by
Sandro Jung
for the English Association**

D. S. BREWER

ESSAYS AND STUDIES 2013
IS VOLUME SIXTY-SIX IN THE NEW SERIES
OF ESSAYS AND STUDIES COLLECTED ON BEHALF OF
THE ENGLISH ASSOCIATION
ISSN 0071–1357

First published 2013
D. S. Brewer, Cambridge

D. S. Brewer is an imprint of Boydell & Brewer Ltd
PO Box 9, Woodbridge, Suffolk IP12 3DF, UK
and of Boydell & Brewer Inc.
668 Mt Hope Avenue, Rochester, NY 14620–2731 USA
website: www.boydellandbrewer.com

ISBN 978–1–84384–343–6

A CIP catalogue record for this book is available
from the British Library

The publisher has no responsibility for the continued existence or
accuracy of URLs for external or third-party internet websites referred to in this book, and does not guarantee that any content
on such websites is, or will remain, accurate or appropriate

Papers used by Boydell & Brewer Ltd are natural, recyclable products
made from wood grown in sustainable forests

Printed and bound in Great Britain by
CPI Group (UK) Ltd, Croydon, CR0 4YY

Contents

List of Illustrations   vii

Notes on Contributors   xiii

Introduction   1
Sandro Jung

Tracing a Genealogy of *Oroonoko* Editions   5
Laura L. Runge

The Pilgrim's Progress, Print Culture and the Dissenting Tradition   33
Nathalie Collé-Bak

Printing for the Author in the Long Eighteenth Century   58
J. A. Downie

Robert Burns's Interleaved *Scots Musical Museum*: A Case-Study
    in the Vagaries of Editors and Owners   78
Gerard Carruthers

Packaging, Design and Colour: From Fine-Printed to Small-
    Format Editions of Thomson's *The Seasons*, 1793–1802   97
Sandro Jung

Print Illustrations and the Cultural Materialism of Scott's
    Waverley Novels   125
Peter Garside

Beyond Usefulness and Ephemerality: The Discursive Almanac,
    1828–60   158
Brian Maidment

The Last Years of a Victorian Monument: The *Athenaeum* after
    Maccoll   195
Marysa Demoor

Index   213

Illustrations

The editor, contributors and publishers are grateful to all the institutions and persons listed for permission to reproduce the materials in which they hold copyright. Every effort has been made to trace the copyright holders; apologies are offered for any omission, and the publishers will be pleased to add any necessary acknowledgement in subsequent editions.

The Pilgrim's Progress, Print Culture and the Dissenting Tradition

Fig. 1: The 'Sleeping Portrait', frontispiece, engraved by Robert White, *The Pilgrim's Progress* (London: printed for Nath. Ponder at the Peacock in the Poultrey near Cornhil, 1678). © The British Library Board. All Rights Reserved (C.37.d.61 & C.25.c.24)   36

Fig. 2a: The 'Sleeping Portrait', frontispiece, *The Pilgrim's Progress*, 14th edition (London: printed for W. P. and are to be sold by Nat. Ponder in London-House-yard, 1695). © The British Library Board. All Rights Reserved (C.111.d.17)   38

Fig. 2b: The 'Sleeping Portrait', frontispiece, *The Pilgrim's Progress*, 19th edition (London: printed for M. Boddington, at the Golden-Ball in Duck Lane, 1718). © John Bunyan Library, Bedford Central Library, Bedford, England   38

Fig. 3a: The 'Sleeping Portrait', frontispiece, *The Pilgrim's Progress*, 3rd edition (London: Nathaniel Ponder, 1679). © The British Library Board. All Rights Reserved (C.70.aa.3)   39

Fig. 3b: The 'Sleeping Portrait', frontispiece, *The Pilgrim's Progress*, 30th edition (London: printed and sold by all the booksellers, 1758). © John Bunyan Library, Bedford Central Library, Bedford, England.   39

Fig. 4: The 'Sleeping Portrait, frontispiece, John Sturt engraver, *The Pilgrim's Progress, Part 2* (London: printed for Nathaniel Ponder at the Peacock in the Poultry, near the Church, 1684). © The British Library Board. All Rights Reserved (C.111.d.8)   42

Fig. 5: Advertisement, *The Pilgrim's Progress*, 5th edition (London: printed for Nath. Ponder, at the Peacock in the Poultrey near the Church, 1680). © The British Library Board. All Rights Reserved (C.58.a.22)   44

Fig. 6: Illustration of the martyrdom of Faithful at Vanity Fair, *The Pilgrim's Progress*, 8th edition (London: printed for Nathanael Ponder at the Peacock in the Poultrey, near the Church, 1682). © John Bunyan Library, Bedford Central Library, Bedford, England   46

Fig. 7a: Illustration of Christiana's pilgrimage, *The Pilgrim's Progress, the Second Part* (London: printed for Nathaniel Ponder at the Peacock in the Poultry, near the Church, 1684). Image reproduced from the 16th edition (London: printed for Robert Ponder, and Sold by Nicholas Boddington in Duck-lane, 1693). © The British Library Board. All Rights Reserved (4415.aaa.10.[2.])   48

Fig. 7b: Illustration of Christiana's pilgrimage; details as for 7a   49

Packaging, Design and Colour: From Fine-Printed to Small-Format Editions of Thomson's The Seasons, *1793–1802*

Plates I–III between pages 114 and 115

Plate I: William Hamilton, 'Celadon and Amelia', engraved by Francesco Bartolozzi, *The Seasons* by James Thomson (London: printed for P.W. Tomkins, 1797). Folio A P 2. Stipple and line engraving printed in colour, Yale Center for British Art, Paul Mellon Collection. Reproduced with permission

Plate II: Francis Chesham, 'Summer' (21.5 × 15.6 cm), engraved by Charles Catton, James Thomson, *The Seasons. A new edition. Adorned with a set of engravings, from original paintings. Together with an original life of the author, and a critical essay on the Seasons. By Robert Heron* (Perth: printed for R. Morison, 1793). Reproduced from a copy in the author's collection.

Plate IIIa: 'Musidora' (8.8 × 6.4 cm), *The Seasons, to which is prefixed, a life of the author. Together with illustrative remarks on The Seasons. By the Rev. J. Evans, A.M. Master of a seminary for a limited number of pupils, Pullin's Row, Islington* (London: printed by J. Cundee, for T. Hurst, 1802). Reproduced from a copy in the author's collection.

Plate IIIb: 'Lavinia's Mother' (8.8 × 6.4 cm), *The Seasons, to which is prefixed, a life of the author. Together with illustrative remarks on The Seasons. By the Rev. J. Evans, A.M. Master of a seminary for a limited number of pupils, Pullin's Row, Islington* (London: printed by J. Cundee, for T. Hurst, 1802). Reproduced from a copy in the author's collection.

Fig. 1: John Opie, 'Damon and Musidora' (52.7 × 40.5 cm). Courtesy of the British Museum 106
Fig. 2: Henry Fuseli, 'Celadon and Amelia' (8.3 × 11.2 cm), *The Seasons* (London: printed for F. J. du Roveray, 1802). Reproduced from a copy in the author's collection. 108
Fig. 3a: William Hamilton, 'Palemon and Lavinia', engraved by Richard Corbould, *The Seasons: A new edition. Adorned with a set of engravings from original designs. To which is prefixed an essay on the plan and character of the poem, by J. Aikin* (London: printed for J. Murray, 1778). Reproduced from a copy in the author's collection. 110
Fig. 3b: William Hamilton, 'Palemon and Lavinia', engraved by Francesco Bartolozzi, *The Seasons by James Thomson* (London: printed for P.W. Tomkins, 1797). Courtesy of the British Museum. 111
Fig. 4: Frontispiece. *The Seasons. A new edition. Adorned with a set of engravings, from original paintings. Together with an original life of the author, and a critical essay on the Seasons. By Robert Heron* (Perth: printed for R. Morison, 1793). Reproduced from a copy in the author's collection. 116

Print Illustrations and the Cultural Materialism of Scott's Waverley Novels

All by kind permission of Edinburgh University Library

Fig. 1: Flora in the Glen of Glennaquoich (1823; reprinted 1832): Charles Robert Leslie; engraved by Charles Heath 130
Fig. 2: 'Landed—landed! . . . swimming with me' [Father Philip and the White Lady of Avenel] (1821): Richard Westall; engraved by Charles Heath 132

Fig. 3. 'They found . . . functions of clerk' [Baron of Bradwardine reading the Service before the Battle of Prestonpans] (1829): Gilbert Stuart Newton; engraved by Charles Rolls   136

Fig. 4: Rebecca (1834): Solomon Alexander Hart; engraved by John Cochran   140

Fig. 5: Fray at Jeanie Mac Alpine's / Fray chez Jeanne Mac Alpine (1836): George Cruikshank   142

Fig. 6: Edinburgh. March of the Highlanders / Edimbourgh. Marche des Montagnards (1836): J. M. W. Turner; engraved by Charles Higham   143

Fig. 7: 'They had accomplished . . . sylvan to flight' [Frank Tyrrel's meeting Clara Mowbray] (1853; reprinted 1877): Abraham Solomon; engraved by Edward Radclyffe   148

Fig. 8: Waverley's Last Visit to Flora Mac-Ivor (1865): Robert Herdman; engraved by Lumb Stocks   152

Fig. 9: The Duel between Halbert and Sir Piercie Shafton (1903): Byam Shaw   155

Beyond Usefulness and Ephemerality: The Discursive Almanac, 1828–60

Fig. 1: Chromolithographed single-sheet almanac for 1864 from an anonymous scrap album. Reproduced from a copy in the author's collection.   160

Fig. 2: Title page of the first volume of The British Almanac (London: Baldwin and Cradock, 1828), showing the Almanac Duty stamp. Reproduced from a copy in the author's collection.   164

Fig. 3: Title page of The Companion to the Almanac (London: Baldwin and Cradock, 1828). Reproduced from a copy in the author's collection.   166

Fig. 4: Title page of The British Working-Man's Almanac for 1836 (London: Charles Knight, 1836). Reproduced from a copy in the author's collection.   170

Fig. 5: Cover page for The Political Almanack for 1836 (London: Effingham Wilson, 1836). Reproduced from a copy in the author's collection.   174

Fig. 6: Title page opening for The Political Almanack for 1836. Reproduced from a copy in the author's collection.   175

Fig. 7: 'August' page from *The Political Almanack for 1836* showing the verse and illustration. Reproduced from a copy in the author's collection.   176

Fig. 8: Title page for the *Illustrated Family Almanack* (London: John Cassell, 1855). Reproduced from a copy in the author's collection.   180

Fig. 9: Double-page spread for 'September' from the *Illustrated Family Almanack* for 1855. Note that the running heading for the page refers to the volume as *Cassell's Family Almanack*, thus reinforcing the publication's close identification with Cassell's brand. Reproduced from a copy in the author's collection.   181

Fig. 10: Title page for the first volume of the *Illustrated London Almanack* for 1845 (London: Office of the *Illustrated London News*, 1845). Reproduced from a copy in the author's collection.   182

Fig. 11: Page 51 of the *Illustrated London Almanack* for 1852. Reproduced from a copy in the author's collection.   184

Fig. 12: Title page from the January 1846 issue of *The Almanack of the Month* (London: Punch Office, 1846). Reproduced from a copy in the author's collection.   188

Fig. 13: 'February' from the *Punch Almanack* for 1842. Reproduced from a copy in the author's collection.   192

The Last Years of a Victorian Monument: The Athenaeum after Maccoll

Fig. 1: *Athenaeum* issue, 2 September 1899 (under Maccoll).   203

Fig. 2: The masthead of the *Athenaeum* under Arthur Greenwood, during the war, December 1917.   206

Notes on Contributors

Gerard Carruthers is Professor of Scottish Literature since 1700 at the University of Glasgow and General Editor of the new Oxford University Press edition of the *Works of Robert Burns*. His publications include the monographs *Scottish Literature, A Critical Guide* (2009) and *Robert Burns* (2006); as editor, *The Edinburgh Companion to Robert Burns* (2009); and, as co-editor, *The Cambridge Companion to Scottish Literature* (2012) and Walter Scott's *Reliquiae Trotcosienses* (2004).

Nathalie Collé-Bak is an associate professor at Université de Lorraine, France. She specialises in the illustration of classics of English literature and has given numerous papers and published many articles on the subject. Her research focuses on the role of illustrations, in their multiple forms, in the production, circulation and reception of texts. She co-edited several books, among which are *Left Out: Texts and Ur-Texts* (2009) and *The Lives of the Book* (2010), and, with colleagues David Ten Eyck and Monica Latham launched a book series in the field of book history and textual scholarship entitled Book Practices and Textual Itineraries. She is also associate editor of the *Revue de la Société d'Études Anglo-Américaines des XVIIe et XVIIIe siècles*.

J. A. Downie is Professor of English at Goldsmiths, University of London. His books include *Robert Harley and the Press* (1979), *Jonathan Swift, Political Writer* (1984), *To Settle the Succession of the State: Literature and Politics, 1678–1750* (1994), and *A Political Biography of Henry Fielding* (2009). He has recently finished editing *The Oxford Handbook of the Eighteenth-Century Novel*.

Marysa Demoor is a Professor in English Literature at Ghent University, Belgium and a life member of Clare Hall, Cambridge, UK. In 2011 she was also the holder of the Van Dyck chair at UCLA. Demoor is the author of *Their Fair Share: Women, Power and Criticism in the Athenaeum, from Millicent Garrett Fawcett to Katherine Mansfield, 1870–1920* (2000) and the editor of *Marketing the Author: Authorial Personae, Narrative Selves and Self-Fashioning, 1880–1930* (2004). With Laurel Brake she edited *The Lure of Illustration in the Nineteenth Century: Picture and Press* (2009) and the *Dictionary of Nineteenth-Century Journalism* (2009).

Peter Garside is Honorary Professorial Fellow at the University of Edinburgh. He has helped provide a number of bibliographical resources relating to print production, including *The English Novel 1770–1829* (2000), and has also edited a variety of texts belonging to the Romantic period, among these James Hogg's *Private Memoirs and Confessions of a Justified Sinner* (2001) and Scott's *Waverley* (2007). Online databases which he has directed include *British Fiction 1800–29* (2004) and *Illustrating Scott, 1814–1901* (2009).

Sandro Jung is Research Professor of Early Modern British Literature and Culture and the Director of the Centre for the Study of Text and Print Culture at Ghent University. The editor of three learned journals, *ANQ*, *Eighteenth-Century Poetry* and the *Journal of the Printing Historical Society*, he is also the author of *David Mallet, Anglo-Scot: Poetry, Politics and Patronage in the Age of Union* (2008) and *The Fragmentary Poetic: Eighteenth-Century Uses of an Experimental Mode* (2009). His most recent book, *James Thomson's 'The Seasons', Print Culture, and Visual Interpretation, 1730–1842*, is forthcoming, and he is in the process of completing a book on the paratexts of Spenserian editions in the eighteenth century.

Brian Maidment is Professor of the History of Print at Liverpool John Moores University and a Visiting Professor at the Centre for the Study of Text and Print Culture, Ghent University. He has written widely on nineteenth-century print culture, especially periodicals, mass-circulation literature and writing by labouring-class writers. Recent work has concentrated on visual culture and the marketplace for print in the early nineteenth century. A new book, *Comedy, Caricature and the Social Order 1820–1850*, was published in 2013.

Laura L. Runge is Professor of English at the University of South Florida, where she specialises in eighteenth-century British literature, women's writing and place studies. She has written several articles on Aphra Behn and *Oroonoko* and she is the editor of *ABO: Interactive Journal for Women in the Arts, 1640–1830*. She is author or editor of six books, including co-editor (with Pat Rogers) of *Producing the Eighteenth-Century Book: Writers and Publishers in England, 1650–1800* (2009).

Introduction

SANDRO JUNG

Print-culture studies is a burgeoning field: it is actively fostered by bibliographical societies worldwide; centres for the study of the history of the book and material text have been founded, and several specialist book series on print culture have produced excellent contributions to the field. These series continuously demonstrate the need to revisit existing histories of print and to include alternative narratives that reveal hitherto neglected, often ephemeral print cultures. It is the recovery of these lesser-known print cultures that is essential for the mapping of cultural production in different knowledge economies and a better understanding of the role that print played in the fashioning of literature. Book-historical perspectives have helped scholars to investigate the cultural mechanisms affecting the production, dissemination and consumption of books in print form; as a discipline book history has expanded beyond the traditional focus on the material book to explore the social, cultural, ideological and economic processes underpinning an explosion of print in the eighteenth century. The flood of print matter that fed consumer demand and encouraged the consumption of all kinds of fashionable objects was closely linked with the rapidly developing visual cultures of society, especially in the eighteenth and nineteenth centuries, when innovations in the printing of illustrations contributed to creating a mass-culture of the visual not possible before. Print culture catered to, and shaped, readers' visual imagination, and literary texts were frequently illustrated. From the 1770s onwards, not only were illustrations issued in printed books, but printsellers produced a large number of affordable prints for collecting and a lesser number of expensive furniture prints (based on major artists' designs) for display in the home.

Illustration studies have become an important research area within current scholarship on print culture and a range of large-scale projects aimed at remapping the history of illustrations in eighteenth-century Europe, such as the *Database of Eighteenth-Century Book Illustration*, are under way. Equally, digital initiatives like *A Database of Cheap Literature, 1837–1860* and the *Database of Mid-Victorian Illustration* have contributed significantly to shedding light on, and to the understanding of the importance of, corpora and illustration techniques that did not feature in traditional accounts of literature and book history. The ongoing *Oxford History of Popular Print Culture* acknowledges the visual as one of the principal forces for the widespread dissemination of literature and cultural literacy more generally.

The study of print culture and literature has in recent years been not only driven by the tireless efforts of institutionalised groups such as the international Society for the History of Authorship, Reading and Publishing (SHARP) and journals such as, among others, *Book History*, *The Journal of the Printing Historical Society*, *Print Quarterly*, *Publications of the Bibliographical Society of America*, *Studies in Bibliography*, *The Library*, and *Word & Image*; rather, each of these journals has promoted different aspects of the study of print as cultural medium which, from the invention of the printing press in the fifteenth century onwards, was appropriated by its promoters for purposes as varied as the religious edification of its users, the improvement of its readers by means of culturally relevant narratives, and the marketing of consumer goods through advertising. To date scholars of print culture have studied the mediation of complex messages by means of type, paper, illustrations and other paratexts involved in the making of mechanically reproducible print objects, but important archives (of paper-based ephemera and media of cheap print, but also of material providing insight into the lives and working practices of those individuals who were responsible for the design and production of print matter) have largely remained unexplored.

From the seventeenth century onwards print objects, as will be seen in this volume of Essays and Studies, could be issued in remarkably different shapes and formats, ranging from affordable editions of John Bunyan's *The Pilgrim's Progress* (featuring religiously interpretive, iconographical narratives in the form of woodcuts or copper engravings) to chapbook versions of the same text. The latter were consumed by a mass-market of readers deriving cultural and religious literacy from redacted and frequently abbreviated versions of Bunyan's work. By contrast, the former accessed an iconographical tradition of religious dream visions that related the work both textually and visually to earlier allegorical productions. The changes that are deliberately introduced in the illustrations of *The Pilgrim's Progress*, and the interpretive matrix of these which forms the basis of Nathalie Collé-Bak's contribution to this volume add much to the meaning of Bunyan's text. As do, for Aphra Behn's *Oroonoko*, the errors that Laura L. Runge discusses in relation to its numerous editions and the ways in which editors affected the reading and reception of the work by retaining the errors of previous editions.

Not only do reprints and novel editions of one and the same text fix textual meaning but, at times, they also erase or obscure meanings by perpetuating errors; print thus serves the function of an agent of supposed semantic and representational stability, even though this fixing of meaning through the printed word may not reflect authorial intention, but compositors' or editors' misreadings and errors. The reconstruction of authorial identity and intention, as well as of the personae that authors fashion, which underpins traditional literary studies concerned with authorship, is made more difficult once books are published without an author's name or at the request of an author who takes on the financial risk of print publication by covering the printing costs of the work to be published. Alan Downie considers the little-studied practice of printing for the author and complicates common views on eighteenth-century authorship and the canon that have come under increasing scrutiny in the past thirty years. Gerard Carruthers examines the instability of print media in that they often do not occur as the sole objects containing textual information but are supplemented by paratextual material such as added leaves (bearing additional textual meaning) in interleaved copies. Carruthers studies a copy of the *Scots Musical Museum* that Robert Burns compiled and traces its history and mobility as an object transformed and edited by its successive owners who revised and reshaped the Burnsian *Ur*-text. The fluidity of textual existence demonstrated in the case of Burns's copy of the *Scots Musical Museum* is reminiscent of the textual condition itself as continuously morphing and autopoietic.

While book-historical studies concerned with textual production in the eighteenth and nineteenth centuries have, to a large degree, focused on material issued for the middle classes, systematic interest in cheap print media is a more recent phenomenon. Equally, the study of subscription editions, ambitious and costly ventures for which a certain number of subscribing supporters needed to be found before the editions could be printed, have remained neglected. The chapter on editions of James Thomson's best-selling long poem *The Seasons* in the 1790s investigates the ways publishers of the text recruited novel technologies such as colour printing to create commodities that promoted their editions as auratic rather than as what Walter Benjamin conceives of as the merely mechanically reproducible print object, which is devoid of aura. Peter Garside's contribution concerns itself with the illustrations of Sir Walter Scott's works; he produces a detailed history of illustrated editions and sheds light on the importance that publishers assigned to the visual medium as a feature that could significantly advance a volume's or series' marketing potential and value.

Brian Maidment and Marysa Demoor's essays engage with print-culture genres – almanacs and Victorian periodicals – that are more ephemeral than the print media introduced by the other contributors. Focused on current affairs and day-to-day matters, the almanac and the *Athenaeum* do not promote the notion of literature as belles-lettres that Thomson's *The Seasons* embodied (as a result of which it featured prominently in the formation of the eighteenth-century canon); rather, the kind of Victorian almanac that Maidment examines is not prophetic or focused on providing a reference work on the agricultural cycle of the year, as earlier examples would have been. It introduces topical discussions, deploys the comic mode and visual satire frequently, and, as frequently, serves as a subversive means to question the validity of social distinctions and the power of institutions. Maidment's almanac is read as socially progressive and as invested with the power to affect readers politically in a way that traditional agricultural almanacs could not. Demoor examines a particular, hitherto neglected phase in the history of the *Athenaeum* and offers information on the editing, editorial practice and the refashioning of a dinosaur (her term) of Victorian print culture.

The subject range of this volume of Essays and Studies indicates some of the varied directions in which print-culture research is developing. While the contributors still use the history of the book and its methodologies to unravel the multifarious meanings and contexts of print culture, they also deploy tools derived from textual studies and visual culture research. It is this combined approach which makes possible the reconsideration of literature and print as not only limited to an artificial and monolithically conceived literary canon. Rather, the meaning and status of literature as an expression of cultural achievement is being redefined as the field of print-culture studies diversifies and 'rediscovers' neglected forms of print, all of which had specific cultural meanings when they were first produced.

My thanks are due to the contributors to this volume. Above all, I would like to thank Elaine Treharne for her support throughout the editing of the volume and to Caroline Palmer and Rohais Haughton for expertly overseeing its production. Finally, my thanks to Samantha Matthews who has been a painstakingly accurate and efficient copy-editor.

Tracing a Genealogy of
Oroonoko *Editions*

LAURA L. RUNGE

ON THE TITLE PAGE of the fifth edition of Aphra Behn's collected novels (1705), someone added the tag 'Corrected from the many Errors of former Impressions'. Whether the phrase was inspired by a sense of pride in work well done or, more likely, a desire to advertise the book's superiority, it advises the modern reader of a number of important things. First, it tells us that the 1705 edition succeeds a number of previous editions, informing us that Behn's novels have a history, a textual history that involves errors. The language refers to the physical action of the hand-press, and it reminds us of those individual hands that set the type that formed the impressions remaining on the page today. The phrase underscores the fact that the text we receive underwent changes well after Behn's death in 1689. Most importantly for this essay, its claim testifies to a widespread and largely unacknowledged textual practice in the transmission of Aphra Behn's most famous short fiction, *Oroonoko*.

Over the course of the eighteenth century, various hands anonymously 'corrected' and 'improved' Behn's text in a gradual accretion of extensive textual corruption. Given the pedagogical prominence *Oroonoko* has assumed in the past twenty years and its overwhelming presence in literary scholarship of the seventeenth and eighteenth centuries, a fitting subtitle to this article might be: 'The Hazards of Choosing an Edition'. As Gerald Duchovnay and Mary Ann O'Donnell have documented, the publication of *Oroonoko* in 1688 was far from free of problems.[1] Since

I thank the following for their help in researching this article: Martine Watson Brownley, J. Paul Hunter, Jenny Keith, Joanna Lipking, Pat Rogers, William Scheuerle, and Janet Todd. I especially thank Mary Ann O'Donnell and David Vandermeulen for corrections and advice on this manuscript. For their assistance, I also thank Joy Pasini, Jessica McKee and Jessica Cook. An overview of the editions examined in this essay is provided in the form of an appendix.

1   Gerald Duchovnay, 'Aphra Behn's *Oroonoko*: A Critical Edition' (unpublished Ph.D. dissertation, Indiana University, 1971), and Mary Ann O'Donnell, *Aphra Behn: An Annotated Bibliography of Primary and Secondary Sources*, second edition (Aldershot and Burlington: Ashgate, 2004).

that time, a history of loose reproduction and frequent, silent emendation – not to mention egregious error – necessitates a careful scrutiny of
Oroonoko texts, for it was not until the 1990s that principles of scholarly
editing were regularly applied to Behn's novel. As a result, the first reliable versions of the story only became available to the mainstream market
within the last two decades. That leaves over three centuries of unexam-
ined, casual and error-filled textual reproduction, which have generated
a tremendous legacy of commercial and scholarly misrepresentation. In
this light, the many errors of former impressions require a careful sorting.

The history of *Oroonoko*'s textual reproduction is of interest now for
a number of reasons.[2] The first is the novel's sheer popularity. Next to
Shakespeare's plays, *Paradise Lost*, and a handful of poems, it is perhaps
the only seventeenth-century English text to achieve 'hypercanonic-
ity', and it is certainly the only such text written by a woman before
Jane Austen.[3] According to O'Donnell, Behn's most thorough bibliographer, *Oroonoko* has been published in at least fourteen different versions and eight translations, between 1985 and 2002.[4] Of these some
are clearly unreliable, while others fare better.[5] It is currently available
in at least seven separate classroom editions, including the heavily
referenced volumes edited by Joanna Lipking (1997) and Catherine
Gallagher (1998) for Norton and Bedford respectively.[6] A full-text version is available in all four of the major British Literature anthologies:
Blackwell's *British Literature 1640–1789*, Longman's *Restoration and
the Eighteenth Century*, Norton's *Anthology of English Literature* and *the*

2   For accounts of the influence and adaptation of Behn's work, see Janet Todd,
The Critical Fortunes of Aphra Behn (Columbia: Camden House, 1998), and Jane
Spencer, *Aphra Behn's Afterlife* (Oxford: Oxford University Press, 2000).
3   Janet Todd, ed., *Aphra Behn Studies* (Cambridge: Cambridge University
Press, 1996), pp. 3–4.
4   O'Donnell, *Annotated Bibliography* accounts for sources published through
2002.
5   See Mary Ann O'Donnell, 'Review of *Oroonoko, or, The Royal Slave: A
Critical Edition*, edited with an introduction by Adelaide P. Amore (Lanham,
MD: University Press of America, 1987)', *Eighteenth-Century Fiction* 1.3 (1989),
248–51; see also *The Scriblerian* 21.1 (1988), 84–5.
6   Duffy (Methuen), Todd (Penguin), Salzman (Oxford), Lipking (Norton) and
Gallagher (Bedford). For full references, see the Appendix; also Janet Todd, *Oroonoko, or, The History of the Royal Slave* (Harmondsworth: Penguin, 2003). Derek
Hughes edited a version for his anthology, *Versions of Blackness: Key Texts on Slavery from the Seventeenth Century* (Cambridge: Cambridge University Press, 2007).

Broadview Anthology of English Literature. A period-specific collection, *Women's Writing of the Early Modern Period, 1588–1688: An Anthology* (Columbia University Press, 2002) carries *Oroonoko*, and it appears in the two leading anthologies of women authors: the *Norton Anthology of Literature by Women* and the Longman *Anthology of Women's Literature.* Finally it is featured in Norton's definitively canon-making collection, *Major Authors.*

It is now also accessible on the web in at least seven hypertext versions as well as in the Chadwyck-Healey English Prose Full-Text Database.[7] For those institutions with subscriptions, students can access original versions on Early English Books Online (EEBO) and Eighteenth Century Collections Online (ECCO).[8] A quick search on Amazon, Barnes and Noble, or iTunes brings up six additional non-scholarly trade paperbacks,[9] and six ebooks – some of which are versions of print books, others not. There are two digital editions available as smartphone apps. Finally there are two audio versions available for free as podcasts.[10]

The current commercial interest in *Oroonoko* relates, of course, to the increasing classroom utility of the text. Its size and content make it a desirable addition to many an undergraduate syllabus. It is a hybrid text aptly suited to the investigation of our triumvirate of critical modalities: gender, race and class. It is also fortuitously poised among

7   For a listing of online editions available in 2002, see O'Donnell, *Annotated Bibliography*, A31.b. Since then it has appeared also on the University of Adelaide Library website, rendered into HTML by Steve Thomas (Adelaide: eBooks@Adelaide, last updated 4 July 2012) http://ebooks.adelaide.edu.au/b/behn/aphra/b420/.

8   In preparing my research for this paper, I discovered the existence of yet another eighteenth-century print edition of *Oroonoko*, from 1791 (Dublin) which is not listed in O'Donnell's bibliography.

9   ReadHowYouWant, 2006; Dodo Press, 2008; CreateSpace, 2010; Cathedral Classics, 2010; Kessinger Publishing Company, 2010; EEBO Editions/ProQuest, 2011.

10   Both Penguin editions are available as ebooks through Amazon, Barnes & Noble, and iTunes; other iTunes ebook options include *Oroonoko* (ReadHowYouWant, 2008), and *Oroonoko* (The Floating Press, 2009). Google eBooks offers the *Works of Aphra Behn, Mobi Collected Works* (MobileReference, 2010, phone app); and *Oroonoko: or, the Royal Slave* (Sunscroll, Publish This LLC, 2009, phone app). Podcasts include *Oroonoko, or The Royal Slave* by LibriVox (2009) and Babblebooks (2008).

fictional and non-fictional genres of increasing interest, including travel narratives, colonial narratives, romance, novels, history and even life-writing. More recently I have found Behn's novel significant for place studies and possibly for ecological criticism as well. Its themes are eminently salacious, mixing the political and the sexual, the violent and the adventurous, slavery and rebellion, love and war. And to crown all, it is written in the voice of an engaging – if not overly precise – first-person female narrator.

Efforts have been made to illustrate – again – the importance of bibliographic studies to the teaching and scholarship of literature. With respect to classroom editions in general, Alexander Pettit has argued that readers can be seriously compromised 'if they do not educate themselves about the contingencies that help define the volume'.[11] The many contingencies in an edition of *Oroonoko* need to be recognised and appreciated for the impact they bear on the meaning of the text. Despite the recent production of reliable editions, any single class might yet be subject to a variety of texts, even when the students apparently purchase the same edition![12] Among the editions, the range of possibilities can lead to a hodgepodge of fundamental textual contradictions. For instance, some texts reproduce Behn's original dedication to the soon-to-be exiled Catholic, Lord Maitland, either with or without the stop-press variant; others leave the letter out altogether. This context affects the political reading of the story because the letter supplies direct evidence of Behn's Catholic, and hence Stuart, allegiance. Some texts represent the narrator reading the 'Lives of the Romans' to Oroonoko and Imoinda together, while others record her giving Plutarch's text to Oroonoko alone and the stories of nuns to Imoinda. More problematically, others have them sharing an imaginary text, the 'loves of the Romans'. While the last is a significant error, it matters who reads Plutarch and who reads stories of the nuns if one is concerned about the gendered and generic implications of the characters' literacy. Some editors of the text retain Behn's curious shift in the gender of tigers, from female to male, while others make the pronouns consistently feminine.[13]

11   Alexander Pettit, *Textual Studies and the Common Reader: Essays on Editing Novels and Novelists* (Athens, Georgia: University of Georgia Press, 2000), p. 5.
12   Joanna Lipking has detailed some of the problems associated with the different Norton editions in Joanna Lipking, 'Letter to the Editors', *Restoration* 26.1 (2002), 50–2.
13   See Eric Miller, 'Aphra Behn's Tigers', *Dalhousie Review* 81.1 (2001), 47–65.

Another factor of importance in this study is the fact that women generally have been subject to far less bibliographical study than have their male counterparts. Pettit writes: 'The imbalance between male and female editors and "editeds" will be clear to anyone who surveys the field. Equally noticeable is the paucity of critical commentary on women and editing, a stark and surprising disavowal of the terms of academic debate.'[14] Critics and editors have been calling for a change in the treatment, particularly of texts by early women authors, for some years now.[15] The tide is beginning to turn, but studies such as this one point to a continuing need.

The problems that *Oroonoko*'s textual legacy generates are manifold. Students continue to be affected by pre-1990s editions because regularly consulted reference works list substandard editions. Many literary dictionaries and encyclopaedias from the 1980s, for instance, refer students to the Montague Summers 1915 collection or Maureen Duffy's 1987 edition. At the time of publication, these were the most reliable editions available, but both are based on corrupt texts. More harm is done by reference to the 1973 Norton trade *Oroonoko* with introduction by Lore Metzger. One of Behn's entries in the *Dictionary of Literary Biography* lists this work as a source, and it incorrectly cites Metzger as its editor.[16] This common misattribution becomes all the more injurious to Metzger's credit when we recognise that the 1973 text itself is significantly flawed and that the copyright page, which states, 'Reprint of the 1688 ed. printed for W. Canning, London', is misleading.

The misunderstanding about Metzger as editor, combined with the misidentification of the textual source, has led scholars to assume the reliability of the 1973 Norton edition, and so without suspecting its corrupt textual base, they pass its errors into critical discourse. The most noteworthy critical miscue along these lines is Laura Brown's reading of Oroonoko as a consumer of the heroic romances that he enacts, having been 'entertained . . . with the Loves of the Romans'.[17] Brown's

---

14   Pettit, *Textual Studies*, p. 10.
15   See Marilyn Butler, 'Editing Women', *Studies in the Novel* 27.3 (1995), 273–83, and Germaine Greer, 'Honest Sam. Briscoe', in *A Genius for Letters: Booksellers and Bookselling from the 16th to the 20th Century*, ed. Michael Harris (Winchester, England: Oak Knoll Press, 1995), pp. 33–48.
16   Jerry C. Beasley, 'Aphra Behn', *Dictionary of Literary Biography: British Novelists, 1660–1800*, ed. Martin C. Battestin (Detroit, Michigan: Gale, 1985), XXXIX, pp. 48–58.
17   Laura Brown, 'The Romance of Empire: *Oroonoko* and the Trade in Slaves',

essay, 'The Romance of Empire: *Oroonoko* and the Trade in Slaves', first published in the ground-breaking collection, *The New Eighteenth Century* (1987), and reproduced as part of her successful book, *The Ends of Empire*, frequently acts as an authority in Behn scholarship.[18] To offer just one prominent example, Stephanie Athey and Daniel Cooper Alarcon in their important article on Imoinda published in *American Literature* (1993) explicitly follow Brown, and they go so far as to adopt the 1973 Norton text for their analysis and thus perpetuate the same errors.[19] Scholarly works published as recently as 2000 have used the 1973 Norton edition as a source for their textual analysis,[20] and so they have passed along the textual corruption and errors of that particular edition.

The nuisance of the Norton 1973 text and earlier corrupt versions of *Oroonoko* remains with us. With the advent of digital reproduction, the standards for editorial practice have retreated since the high mark of the 1990s, and we are meeting with many of the same issues of textual instability we saw prior to that. Indeed, we are seeing the return of some of the problematic texts themselves. Of the three ebooks that I reviewed, two are based directly on the 1973 Norton text, complete with errors like the 'loves of the Romans'. Both the mobile references – downloaded to my Android phone – are based on the Montague Summers 1915 *Works*.

The history of *Oroonoko* editions reveals many variants and poses some compelling mysteries. Beyond the obvious discrepancies among the editions lie the subtler but equally significant editorial choices of emendation, normalisation and modernisation. More remote and yet more crucial is the central question of copy-text, an identification that twentieth-century editions frequently fail to make and sometimes misrepresent. If the 1973 text by Norton is not a reprint of the 1688 original, than what text is it? Where in the three-hundred-year history of the text does the 'loves of the Romans' first appear? Is there a textual basis for any of the emendations incorporated, or are they accidental

The New Eighteenth Century: Theory, Politics, English Literature, ed. Laura Brown (New York: Methuen, 1987), p. 51.
18   See Laura Brown, *The Ends of Empire: Women and Ideology in Early Eighteenth-Century English Literature* (Ithaca: Cornell University Press, 1993).
19   See Stephanie Athey and Daniel Cooper Alarcon, '*Oroonoko*'s Gendered Economies of Honor/Horror: Reframing Colonial Discourse Studies in the Americas', *American Literature* 65.3 (1993): 415–43.
20   See Daniel Punday, 'A Corporeal Narratology?', *Style* 34.2 (2000): 227–42.

variants? My study suggests that the answers to these questions lie in the editing of the nine editions of Behn's *All the Histories and Novels* in the early part of the eighteenth century. This long train of editions yields a number of twentieth-century offspring without any assessment of the corruptions introduced. The primary objective of this study is to establish a reasonable line of descent for *Oroonoko* texts in English and so establish some context for the authority of editing decisions for a very popular classroom text.

Methods of Genealogy

In establishing the line of descent for *Oroonoko* texts, I am greatly indebted to the bibliographic scholarship of Mary Ann O'Donnell and, to a lesser degree, Gerald Duchovnay. The former identifies extant *Oroonoko* texts in her *Annotated Bibliography*, which includes a collation of the earliest versions of Behn's collected *Histories and Novels*, many of which are available in only a handful of research libraries. Duchovnay's 'Aphra Behn's *Oroonoko*: A Critical Edition' provides a detailed bibliographical analysis of the original edition, as well as an account of the relationships among the first four editions of the collected *Histories and Novels*. My study benefits from and moves beyond their work with a fuller analysis of later editions of *Oroonoko*, thereby establishing a more complete and useful genealogy of textual descent.[21]

At the outset, let me acknowledge that my methods are intended to establish minimal, though reasonable, evidence of descent. Counting the original 1688 edition, there are at least thirty-six different versions of *Oroonoko* in English published up to the year 2000, not including reissues and modern reprints. I created a chart of variants using the first four pages of the original 1688 edition of *Oroonoko*, in which I have compared all thirty-six subsequent editions. I do not include versions that have been established as reissues, such as the second issue – sometimes called the second edition – of the 1696 edition for S. Briscoe and R. Wellington. I used the information from the chart of variants to create a stemma, which represents a full genealogy of all the known texts of Behn's *Oroonoko* in English from 1688 to 2000.

21   Most of these books I have examined in hand, but when these artifacts have been unavailable to me, I have used microfilm copies, as in the case of the original 1688 version, the 1696, 1698, 1735 and 1753 editions.

In addition to the chart of variants, I have examined four separate
textual cruxes, usually where problems with the original made editing
decisions necessary. As Duchovnay and O'Donnell have shown, the
original publication of *Oroonoko* appears to have been the work of two
compositors; Compositor II apparently began after H8v – numbered
page 112; an entire signing is dropped without loss of text and the pages
follow with signature K, beginning with numbered page 129. The typeface is larger and the number of lines per page shifts from twenty-three
to twenty-two, and there are new variations in spelling and italics.[22] The
textual cruxes I examined fall within the early pages of what appears to
be the work of a second compositor. On page 133, line 13, the original
includes the confusing phrase 'Dog, that *Clemene* had presented / her'.
On page 141, lines 18 and 19 include the following phrase, corrupted
in several significant ways already alluded to: 'entertain'd him with the
Lives of the / Romans, and great Men'. Page 153 contains the following
much commented upon lines: 'Forms and Colours, that the Pro-/spect
was the most raving that / Sands can create' (1–3) and 'Orange and
Limon Trees, about / half the length of the Marl hear, / whose Flowery
and Fruity bear / Branches meet at the top' (6–9). Finally, I examined
the passage where Oroonoko kills the legendary tiger because the 1688
original intriguingly shifts the gender of the pronoun referring to it: 'he
shot her just into / the Eye, and the Arrow was / sent with so good a will,
and so / sure a hand, that it stuck in her / Brain, and made her caper, and
/ become mad for a moment or / two; but being seconded by / another
Arrow, he fell dead up- / on the Prey: *Caesar* cut him Open / with a
Knife, to see where those / Wounds were that had been re- / ported to
him, and why he did / not Die of 'em' (161). Most of these problems
were emended, in different ways, in the early editions of the novel, and
so provide a second index of genealogy.

Oroonoko *Texts in the Seventeenth and Eighteenth Centuries*

Duchovnay estimates that the first edition of *Oroonoko* was published in
April or May of 1688 by William Canning (O'Donnell A31.1a), and re-
issued in a collection of her novels entitled *Three Histories* (O'Donnell
A32) in July of the same year. With the exception of a stop-press variant
in the Dedication to Lord Maitland with lines praising his Catholicism,

22   Duchovnay, 'Aphra Behn's *Oroonoko*', cxxv–cxxvii.

found only in the Bodleian library copy, the texts of *Oroonoko* are the same in these two versions.[23] The next edition of Behn's novella appears in 1696's *The Histories and Novels of the Late Ingenious Mrs. Behn, in one volume* (O'Donnell A40.1a), published by Sam Briscoe, with a second issue shared with printer-bookseller Richard Wellington (O'Donnell A40.1b). O'Donnell explains that this second issue functions, if not technically then in practice, as the second edition of *The Histories and Novels*. 'Although this issue is clearly not a new edition, Briscoe seems to have considered it as such when he published the designated "Third Edition" in 1698 (A40.3a and b).'[24] Here, and in all subsequent editions of her collected novels until Summers' 1915 *Works, Oroonoko* is given precedence as the lead item.

Because of the length of time between the first edition (1688) and the edition of 1696, and because Behn died in 1689 and thus could have had no say in the changes of the 1696 text, Duchovnay and later editors conclude that only the 1688 edition is textually authoritative, but it remains nonetheless problematic.[25] Germaine Greer and Duchovnay both find evidence that the copy-text for the 1696 volume was the 1688 edition.[26] O'Donnell disagrees (A40.1a) and argues that the 1696 text is a reprint of 1688. All accounts agree on the direct relationship between the 1688 and 1696 versions.

The 1698 edition, or the 'Third edition, with large additions' (O'Donnell A40.3a), shows a clearer editorial presence. This collection, entitled *All the Histories and Novels Written by the Late Ingenious Mrs. Behn, Entire in one Volume*, adds three stories and replaces the dedication to Maitland with a letter to Sir Simon Scroop, signed by Charles Gildon. The memoir 'By one of the Fair Sex' is bulked up to sixty pages with additional discussion of Behn's purported amours. This collection is reprinted in 1699 as volume one of the 'fourth edition' (O'Donnell A40.4a) and reissued with a cancel title page in 1700 and probably sold with Briscoe's second volume containing Behn's translations (O'Donnell A40.4b).[27] Gildon's dedication to Scroop, the memoir, and

23   Duchovnay, 'Aphra Behn's *Oroonoko*', cxx–cxxi; O'Donnell, *Annotated Bibliography*, p. 147. See O'Donnell, *Annotated Bibliography*, A32.
24   O'Donnell, *Annotated Bibliography*, p. 150.
25   Duchovnay, 'Aphra Behn's *Oroonoko*', p. cxxiii.
26   Greer, 'Honest Sam. Briscoe', p. 36. Duchovnay, 'Aphra Behn's *Oroonoko*', p. cxxx.
27   For a fuller account of the complicated history of publishing these volumes, see O'Donnell, *Annotated Bibliography*, A40.3a and b, and A40.4a and b.

the love-letters preface the collection of novels, despite their other variations, from this point through to the 1751 edition. Pearson similarly
includes them in his 1871 reprint of the 1735 edition. Consequently,
Gildon's name has long-lasting association with *Oroonoko*, although his
role in the transmission of the text is unclear.

The 1698 edition represents the first major step in the gradual introduction of silent emendation and corruption of the text. Gildon's
self-identification in the dedicatory letter tempts us to consider him
as the figure responsible for changes to the text, which are extensive
and substantial enough to indicate they are not simply the result of
compositors' habits. According to Duchovnay, the 1698 edition 'generally follows line for line and page for page the second [issue of 1696],
except there is greater editorial intervention in the third [1698]'.[28] I
recorded fourteen variants in the 1698 text, whereas there is only one in
the 1696 edition. The emendations reflect a desire for textual consist-
ency or normalisation and clarification of the language. Unsurprisingly,
the changes also bring some errors. Four of the five problematic textual
cruxes are changed here in ways that influence most of the later texts.
The passage on the 'Lives of the Romans' includes a key change from
the original 'entertain'd him' to the plural 'entertain'd 'em', which in
subsequent editions easily becomes 'them' (1698 edn, p. 61). In the
'Prospect was the most raving that Sands can create', the 1698 edition
sensibly replaces 'raving' with 'ravishing' (1698 edn, p. 66). Greatly altering the confusing lines in the original passage on fruit groves, this
version prints 'Orange and Limon-Trees, about half the length of the
Mall here, whose Flowery and Fruit-bearing Branches met at the top'
(1698 edn, p. 66). Finally, this edition makes feminine all the pronouns
that refer to Oroonoko's tiger (1698 edn, p. 69). Because these changes
are frequently adopted or adapted in later editions, they become significant in dating the unacknowledged sources. The 1699/1700 edition
of *All the Histories and Novels* (A40.4a–b) claims on its title page to be
the fourth edition. Duchovnay argues that 'the fourth edition follows
the third except for a continued corruption of the text', and I found no
reason to question that claim.

During the eighteenth century, *Oroonoko* was published as the first

---

28   'There are corrections of obvious misprints and mistakes, such as the mis-
pagination of the second [issue], which could be expected, but there is also a noticeable normalizing of spellings, such as "intreat" to "entreat," "loosing" to "losing," and "chus'd" to "chose" ' (Duchovnay, 'Aphra Behn's *Oroonoko*', cxxxi).

fiction in *All the Histories and Novels* in octavo in 1705 and 1718, and in duodecimo in 1722, 1735 and 1751. In 1770 a tiny version of *Oroonoko* taken from the ninth edition of 1751 is published solo by C. Plummer in Doncaster. The copy from The Eighteenth Century microfilm collection indicates that the volume is in octodecimo. The novella was printed in the *Oxford Magazine* in 1736 (no copy is extant), and it was serialised in the *Ladies Magazine* in 1753. In 1777 Elizabeth Griffith revised the novel as part of her duodecimo *A Collection of Novels*, and she later abridged this *Oroonoko* and printed it on its own as *English Nights Entertainments. The History of Oroonoko*, in 1800. The trend reflects Behn's popularity in the first half of the eighteenth century, with an edition of her novels in each of the first four decades and the move to the more portable and popular duodecimo form. The record also indicates the reading public's waning interest after 1740. Despite the recognised fame of *Oroonoko*, which Griffith claims 'has been long so popular, that the Editor of this work could not be excused from admitting it into the Collection' (1777 edn, p. 199), the novel falls into obscurity with the rest of Behn's works until the late nineteenth century.

However, the transmission of *Oroonoko* before this decline requires further comment. With the fifth edition of *All the Histories and Novels* in 1705 (O'Donnell 1705), Behn's texts temporarily fall under the sole province of Richard Wellington, who had played a partial role in the publication of the 1696 second issue. While it claims on the title page to be 'Corrected from the many Errors of former Impressions', this edition of *Oroonoko*, at least, appears to be another stage in the gradual refinement or deterioration – depending upon the perspective – of the text. It reproduces, and emends, Gildon's letter to Scroop; for example, for the passage in 1698: 'that without her Name we might discover the Author, as *Protegenes* did *Apelles*, by the Stroak of her Pencil' (A4v), this edition substitutes 'by the stroak of his pencil' (1705: n.p.). The edition adopts all but two of the changes made in the previous edition and introduces five additional changes, primarily to create more grammatical or smoother sentences. Similarly, this edition reproduces verbatim the emendations to the textual cruxes introduced in the third edition of 1698 and passed on to the 1699/1700 volume. Consequently, we can conclude that this 1705 edition is based on the 1699/1700 edition and is a lineal descendant of 1688 with continued minor changes.

The 1718 edition (O'Donnell 1718a) is the last to produce *All the Histories and Novels* in octavo and is important because it ultimately serves as a source for several twentieth-century versions, including Henderson's 1930 Everyman's edition. It is a clear descendant from the

1705 fifth edition, claiming on its title page to be 'The Sixth Edition, Corrected'. An editor or compositor includes all of the previous emendations in the first four pages, and he or she introduces several substantive changes that are passed on to most later editions. In the original 1688 edition, the sentence on page 3, lines 11–15 reads: ''tis fit I tell you the manner of bringing them to these new *Colonies*; for those they make use of there, are not *Natives* of the place'. The revision drops 'for' and changes 'are not *Natives*' to 'not being *Natives*' (1718 edn, p. 54). A similar elision takes place on the following page; the narrator describes the marmoset in 1688: it 'has Face and Hands like an Humane Creature:'. The revision cleans up spelling and punctuation and alters the phrasing to read: 'having Face and Hands like a Human Creature;' (1718 edn, p. 54). In the textual cruxes, only one significant emendation is made: The 1718 edition expands the contraction ''em': 'I entertained them with the Lives of the *Romans*' (1718 edn, p. 104). Although like the other seventeenth- and eighteenth-century editions, this contains no explicit statement on emendations, the text shows evidence of attempts to create smoothness, and alter punctuation, spelling and emphases.

The 1722 seventh edition of *All the Histories and Novels* (O'Donnell 1722) is the first to be published in duodecimo, and it is the first to include Gildon's name on the title page. While the line 'Published by Mr. Charles Gildon' suggests his authority over the text, Gildon was reportedly blind and infirm by 1721.[29] He would die in 1724, but the line claiming his role would continue to grace the title pages of the 1735, 1751 and 1770 editions of *Oroonoko*. This, with the signed letter written to Scroop, attests to his involvement over the years in Behn's novel, although it in no way clarifies the nature of his role. This volume reproduces the novels published in Gildon's 1698 edition, but includes illustrations for the first time and separates the collection into two volumes. This division of stories, due presumably to the duodecimo format, would be duplicated in the 1735, 1751 and 1871 editions. Some changes made to the 1722 edition alter the celebrated 'oral' style of the tale with grammar that increases sentence length. For example, in the passages examined, there are two instances of changing a period to a colon, creating one long sentence from the three original (page 3, line 10 through page 4, line 23). These changes are retained in many of the editions descending from this and so help to determine the specific source for later texts.

29 Greer, 'Honest Sam. Briscoe', p. 43.

The eighth edition, 'corrected and illustrated with cuts', in 1735 (O'Donnell 1735) is reprinted in 1871 by John Pearson, and thus it contributes directly to Victorian debates about Behn and *Oroonoko*. It is a descendant of the seventh edition, including all accidental and substantive changes to date, but this edition shows a greater idiosyncrasy in capitalisation and other minor changes (such as hyphenating 'three-score' from page 4, line 16). It is the first edition to combine the words 'my' and 'self' (both on page 2, line 8 and page 4, line 21).

The 1751 edition of *All the Histories and Novels* (O'Donnell 1751) appears to be the last in the long line of gradual changes to Behn's text and its first thorough modernisation. It appears to be a direct descendant of the 1735 text, although there are pervasive changes. All the substantive changes in the passages examined in 1735 are retained with the exception of the hyphenation of 'three-score', which reads 'three score' as in the original (page 4, line 16). The combination of 'my' and 'self' in two places is retained, but this could be the effect of normalising spelling. The extensive emendation appears to bring the text in line with modern printing practices of the mid-century, minimising capitalisation and italics, and employing modern word divisions.

Although the editions of 1770 and 1777 do not serve as source texts for later editions, they merit brief mention for their particularities. The tiny 1770 version of *Oroonoko* is a rare instance of the novel appearing on its own outside of serialisation in the eighteenth century (O'Donnell 1759).[30] The title page claims that it is 'Published by Charles Gildon. The Ninth Edition corrected', and there is no reason to challenge its descent from the 1751 edition. The text of 1770 is normalised in spelling, and, following 1751, in capitals and italics. However, it includes no letter, memoir or frontispiece, and there are frequent changes to substantives not seen elsewhere. The book is of interest because Summers mentions it in his spotty bibliography of *Oroonoko* in the *Works*, which suggests that it may have played a role in his editing of the novel, but I found no other evidence to support this.[31]

---

30   O'Donnell lists this as published in 1759 and states that 'The Eighteenth Century Microfilm Project (18th c to 198:2) shows the date on the title page changed by hand from MDCCLIX to MDCCLXX' (p. 124). Summers (V, pp. 127, 128) also refers to it as published in 1759. The microfilm copy from the British Library shows the title-page imprint to read MDCCLXX; it is blurred but it does not appear to be altered. The card catalogue and the listing on ECCO accept the 1770 date.

31   *Works of Aphra Behn*, 5 vols., ed. Montague Summers (London: Heine-

There is, however, some evidence that Griffith's much revised version of *Oroonoko* plays a role in later editions, albeit in a minor way. Griffith's text appears to be direct descendant of 1751, but she makes many substitutions for words. Significantly, she changes Oroonoko's nomenclature from 'gallant slave' to 'gallant Moor'. In her introduction to the 1777 collection, Griffith makes the first explicit editorial statement by a Behn editor, restricting herself: 'to correct or cancel improper passages, or to clear up obscurities in the text or language, by giving a different turn to the thought or expression' (1777: A4v). For the most part, her emendations follow the trends of normalisation seen in 1751, but she adds her own idiosyncratic editing. Notably, the language of the passage on the prospect from St. John's Hill apparently needed clarification, because she introduces the change from 'sands' to 'fancy': 'the prospect was the most ravishing that fancy can create' (1777 edn, p. 249). This substitution gains lasting presence in the later emendations of Pearson, Baker and others, including Lipking. Griffith's 1800 edition maintains many of the changes she made in 1777 with the addition of significant abridgments to the text.

Victorian Texts

With Griffith's abridgment in 1800, we end *Oroonoko's* period of continued fame; England does not see another edition of the text until 1871, and that is an antiquarian's reproduction of the 1735 eighth edition of *All the Histories and Novels*. In *The Plays, Histories, and Novels of the Ingenious Mrs. Aphra Behn with Life and Memoirs* (O'Donnell 1871), John Pearson resets the eighteenth-century text, with every attempt to reproduce the original. He includes the engravings, the pagination and the typeface with the long 's'. For the novels, he reproduces the 1735 title page and all of the contents in two volumes. While there is no statement of editorial practice or textual source, the chart of variants indicates that Pearson closely follows the 1735 edition. Pearson does include one significant change in the textual cruxes, as mentioned above, substituting 'fancy' for 'sands' (1871 edn, p. 155). This is the only significant departure from the 1735 text that I noted, but it indicates the possibility that he introduced additional errors and changes elsewhere. Pearson's elaborate six-volume collection instigated heated debate in

mann, 1915), I, p. 127.

the literary journals about the value of Behn's works that subsequently shaped the understanding of audience and censorship for Baker's and Summers' editions.[32]

There is only one other nineteenth-century edition of the novel, published fifteen years after Pearson. In 1886 the Temple Company publishes a heavily edited, solo edition of *Oroonoko*, presumably for the casual reader. This edition modernises the language and regularises italics, capitals, irregular spellings and contractions but does so with apparent fidelity to the original source. Temple confusingly identifies its source on the title page as 'a reprint from the original in the British Museum'. It is unclear which original was used, but is likely to have been the 1751 edition.

Early Twentieth-Century Editions

With Ernest Baker's edition of *The Novels of Mrs. Aphra Behn* (O'Donnell 1905), we come upon the first modern edition of *Oroonoko* with enduring influence. Published by Routledge and Dutton in 1905, it was reprinted by both in 1913 and again by Greenwood Press in 1969. In direct response to Pearson's uncensored reproduction of the plays and novels, Baker famously justifies the publication of only Behn's novels, 'not because they are more clever, but because they are less offensive to modern taste than her comedies'.[33] While he makes no overt claims, he apparently adapts Behn for the student of literature. Like the 1886 edition, Baker normalises the text with modern spelling and grammatical usage, but I would argue against a direct descent both because of subtle differences in the chart of variants and because Baker's volume includes nine fictions in addition to *Oroonoko*, and the 1886 Temple *Oroonoko* is a solo text. Baker does not identify his source text, but the variants identified in the chart that could not be explained by normalisation suggest that he used a 1722 edition or later. It is possible that he

---

32 See 'Literary Garbage', *The Saturday Review* (27 January 1872), 109–10; *The Examiner* (20 January 1872), 74–5, 217, 301–3; John Pearson, 'Aphra Behn and "Literary Garbage" ', *The Examiner* (1872), 151; Laura L. Runge, 'Editions of Oroonoko, 1688–2000: A Historical Perspective', in *Aphra Behn (1640–1689): Le Modèle européen*, ed. Bernard Dhuicq (Entrevaux, France: Bilingua GA Editions, 2005), pp. 142–53.

33 *The Novels of Mrs. Aphra Behn*, ed. Ernest Baker (London: Routledge, 1905), vii.

used Pearson's text, which he mentions obliquely in his opening.[34] We can date the source text based on key changes. For example, Baker includes the omission of 'though' on page 2, line 15, which is first seen in 1722. Because he incorporates the changes first seen in 1722 and 1735, I would argue for a source in either the seventh or eighth editions of *All the Histories and Novels*. Because he does include the substitution of 'fancy' for 'sands' as in Pearson, it also seems likely that the 1871 reproduction influenced him.

Because of its recognised standing as the first edited collection, Montague Summers' 1915 *Works of Aphra Behn* (O'Donnell 1915[a]), reprinted by Phaeton and Benjamin Blom in 1967, provides the most influential of the *Oroonoko* texts of the early twentieth century. But, like Baker, Summers is not clear about his textual source. Duchovnay claims that Summers 'used the 1698 edition as his copy-text, but "corrected" and modernised freely and silently' (p. cxxxvi). Alternatively, I would argue, based on the chart of variants and the cruxes examined, that Summers used either a 1722 or 1735 edition and reproduced the text with little emendation. The corrections and modernisation that Duchovnay identifies actually appear in these later eighteenth-century editions, which Duchovnay does not include in his collation. The text of the first four pages from the original in Summers is identical to Pearson's 1735 reproduction, with two slight exceptions. While we might conclude that Summers used the readily available edition by Pearson, two points rule against it. First, Summers does not include the substitution of 'fancy' for 'sands' but reproduces the sentence as it appears in the 1722 and 1735 editions.[35] This is the most significant departure from Pearson of the three I discovered, and it indicates an earlier text. Second, he claims to have used the earliest editions available, and so using a nineteenth-century reprint seems more than a little duplicitous. While it is not conclusive, evidence suggests that Summers used the 1722 edition of *All the Histories and Novels* as his text for *Oroonoko*, and he may have checked this against either the 1735 or Pearson's edition. This assessment alters Duchovnay's view of Summers as an editor of the novella, in that he appears to have reproduced faithfully the seventh or eighth edition of the text. Unfortunately, it is a corrupt text faithfully reproduced.

---

34   Ibid., vii.
35   *Works of Aphra Behn*, ed. Summers, I, p. 179.

The Problem Texts: 1930–87

Philip Henderson's Everyman's *Shorter Novels: Jacobean and Restoration* (O'Donnell 1930a) is significant because it appears to be the source of the popular Norton Library edition from 1973.[36] Henderson does not acknowledge his sources for the volume, but he does reproduce the 1688 title page for *Oroonoko*. That he does not include the dedicatory letter to Lord Maitland (available in the 1688 and 1696 editions only) is just the first indication that this text is not based on the original of 1688. His copy-text is arguably the sixth edition of 1718, because the emendations he includes either begin or end with that version of the tale. For instance, Henderson includes 'though' in 'And though I shall omit', whereas editions from 1722 and following omit it. The emendations to two phrases introduced in 1718 mentioned earlier, 'not being Natives' and 'having face and hands like a human creature;' are both followed in Henderson. He opts not to hyphenate 'three-score' as is done in 1735, and he similarly does not follow the 1735 in combining 'my' and 'self' from page 4, line 21, despite the thorough modernisation of the text. These argue for a copy-text earlier than 1735 and even 1722. Henderson normalises capitals and italics and spelling in keeping with Everyman's mission. But he also introduces many substantive errors, the most notorious being the first instance of 'the loves of the Romans'. Recall that the original in 1688 reads: 'entertain'd him with the Lives of the / Romans, and great Men'. The 1718 edition expands the contraction of the plural pronoun ''em' introduced in 1698 to 'them'. Henderson's text reads: 'I entertained them with the loves of the *Romans*, and great men'.[37] Another major error of omission occurs in the lines on the fruit trees: 'about half the length of the *Mall* here, flowery and fruit-bearing branches met at the top'.[38] Henderson leaves out the word 'whose' before 'flowery', an error that is only followed in Moore's 1934, the Norton 1973 and Sey's 1977 editions, further suggesting their direct descent from this text. By far the most careless of the modern editions, this version of *Oroonoko* introduces numerous errors in substantives and accidentals to a corrupt source masquerading as the original edition. Henderson provides no editorial statement, but the

36   This source was first identified to me by Joanna Lipking.
37   Philip Henderson, ed., *Shorter Novels: Jacobean and Restoration* (London: Dent, 1930), p. 192.
38   Ibid., p. 196.

deviations from the 1718 edition appear to be the product of poor methodology, not forethought.

Before moving on to the texts directly influenced by Henderson's flawed edition, another 1930 version of *Oroonoko* deserves mention. Everyman's competitor, Nelson's English Series under the general editorship of Ernest Bernbaum, produced a collection entitled *Malory to Mrs. Behn: Specimens of Early Prose Fiction* (O'Donnell 1930b) in the same year as Henderson's *Shorter Novels*. Edited by Albert Morton Turner and Percie Hopkins Turner, both of the University of Maine, this edition of *Oroonoko* might be called the first American version, published by Thomas Nelson and Sons in New York and based on texts provided by Harvard Library. It is unique in its claim to follow the 1688 edition included in *Three Histories* and in *apparently doing so*, despite modernisation and Americanised spellings. This text makes no attempt to identify emendations, and they are rife throughout. In fact, in the passages examined, this text includes most of the variants seen in the seventh and eighth editions of *All the Histories and Novels*. In the textual crux describing the prospect at St. John's Hill, they substitute the term 'fancy' for 'sands', which argues for the influence of only a handful of texts – Griffith's, Pearson's, Temple's and Baker's.[39] Given the mention of Baker's text in the brief bibliography they include, I argue for the influence of Baker's edition on the editing of this text. Many of the accidentals and substantive changes in the first four pages are similar or identical to Baker's, which also modernises the text. The Turners intervene a great deal more in punctuation, however; they freely cut sentences, replace semicolons and colons with either commas or periods and omit commas in many places as well. Despite the probability that the Turners consulted later editions, there is evidence that they adapted an original 1688 version. Their edition includes two significant examples from the original that would be changed in editions as early as 1698: the use of the singular masculine pronoun 'him' in the passage 'entertained him with the lives of the Romans and great men'[40] and the shifting gender of the tiger that Oroonoko kills.[41] With its editorial statement, use of original text, endnotes and bibliography, and the seemingly standard practice of silent borrowings, emendations and errors, the result is a curious but unreliable text.

39   *Malory to Mrs. Behn*, ed. Albert and Percie Turner (New York: Nelson, 1930), p. 371.
40   Ibid., p. 367.
41   Ibid., p. 374.

With the 1934 text edited by Cecil A. Moore, appearing in the anthology *Restoration Literature: Poetry and Prose 1660–1700* published by Appleton-Century-Crofts in New York, we witness the first ill-effects of Henderson's edition.[42] Like the Turners, Moore acknowledges new editorial customs by providing a statement of editorial practice in his preface: 'The texts are the most authentic I could procure, although I should explain that I have not made a fetish of best editions to the point of slavishly copying an obvious error from an approved text when it might be corrected by reference to another.'[43] He might have had more success in his edition if he had procured virtually any other text because he does in fact copy many 'obvious' errors from the Everyman's edition that might have been corrected by reference to another. He incorporates all the errors that belong uniquely to Henderson's text. The only differences between Moore's and Henderson's lie in changes to spelling in preference to the American lexicon and some deletions of commas. With the Norton 1973 and Sey's texts, this forms a family of silent descendants from Henderson.

As a direct descendant of the Henderson text, the 1973 Norton Library edition of *Oroonoko* (O'Donnell 1973) is most problematic. Although stating on its copyright page, 'Reprint of the 1688 ed. printed for W. Canning, London', and reproducing the title page of the same, the 1973 Norton edition is clearly not what it claims to be. The Henderson edition, which is itself probably based on the 1718 sixth edition of *All the Histories and Novels*, most likely serves as the source for the novel put out by Norton. The text, lineation, setting of text (13.5 cm) and font ('old style') appear to be the same as the Henderson edition, suggesting the possibility of a photographic reproduction, such as photolithography; however, the Norton 1973 edition oddly possesses one significant difference that obviates that possibility.[44] While the trend in twentieth-century editions moves toward modernising spelling and normalising capitals and italics, the 1973 Norton edition returns some of the 'strangeness' of the old text by bringing back the use of capitalisa-

---

42   I thank Violetta Trofimova for identifying this version of *Oroonoko*, which is not listed in O'Donnell's bibliography.

43   Cecil A. Moore, ed., *Restoration Literature: Poetry and Prose 1660–1700* (New York: Appelton-Century Crofts, 1934), p. v.

44   My thanks to Pat Rogers for help in identifying the font and settings of the Everyman's edition.

tion and italics for proper names and speeches. If we accept Henderson's as the copy-text, there are no emendations or errors among the variants examined that cannot be explained by this reversal of modernisation. The 1973 Norton appears to follow earlier versions of *Oroonoko* in its use of capitals and italics without significant exceptions. This suggests that an in-house compositor copied Henderson's text, including the rare error of 'Loves of the Romans' and the substantive omission of 'whose' in the phrase '^ flowery and fruit-bearing Branches met at the top' (Norton 1973 edn, p. 46, 50), but may have consulted an earlier edition for the use of capitals and italics. There does not appear to be a different source for Henderson that may have come into the hands of the Norton team. The 1934 Moore edition, which also descends directly from Henderson's, moves toward modernisation. None of the other known editions bears significant resemblance.

It should be noted that this poor precedent for Norton has been all but erased by later efforts by the publisher to establish reliable editions of the novel both in the Norton Anthologies and in the Norton Critical edition. The publisher has made good-faith efforts to eliminate the corrupt text and replace it with the trustworthy text edited by Lipking.

The 1980s witnessed two versions of *Oroonoko* that evidence the shift in interest to the woman writer as such. In 1986 Methuen published a collection of Behn's works edited by Behn's biographer, Maureen Duffy, and in 1987 Meridian included *Oroonoko* in their *Anthology of Early Women Writers* (O'Donnell 1987b), edited by Katharine M. Rogers and William McCarthy. While both identify their source text, neither is unproblematic. Duffy continues to give Behn's novella pride of place in the volume entitled *Oroonoko and Other Stories* (O'Donnell 1986). She situates the book as a recovery project and modernises and normalises the text in the hope that she will 'rekindle for [Behn] a proper appreciation of her place in the history of English fiction'.[45] Duffy's is the first edition since 1696 to include the dedication to Maitland before the novel, noting the stop-press variant, but she does not indicate what source provides the text.[46] Her own copy-text is acknowledged to be the 1718, sixth edition of *All the Histories and Novels*. The Meridian editors follow in the same feminist spirit as Duffy by placing Behn at the head

45   Maureen Duffy, ed., *Oroonoko and Other Stories* (London: Methuen, 1986), p. 22.
46   Summers includes the letter as a late addition in his appendix to the volume (*Works of Aphra Behn*, ed. Summers, V, p. 524).

of what they want to label 'The Age of the Emerging Woman Writer' (p. xiii). Rogers and McCarthy note that they use Summers' 1915 collected *Works* as their copy-text, but they modernise and Americanise spelling and punctuation. The Meridian version includes the rare error of 'the loves of the Romans' (p. 51), which suggests that there may be other substantive or accidental errors not introduced by Summers. Both versions of *Oroonoko* from the 1980s evince an attitude toward greater editorial responsibility, but because of mistakes and the unreliability of the sources, these editions continue the circulation of corrupt texts.

One additional text from that decade, Adelaide P. Amore's 1987 *Oroonoko, or, The Royal Slave: A Critical Edition*, needs mention due to the misleading nature of its title and its widespread availability in university libraries. O'Donnell's responsible review of this edition in *Eighteenth-Century Fiction* makes clear that this seriously flawed text should be avoided by scholars and students alike.[47]

Contemporary Editions based on the 1688 Original

The 1990s heralded a new age for *Oroonoko* editions based on the textually authoritative source from 1688. Significantly, most of these texts benefit from the scholarship of Duchovnay and O'Donnell, indicating the importance of bibliographic work for editing, whether the editions are intended for the serious scholar or the undergraduate reader. The versions by Todd in 1992 and 1995, Salzman in 1994, and Lipking in 1993 and 1997 all begin with the original 1688 text, and although each emends, edits and annotates in different ways, each provides a reasonably accurate account of these editing choices.

Todd's 1992 collection from Penguin, entitled *Oroonoko, The Rover and Other Works* (O'Donnell 1992a) (reprinted with corrections and a new chronology in 2003), contains a cautiously modernised version of the story. Joanna Lipking edited the next important *Oroonoko* edition for Norton in 1993, producing the modernised version that has been adopted in all the anthologies as well as the trade paperback. This text ultimately replaced the flawed trade version first introduced by Lore Metzger. As indicated by footnote, Lipking uses the 1688 edition as her source and consults Duchovnay's thesis.[48]

47 O'Donnell, 'Review'.
48 *Norton Anthology*, p. 1866.

Although also based on the original, Todd's version of *Oroonoko* included in the Pickering and Chatto collection of *The Works of Aphra Behn* has been re-edited for scholarly purposes (O'Donnell 1995a). Generally hailed as an important landmark in Behn studies, this collection met with mixed reviews.[49] Notably, it received an excessively harsh evaluation on textual criticism from Alexander Pettit, who claims 'only arguably does the edition supersede Montague Summer's six-volume edition of 1915'.[50] With respect to *Oroonoko*, Todd's text clearly replaces Summers' corrupt version. Based on the Bodleian copy of the 1688 *Three Histories*, Todd's text includes the dedication to Maitland with the stop-press variant, and like the 1992 Penguin, includes references to later emendations in the endnotes. The list of her own emendations on page 468 includes only eight references to *Oroonoko*, suggesting a very light hand for the scholarly edition. This text was adopted by Bedford in its Cultural Editions volume of *Oroonoko*, edited by Catherine Gallagher and Simon Stern.

As a mark of the growing interest in Behn by 1994, Salzman writes confidently of her status in literary history. His collection, entitled *Oroonoko and Other Writings* (O'Donnell 1994a), published by Oxford University Press, includes six works of prose fiction and thirty poems. His statement of copy-text is explicit: for *Oroonoko* 'the text is taken from the first edition of 1688 (O'Donnell, A31.1a), checked against a copy of the *Three Histories* (1688), (O'Donnell, 32), in which *Oroonoko* was reissued' (p. 269). Like Todd's 1992 Penguin edition, this volume is adapted for the general reader.

The edition of *Oroonoko* included in Blackwell's *British Literature 1640–1789* (O'Donnell 1996) is likewise based on the first edition of 1688. Robert DeMaria Jr. cites Todd's *Works of Aphra Behn* as a source for his annotation, but he newly edits the text. Based on the chart of variants, the editing appears to be principally concerned with expanding contractions (as in 'cou'd', 'charm'd', ''em') and correcting obvious errors, such as 'Poet's' for 'Poets' in the opening

---

49   For examples, see *The Scriblerian* 28.1–2 (1995–6), 88–9; Ros Ballaster, 'Astrea, Who Puts All to Bed', *Times Literary Supplement* (6 December 1996), 18; Catherine Gallagher, 'The Networking Muse', *Times Literary Supplement* (10 September 1993), 3–4; Judith Hawley, 'The Candour of Aphra Behn', *Times Literary Supplement* (17 November 1995), 30; and Jessica Munns, *The Scriblerian* 29–30.2–1 (1997), 233–5.
50   Pettit, 'Aphra's Bane', *Seventeenth-Century News* 56 (1998), 1–5.

paragraph. The passage on the killing of the tiger retains and aug-
ments some of the original's confusion: 'he shot her just into the
Eye, and the Arrow was sent with so good a will, and so sure a hand,
that it stuck in her Brain, and made her caper, and become mad for
a moment or two; but being seconded by another Arrow, he fell dead
upon the Prey. *Cæsar* cut him open with a Knife, to see where those
Wounds were that had been reported to him, and why she did not
Die of them'.[51] After the first instance of the masculine pronoun
here, DeMaria notes 'the referent is unclear to me'. DeMaria silently
emends the passage by changing the final pronoun in reference to
the tiger to 'she' when in the original the tiger remains masculine
after he is killed. DeMaria's version of *Oroonoko* thus compromises
between reproduction of the original and silent emendation for the
modern reader.

In the 1997 Norton Critical Edition of *Oroonoko* (O'Donnell
1997a), Lipking returns to the text and edits it anew. She describes
her editorial decisions: 'To provide a readable classroom text, spellings and punctuation that are distracting or confusing have been
emended, in most cases following the small corrections (but not the
guesswork) of the second and third editions', by which she means
the 1696 edition of *The Histories and Novels* and the 1698 edition of
All the Histories and Novels. At 126 the number of her emendations
is far more extensive than Todd's eight. Any significant emendations
are noted with reference to later editions, and these suggest that
Lipking favours greater intervention for the sake of readability. As
a classroom text, this edition differs considerably from the others
in that it only includes Behn's one novella, and it offers substantial
outside historical and critical matter. In this respect, it compares
best with the Bedford Cultural Edition, which uses Todd's 1995
text.

The 1999 *Longman Anthology of British Literature*, edited by David
Damrosch, includes a full-text version of *Oroonoko* based on the original 1688 but clearly influenced by the editing of Todd and Lipking,
whose works he lists in the bibliography.[52] This modernised text closely follows Lipking's 1993 version in substantive changes, although the
chart of variants reveals similarities with Todd's 1992 emendations as

---

51   Robert DeMaria, ed., *British Literature 1640–1789: An Anthology* (Oxford:
Blackwell, 1996), p. 448.
52   I thank Lawrence Lipking for drawing my attention to this work.

well. The annotations similarly reflect the work of Todd (1993, 1995) and Lipking (1997). Thus while the editorial work appears derivative, it is reliable.

Despite the apparent ease with which *Oroonoko* editions issue forth from the press, it is not an easy text to edit. Having been first published in the final year of Aphra Behn's life, when she was reportedly in desperate need of money and suffering from crippling disease, *Oroonoko* was hardly confident in its textual debut. In her letter to Maitland she claims to have written the story in a matter of hours, which is more believable when we recall what Gildon mentions in his dedication, that it was a story she frequently told in conversation.[53] Furthermore, there are no existing drafts or corrected settings of *Oroonoko* in Behn's hand, and so like scholars of many Renaissance writers, the editor of *Oroonoko* has to rely on the first published version as the default authoritative text. Given the state of London publishing in the 1680s and 1690s, with Jacobite booksellers like William Canning hampered by the threat of censorship as well as the relatively common, practical need for piecing out the labour of typesetting, the original publication of *Oroonoko* is unsurprisingly riddled with problems, as later editors were quick to realise. These conditions prepare the way for the long history of textual intervention detailed above.

This research establishes for the first time a provisional genealogy of *Oroonoko* texts, a history that is particularly important because prior to the 1990s source attributions in editions of *Oroonoko* are rare and frequently erroneous. While some mysteries have been solved by establishing the genealogy of texts, others have emerged. Chief among these is the role of Charles Gildon in altering Behn's texts. How far does the influence of this Grub-street hack extend in *All the Histories and Novels of the Late Ingenious Mrs. Behn*? A fuller analysis of Elizabeth Griffith's late eighteenth-century revisions of *Oroonoko* is due, as is some understanding of how these changes affected Victorian readers. More light might be shed on the relationships between the late nineteenth- and early twentieth-century editors: Pearson, the editor for Temple, Baker, and their successors, Summers, Henderson, Moore and the Turners. Greater knowledge of Henderson's task in the Everyman's series might clarify the production of such a flawed text.

53   Janet Todd, *The Secret Life of Aphra Behn* (London: Pandora Press, 1996, 2000), p. 417.

The generation of errors from these early editions at some point ought to be accounted for, at least in current scholarship that uses criticism based on these editions.

Gender is a central element to factor into this history. In response to the scholarly interest in early women writers, publishers have produced new editions, perhaps more quickly than care calls for. As the history of *Oroonoko* texts makes clear, the push to make available classroom editions of 'recovered' writers is neither intellectually nor ideologically neutral. On the one hand, *Oroonoko*'s history raises awareness of the imperatives of solid textual editing, but on the other it raises questions about the social, political and economic factors that shape the editing process. Because we are finally gaining widespread access to literature by women, we have reached a point in the recovery of women authors where feminist critics can afford to assess and become critical of the textual status of editions, and much work remains to be done.

Appendix: A Timeline of Editions of Oroonoko (1688–2010)

(Place of publication is London unless indicated otherwise.)

1688   *Oroonoko; Or, the Royal Slave* (O'Donnell A31.1a)

1688   *Three Histories* (O'Donnell A32)

1696   *The Histories and Novels of the late Ingenious Mrs. Behn* (O'Donnell A40.1a)

1696   *The Histories and Novels*, 2nd edition (?) (O'Donnell A40.1b)

1698   *All the Histories and Novels by the Late Ingenious Mrs. Behn*, 3rd edition (O'Donnell A40.3a)

1699/1700   *All the Histories*, 4th edition (O'Donnell A40.4a-b)

1705   *All the Histories*, 5th edition (O'Donnell A40.1705)

1718   *All the Histories*, 6th edition (O'Donnell A40.1718a)

1722   *All the Histories*, 7th edition (O'Donnell A40.1722)

1735   *All the Histories*, 8th edition (O'Donnell A40.1735)

1751   *All the Histories*, 9th edition (O'Donnell A40.1751)

1753   *Oroonoko*. Serialized in *The Ladies Magazine*, vol. 4, numbers 9–23, April 14–November 10, 1753. (O'Donnell A31.1753)

1770 (1759?)   *The History of Oroonoko*, from the ninth edition (O'Donnell A31.1759)

1777   *A Collection of Novels Selected and Revised by Mrs. Griffith*, ed. Elizabeth Griffith (O'Donnell A31.1777)

1791   *Royal Novels: Or, A New Collection of Entertaining Histories and Tragical Stories*. Dublin

1800   *English Nights Entertainment. The History of Oroonoko*, ed. Elizabeth Griffith (O'Donnell A31.1800)

1871   *The Plays Histories, and Novels of the Ingenious Mrs. Aphra Behn*, 6 vols., John Pearson (O'Donnell A31.1871)

1886   *Oroonoko; or, The History of the Royal Slave*, Temple Company (O'Donnell A31.1886)

1905   *The Novels of Mrs. Aphra Behn*, ed. Ernest Baker, Routledge (O'Donnell A31.1905)

1913   reprint of Baker 1905

1915   *Works of Aphra Behn*, 5 vols., ed. Montague Summers, Heinemann (O'Donnell A31.1915a)

1930   *Shorter Novels: Jacobean and Restoration*, ed. Philip Henderson, Dent (O'Donnell A31.1930a)

1930   *Malory to Mrs. Behn*, ed. Albert and Percie Turner, New York: Nelson (O'Donnell A31.1930b)

1934   *Restoration Literature: Poetry and Prose 1660–1700*, ed. Cecil A. Moore, New York: Appelton-Century Crofts (not listed in O'Donnell)

1949   reprint Henderson (O'Donnell A31.1930a)

1953   *Two Tales: The Royal Slave and The Fair Jilt*, Folio Society (O'Donnell A31.1953)

1967   reprint Summers 1915a; also issued in: *Oroonoko & Other Prose Narratives by Aphra Behn*, ed. Montague Summers, New York: Benjamin Blom, 1967

1969   reprint Baker 1905

1971   'Aphra Behn's *Oroonoko*: A Critical Edition', ed. Gerald Duchovnay, Ph.D. Dissertation, Bloomington: Indiana University (O'Donnell A31.1971)

1973   *Oroonoko; Or, the Royal Slave*, introd. by Lore Metzger, New York: Norton (O'Donnell A31.1973)

1977   *Aphra Behn's Oroonoko or The History of Royal Slave*, ed. K. A. Sey, Tema: Ghana Publishing (O'Donnell A31.1977)

1986   *Oroonoko and Other Stories*, ed. Maureen Duffy, Methuen (O'Donnell A31.1986)

1987   *Oroonoko, or, The Royal Slave: A Critical Edition*, ed. Adelaide Amore, Lanham, Maryland: University Press of America (O'Donnell A31.1987a)

1987   *The Meridian Anthology of Early Women Writers*, ed. Katherine Rogers and William McCarthy, New York: Meridian

(O'Donnell A31.1987b)

1992   *Oroonoko, The Rover and Other Works*, ed. Janet Todd, Harmondsworth: Penguin (O'Donnell A31.1992a)

1993   *Norton Anthology of English Literature*, 6th edition, volume 1C, New York: Norton; text edited and modernized by Joanna Lipking.

1994   *Oroonoko and Other Writings*, ed. Paul Salzman, Oxford: Oxford University Press (O'Donnell A31.1994)

1995   *The Works of Aphra Behn*, vol. 3, *The Fair Jilt and Other Stories*, ed. Janet Todd, Pickering and Chatto (O'Donnell A31.1995a)

1996   *British Literature 1640–1789: An Anthology*, ed. Robert DeMaria, Oxford: Blackwell (O'Donnell A31.1996)

1996   *Norton Anthology of Literature by Women*, New York: Norton (2nd edition) (O'Donnell A31.1994b)

1997   *Oroonoko: An Authoritative Text, Historical Backgrounds, Criticism*, ed. Joanna Lipking, New York: Norton (O'Donnell A31.1997a)

1997   reprint of Norton (O'Donnell A31.1973)

1999   *Oroonoko and Other Stores*, ed. Michael Hulse, Cologne: Könemann (O'Donnell A31.1999)

1999   *Longman Anthology of British Literature*, vol. 1, ed. David Damrosch, New York: Longman (second edition 2003) (O'Donnell A31.1999a)

2000   *Oroonoko; or the Royal Slave*, ed. Catherine Gallagher and Simon Stern, Boston: Bedford/St. Martin's (O'Donnell A31.2000a)

2000   *Norton Anthology of English Literature*, 7th edition, part 1C Restoration and Eighteenth Century, New York: Norton; text edited and modernized by Joanna Lipking

2000   *Oroonoko; or the Royal Slave*, ed. Joanna Lipking, New York: Norton (O'Donnell A31.2000c) based on Lipking 1997

2006   *The Broadview Anthology of British Literature: Volume 3: The Restoration and the Eighteenth Century*, ed. Joseph Black et al. Peterborough, ON: Broadview, 2006.

2007   *Versions of Blackness: Key Texts on Slavery from the Seventeenth Century*, ed. Derek Hughes, Cambridge: Cambridge University Press, 2007

2008   *Oroonoko: or The Royal Slave*, Evergreen Review. Kindle edition.

2008   *Oroonoko*, ReadHowYouWant. (Unknown file format distributed by iTunes.)

2008   *Oroonoko, or The Royal Slave*, Babblebooks. Podcast

2009   *Oroonoko, or The Royal Slave by Aphra Behn*, LibriVox, 26 August. Podcast

2009   *Oroonoko*. The Floating Press. (Unknown file format distributed by iTunes.)

2009   *Oroonoko, or The Royal Slave*, MobileReference. Kindle edition

2009   *Oroonoko: or, The Royal Slave*, Buki. Kindle edition

2009   *Oroonoko: or, the Royal Slave*, SunScroll. Publish This LLC. Phone app

2010   *Oroonoko*. No publisher. Kindle edition.

2010   *The Works of Aphra Behn*, *Mobi Collected Works*, MobileReference. Phone app

The Pilgrim's Progress, *Print Culture* and the Dissenting Tradition

NATHALIE COLLÉ-BAK

IN *The what-d'ye-call-it: a tragi-comi-pastoral farce* (1715), English poet and dramatist John Gay satirised the popularity of John Bunyan's *Pilgrim's Progress* (Part 1, 1678; Part 2, 1684) in a scene where a condemned sinner is offered a prayer book and urged to make use of it:

> COUNTRYMAN: ————————————Repent thine ill,
> And Pray in this good Book. —— 		[*Gives him a Book.*
> PEASCOD: ————————————I will! I will!
> Lend me thy Handkercher—— *The Pilgrim's Pro*—
> 						[*Reads and weeps.*
> (I cannot see for Tears) *Pro—Progress—*Oh!
> *—The Pilgrim's Progress—Eighth---Edi—ti—on,*
> *Lon--don--Print--ed--for--Ni--cho--las Bod--ding--ton:*
> *With new Ad--di--tions never made be-fore,*
> –Oh! 'tis so moving, I can read no more. 	[*Drops the Book.*[1]

While Bunyan's allegory of the Christian life on earth was immediately successful, his reputation as a Nonconformist writer of lowly origin held him in disrepute among the literati of his time. Besides Bunyan's varied reception, Gay's humorous, if not inaccurate, account reflects many facets of the late seventeenth- and early eighteenth-century

---

1   John Gay, *The what-d'ye-call-it: a tragi-comi-pastoral farce* (London: Henry Lintot, 1715), II, 1, pp. 24–33, cited in Roger Sharrock, ed., *Bunyan, 'The Pilgrim's Progress': A Casebook* (London: Macmillan, 1976), p. 49. Gay was not a very accurate bibliographer, as the name of Nicholas Boddington actually appeared for the first time on the imprint of the thirteenth edition of *The Pilgrim's Progress*, 'with additions, and the cuts, printed for Robert Ponder, and are to be sold by Nich. Boddington, at the Golden Ball, in Duck-lane, 1693'. The sixteenth edition, 'with additions of new cuts', was in fact the first edition of Part 1 to have been 'Printed for N. Boddington, at the Golden Ball in Duck-Lane', in 1707.

book trade on the whole, and some of the factors by which a work then became and remained a best-seller. Published in the material form of a book, having gone through several editions, printed for a publisher who was also its editor, and advertised as having been newly expanded, *The Pilgrim's Progress* had, by the early eighteenth century already, passed through the hands of a number of publishers, printers and readers. It had already lived an eventful life on the London book market and in the homes of many. As a matter of fact, Bunyan's work was so rapidly popular that, by the time he died in 1688, thirteen editions of the first part (including two non-concurrent impressions of the fifth and ninth)[2] and two editions of the second part had been published in London, alongside several provincial – and possibly pirated – editions, published notably in Edinburgh,[3] as well as a number of imitations.

What the dialogue from Gay's play does not tell us, however, is that, very quickly after it appeared on the book market, *The Pilgrim's Progress* consisted not only of Bunyan's text, but also of a frontispiece and a set of engraved images illustrating that text. Nathaniel Ponder was indeed not simply the first publisher of the work; he was also the initiator of a long and rich iconographic tradition which was to accompany that work through the centuries and throughout the world until today and as far as Canada, Africa or Asia.

I have traced elsewhere the history and development of the massive corpus of illustrations born of *The Pilgrim's Progress* in light of the contemporaneous book market and publishing as well as illustrating practices.[4] This corpus took the form of woodcuts and copper (and, oc-

---

2   More precisely, by 1688, the work had gone through eleven successive editions plus two concurrent editions, the fifth and the ninth having each been through two impressions (the fifth edition in 1680 and 1682, and the ninth edition in 1683 and 1684).

3   The fifth edition, 'with additions, Edinburgh, printed by Iohn [*sic*] Cairns, bookseller, and are to be sold at his chope [*sic*], [. . .] 1680', and the sixth edition, 'with additions, printed by John Reid, and are to be sold at his printing-house, in Bells-Wynd, 1683'. According to the notes to *The Pilgrim's Progress From This World to That Which Is to Come, by John Bunyan*, ed. James Blanton Wharey, rev. Roger Sharrock (1928; Oxford: Clarendon Press, 1960), p. 1, n. 1, the copy of the fifth edition printed by Cairns 'bears no resemblance to any copies of the genuine fifth'.

4   See especially, Nathalie Collé-Bak, 'La Destinée éditoriale et iconographique de *The Pilgrim's Progress* de John Bunyan, de 1678 à 1850: les enjeux d'une mise en images' (unpublished doctoral dissertation, Université Nancy 2, 2002).

casionally, steel) engravings in illustrated editions of all types and formats. It also occasionally took the form of drawings and prints that were originally conceived independently of any edition, as was the case with Thomas Stothard's (c.1788) and John Flaxman's drawings (c.1792), or William Blake's water-colours (c.1824). I have also traced the evolution and after-life of these illustrations into other pictorial forms (such as a gigantic moving panorama, church murals or stained-glass windows), three-dimensional forms of representation (wood sculptures, sculpted bronze door panels or church displays), as well as marketable by-products (card games, board games, postcards and greeting cards, or even mobile-phone cases).[5] My interest has been to show that all these 'illustrations', in the broad sense of the term, have not just been secondary components of Bunyan's work, but rather, agents of its production, circulation and reception worldwide, and of its long-lasting popularity.[6]

In this essay, I would like to outline the early stages in the iconographic tradition inspired by Bunyan's allegory and present its foundational elements, relating them to the historical and publishing contexts in which they were produced. Looking at the material embodiment of a seventeenth-century religious prose allegory – one that has survived the erosion of faith and continued to be published in multiple forms until today – will enlighten the relationship between literature and print culture in late seventeenth- and early eighteenth-century England, during the troubled time of religious Dissent. It will illustrate the interaction between a Puritan author, his first publisher and their reading public, and between a text and its immediate context of publication and reception. It will finally reveal the role of the early *Pilgrim's Progress* il-

5   Nathalie Collé-Bak, 'Bunyan's Pilgrims on Canvas, on Stage, in the Cellar, and in the Art Gallery: The History, Loss and Renaissance of the *Moving Panorama of Pilgrim's Progress*', *Bunyan Studies: John Bunyan and His Times* 15 (2012), 112–28; Nathalie Collé-Bak, 'Wayfaring Images: *The Pilgrim's Progress* Pictorial Journey through Time', *The Oxford Handbook of John Bunyan*, ed. Michael Davies (forthcoming).
6   See, for instance, Nathalie Collé-Bak, 'The Role of Illustrations in the Reception of *The Pilgrim's Progress*', in *Reception, Appropriation, Recollection: Bunyan's 'Pilgrim's Progress'*, ed. W. R. Owens and Stuart Sim (Bern: Peter Lang, 2007), pp. 81–98, and Nathalie Collé-Bak, 'Spreading the Written Word through Images: The Circulation of *The Pilgrim's Progress* via its Illustrations', *Revue de la Société d'Études Anglo-Américaines des XVIIe et XVIIIe siècles* Hors Série no. 2 (2010), 223–46.

Fig. 1: The 'Sleeping Portrait', frontispiece, engraved by Robert White, from *The Pilgrim's Progress* (London: printed for Nath. Ponder at the Peacock in the Poultrey near Cornhil, 1678)

lustrations in promoting that text and, more generally, the function of printed images in the production and popularity of literary texts.

At the Threshold of the Text: Robert White's 'Sleeping Portrait' and Its Variants

Nathaniel Ponder from Rothwell (1640–99), a Nonconformist publisher, printer and bookseller whose name was associated particularly with the works of John Owen, Andrew Marvell and John Bunyan, entered *The Pilgrim's Progress* into the Stationers' Register on 22 December 1677. On 18 February 1678, Bunyan's work was licensed and entered in the Term Catalogue, and published that year 'at the Peacock in the Poultrey near Cornhil' in London. It was thereafter issued in an impressive number and a wide variety of editions, formats and bindings, and with as impressive a number and as wide a variety of illustrations. Among the various extant copies of the first edition is one known as the Palmer–Nash copy, which is unique in its kind in that it contains as a frontispiece the now famous portrait of the 'Dreamer', or 'Sleeping Portrait', engraved by English draftsman and engraver Robert White (1645–1704) (Fig. 1). This allegorical frontispiece, which represents the author–narrator dreaming his dream of the pilgrim,[7] was the very first *Pilgrim's Progress* image to have ever been bound and published with Bunyan's text.[8]

Certainly commissioned by Ponder, the Sleeping Portrait reappeared in most of his later editions of the work, albeit with intriguing variations.[9] It was also copied, imitated and re-interpreted in still later editions published by Ponder's successors, as well as in concurrent – at times pirated – editions by his fellow publishers (Figs. 2a and 2b). By themselves, and notwithstanding the illustrations which have been in-

---

7   As Anne Dunan-Page remarked in 'Portraits of Dreamers', in *Grace Overwhelming: John Bunyan, 'The Pilgrim's Progress' and the Extremes of the Baptist Mind* (Bern: Peter Lang, 2006), p. 140, 'White's Bunyan is not just a dreamer: he is a dreaming minister and a dreaming author'.

8   As recalled in Wharey's edition of *The Pilgrim's Progress*, p. xxxix, and as John Brown first contended in 'Editions, Versions, Illustrations, and Imitations of *The Pilgrim's Progress*', *John Bunyan (1628–1688): His Life, Times, and Work*, rev. edn ed. F. M. Harrison (1885; London: Hulbert Publishing Company, 1928), p. 440, it 'may, however, have been added when the book was rebound'.

9   For details on these, see Brown, 'Editions, Versions, Illustrations', and *The Pilgrim's Progress*, ed. Wharey, pp. v–ciii.

Fig. 2a (above left): The 'Sleeping Portrait', frontispiece from *The Pilgrim's Progress*, 14th edition (London: printed for W. P. and are to be sold by Nat. Ponder in London-House-yard, 1695)

Fig. 2b (above right): The 'Sleeping Portrait', frontispiece from *The Pilgrim's Progress*, 19th edition (London: printed for M. Boddington, at the Golden-Ball in Duck Lane, 1718)

corporated into Bunyan's text ever since, the various Sleeping Portraits produced over time give us precious information about the handling and production of that text, and about its popular and critical reception.

First, the fact that the original version of the portrait appeared in only one copy of the first edition but did not figure in any copy of the second edition (which was also published by Ponder, also in 1678, and also printed at the Peacock), and then reappeared in some copies of the third (1679) and subsequent editions, notably the fifth (1682), with noticeable alterations, suggests that it was temporarily withdrawn or

Fig. 3a (above left): The 'Sleeping Portrait', frontispiece from *The Pilgrim's Progress*, 3rd edition (London: Nathaniel Ponder, 1679)

Fig. 3b (above right): The 'Sleeping Portrait', frontispiece from *The Pilgrim's Progress*, 30th edition (London: printed and sold by all the booksellers, 1758)

lost (Figs. 3a and 3b).[10] This is evidence of editorial intervention, or reader practices, or both: Bunyan's early publishers took the initiative to supply, modify and withdraw the Sleeping Portrait, while some of his readers (or perhaps simply print collectors) took the freedom to remove it from the volumes that passed into their hands. Whatever the explanation to these variations, concrete, physical interaction between a text and its producers and readers is evinced.

Second, the fact that the allegorical portrait of the Dreamer was largely preferred to portraits of the author in early editions of *The*

10   See Brown, 'Editions, Versions, Illustrations', and *The Pilgrim's Progress*, ed. Wharey.

Pilgrim's Progress seems to indicate that readers were interested more in the story of Christian's pilgrimage than in the literary status of its creator or, at least, that Bunyan's publishers were more eager to promote the work via its narrative framework and allegorical contents than via the figure of the tinker-cum-writer. This preference also implies that, as an entry into a text of this kind, an allegorical frontispiece representing key aspects of the story – including the figure of the narrator in the traits of Bunyan dreaming his dream of the pilgrim – was more appealing than a more conventional portrait of its author.

Finally, the fact that the Sleeping Portrait was repeatedly copied or imitated, and simplified in cheap editions and in chapbook versions of the work, attests to its capacity to inspire engravers working with all sorts of publishers and for all types of reading publics. The original version by White was modulated according to the engravers who produced the variants, the publishers who commissioned them, and the readers for whom they were intended. Here, as with any other text, the nature of the publishing venture naturally conditioned the features of the image.

The question of the origin and history of White's allegorical frontispiece has never been fully settled, simply due to the lack of material evidence regarding its initial composition and erratic alteration. This question is of critical importance, however, in that the creation and transformation of the portrait inform us about the concerns and practices of late seventeenth- and early eighteenth-century London engravers, printers and publishers, and consequently about the functioning of the book trade. The fate of the portrait also testifies to prevailing reading tastes and habits of the time. In addition, it attests to the mutability, if not of Bunyan's text (which was pretty much fixed by the third edition[11]), at least of the paratext with which it has been packaged, circulated and read. It therefore proves the importance of paratextual elements in producing a work, promoting it, and sustaining its popularity. For many readers, the Sleeping Portrait in its various forms has become emblematic of Bunyan's allegory.

White's allegorical portrait has been approached mainly from two angles: one bibliographical, notably by James Blanton Wharey in his introduction to the 1928 Clarendon Press edition of *The Pilgrim's*

---

11   As noted in Wharey's edition of *The Pilgrim's Progress*, p. xlvi, '[t]he third edition enjoys the distinction of being virtually the first complete edition of *The Pilgrim's Progress*. [. . .] After the third edition the additions consist of a few phrases inserted in text, and marginal notes, and scripture references'.

Progress,[12] and the other biographical and theological by Anne Dunan-Page.[13] Its iconographic contents have only been dealt with in passing, though, through occasional comments originating from analyses of the text or its contexts of production rather than from close examination of the picture itself and of its variants. Sharon Achinstein, for instance, has commented on the frontispiece to the second part of *The Pilgrim's Progress*, engraved by John Sturt and published in 1684 with the very first edition, in the course of an analysis of the evolution of the public and private spheres of action of Dissenters through and beyond the Puritan Revolution (Fig. 4). In her account she notes that

> [t]he Puritan Revolution may have been most successful in trans-forming the home. Especially when their public roles were denied them, Dissenters created their resistance within the space of the family. The meaning of 'public' and 'private', indeed, underwent change during a time when non-conformist 'public' worship was outlawed; the domestic spaces of the family home took up the roles previously performed by the church. Bunyan emphasizes the family as a little religious community in diaspora in the second part of his *Pilgrim's Progress*, where Christiana travels with her children toward the Celestial City (see Figure 11).[14]

As in most Bunyan criticism, the engraving she cites – '(see Figure 11)' – is used literally as an illustration of aspects of the text, rather than as a significant mode of expression in itself. In her survey of *Literature and Dissent in Milton's England*, Achinstein examines the Dissenting tradition via certain literary works, focusing particularly on Milton, Bunyan, Richard Baxter, Mary Mollineux, John Dryden, Andrew Marvell, Elizabeth Singer Rowe and Isaac Watts, but also on lesser-known writers. She argues for the existence of a literary tradition of Dissent and shows how a distinctive Dissenting cultural legacy took shape in Restoration England. Yet her study gives more weight to literary texts than to the illustrations they have inspired.

---

12 *The Pilgrim's Progress*, ed. Wharey.
13 Dunan-Page, 'Portraits of Dreamers', and A. Dunan-Page, ' "The Portraiture of John Bunyan" Revisited: Robert White and Images of the Author', *Bunyan Studies: John Bunyan and His Times* 13 (2008–9), 7–39.
14 Sharon Achinstein, *Literature and Dissent in Milton's England* (Cambridge: Cambridge University Press, 2003), p. 223.

Fig. 4: The 'Sleeping Portrait' frontispiece, engraved by John Sturt, from *The Pilgrim's Progress, Part 2* (London: printed for Nathaniel Ponder at the Peacock in the Poultry, near the Church, 1684)

The iconic composition of the Dreamer, however, leaves little doubt as to its political content and intent. The representation of what Bunyan calls the 'Denn' (and which he glossed in the margin of the text from the third edition (1679) onward as 'the Goal'[15]), the presence of

15   John Bunyan, *The Pilgrim's Progress*, ed. W. R. Owens (Oxford: Oxford

the prison bars, and the dual symbolism of the lion (signifying strength and perseverance in times of trouble, as well as 'the civil and ecclesiastical persecution of Dissenters'[16] and the 'cruelties of persecution'[17]) all evoke freedom and detention, and the intermittent persecution of Nonconformists under the Clarendon Code. The foreground of the engraving therefore suggests the troubled historical context of the writing and publishing of the text plus the device of the dream vision narrative, while the background represents the central motif of the dream – that of the pilgrimage.

Sturt's reworking of the Sleeping Portrait for the first edition of the second part of the pilgrimage keeps the figure of the dreamer in the foreground but leaves out the den, the prison bars and the lion. Perhaps Sturt's intention was to indicate that the second part had been written and published by a free man rather than by an imprisoned Dissenter. Yet such a reworking of the original design seems to disregard the political context of those years, and notably the fact that the persecution of Dissenters had intensified in the early 1680s, up until the Declaration of Indulgence in 1687. The contents of the dream, more so than its context of production, were put to the fore by the designer of the second frontispiece of the work.

It should be kept in mind that *The Pilgrim's Progress* was mostly a prison book, written in the course of Bunyan's twelve-year imprisonment (and possibly finished in the course of his second, shorter one of six months) for unauthorised preaching and refusal to conform to the Act of Uniformity. Arrested in November 1660, Bunyan turned from forms of oral address to the pen. As N. H. Keeble writes, '[i]ncarceration provided him with additional incentives to write'. For Bunyan, 'separated from his people by prison, writing was the one way he could continue his ministry. "*Taken from you in presence*" and unable in person to "*perform that duty that from God doth lie upon me, to you-ward*", through print he could yet address his congregation and the wider community'.[18] Very quickly for Bunyan's congregation, as well as for the wider community,

University Press, 2003), p. 293.

16   Ibid., p. 297.

17   N. H. Keeble, 'John Bunyan's Literary Life', *The Cambridge Companion to Bunyan*, ed. Anne Dunan-Page (Cambridge: Cambridge University Press, 2010), p. 22.

18   Ibid., p. 22, with quotations from Bunyan's *Grace Abounding to the Chief of Sinners*, ed. Roger Sharrock (Oxford: Clarendon Press, 1962), p. 1.

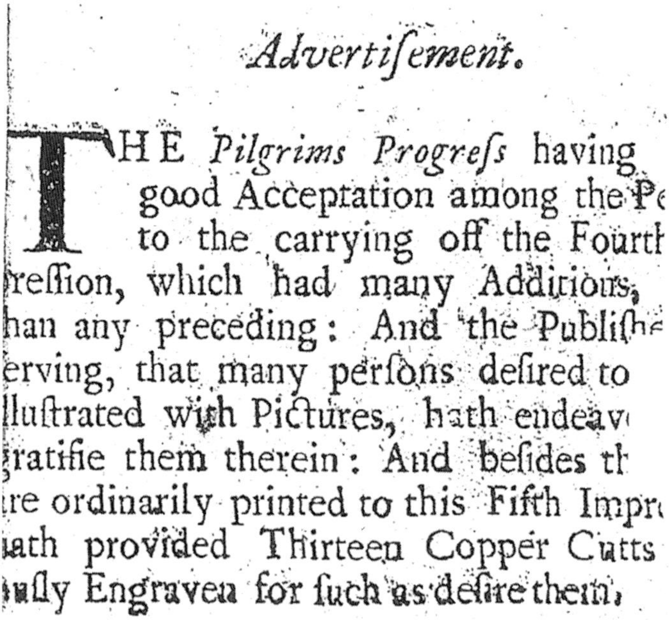

Advertifement.

THE *Pilgrims Progrefs* having
good Acceptation among the Pe
to the carrying off the Fourth
preffion, which had many Additions,
han any preceding : And the Publishe
erving, that many perfons defired to
lluftrated with Pictures, hath endeavo
gratifie them therein : And befides th
re ordinarily printed to this Fifth Impre
hath provided Thirteen Copper Cutts
iufly Engraven for fuch as defire them,

Fig. 5: Advertisement for the fifth edition of *The Pilgrim's Progress* (London:
printed for Nath. Ponder, at the Peacock in the Poultrey near the Church, 1680)

The Pilgrim's Progress consisted in the printed text of its author as well as
the printed images of its early illustrators.

Images on Their Way into the Book

After the introduction of the Sleeping Portrait, the next notable
stage in the development of the corpus of illustrations for *The Pilgrim's
Progress* is to be found in the fifth edition, published in 1680.[19] Along
with the frontispiece, this edition contained an advertisement which
announced the existence of a set of thirteen copper engravings. These
were available for an extra shilling for those readers who wanted to

19   There was another 'fifth' edition, 'printed for Nath. Ponder, at the Peacock
in the Poultrey near the Church', and published in 1682.

purchase them. They were first sold separately from and additionally to the text, and only gradually inserted in and sold with that text, from the fifth (1680) to the eleventh (1688) editions. The gradual and erratic appearance of this original set of illustrations in the regular editions of the work is quite disconcerting. Some copies of the same edition contain different illustrations, or a different number of illustrations, based on the original set of copper engravings announced in the advertisement by Ponder. The original images, first produced on copper, were indeed reproduced on wood in order to be printed with the text in the early illustrated editions.

In the advertisement Ponder claimed that, in providing such 'pictures', he had endeavoured to please the public's 'desire' for them (Fig. 5).[20] Ponder never specified the motivations that lay behind such a desire for illustrations, nor the type of public he had in mind, but his advertisement is significant evidence of the early reception and popularity of the work. It also testifies to the readers' taste for pictures, and to the place of iconographic print culture in the field of literary production. Bunyan's story pleased its readers, but it pleased them even more with pictures, at least if Ponder is to be trusted; he might also have been concerned with capitalising on his investment and making the most of the popularity of the text by republishing it in new forms and with new, attractive features such as illustrations. In any case, the rapid succession and long-lasting popularity of the illustrated editions of the work from the end of the seventeenth century onward have justified his claim.

The fact that Ponder took the initiative to provide the first frontispieces, as well as the first set of illustrations for *The Pilgrim's Progress*, is worthy of note. The fact that he should have commissioned renowned engravers for the frontispieces of Parts 1 and 2, but provided anonymous engravings for the text, is somewhat intriguing. Yet his was a time when the production of illustrated books was financially risky, and when book illustration was not yet considered a distinct form. Ponder might simply have been careful to limit the cost of the venture, satisfying his reading public with, first, an allegorical frontispiece, and second, a full set of illustrations – one which he only reproduced in its entirety once he had been assured of the success of the enterprise, after having tested the readers' appetite for Bunyan's text and its related images.

---

20   John Bunyan, *The Pilgrim's Progress*, the fifth edition with additions (London: Printed for Nath. Ponder, at the Peacock in the Poultrey near the Church, 1680).

ave *Faithful*, Bravely done in word and deed :
dge, Witnesses, and Jury, have insteed
overcoming thee, but shewn their rage,
nen they are dead, thou'lt live, from age to age.

G

him)

Fig. 6: Illustration of the martyrdom of Faithful at Vanity Fair from the eighth edition of *The Pilgrim's Progress* (London: printed for Nathanael Ponder at the Peacock in the Poultrey, near the Church, 1682)

Also important with respect to the history of *The Pilgrim's Progress* images is the fact that the very first illustration bound in a regular edition of the work was one representing the burning of Faithful at Vanity Fair (Fig. 6). The martyrological tradition inherited from John Foxe's heavily illustrated *Actes and Monuments*, or *Book of Martyrs* – which was first published in 1563 and re-published three times during the author's lifetime (in 1570, 1576 and 1583) – surely found its way into the iconographic tradition taking shape with *The Pilgrim's Progress*. With the illustration of Faithful's tormented death, heroic Protestant martyrdom was thus the first subject submitted to the eyes, minds and memories of Bunyan's readers, after that of the Christian pilgrimage on earth in the early frontispieces. This is perhaps because, '[t]o those inside Dissent', as Achinstein observes, 'their story was one of heroic martyrdom, social suffering, and patience, relieved by divine providence in the Glorious Revolution of 1688'.[21] As she recalls,

> [t]he generation of 1662, those ejected from their posts by the edict of Uniformity, were written about, pictured in frontispiece portraits, had their works reprinted in pirated and official editions, and their sayings excerpted to be hung on household walls for inspiration. The political stakes of the Dissenting martyrologies proliferating in the press were clear.[22]

Bunyan's allegory was obviously not a martyrology, but the fact that the first illustration to have appeared in the text was one representing a scene of martyrdom is not insignificant. It attests to the vitality of the iconographic tradition inherited from Foxe, but also to the symbolic bond between Foxe and Bunyan, as well as to the political agenda of Ponder. As John N. King rightly notes, Bunyan, like William Prynne, 'pored over the expanded three-volume version of *The Book of Martyrs* during his imprisonment for nonconformity'.[23] Unlike Foxe, however, who 'demonstrates his involvement in the process of illustration by commenting within the text on the function of the portrayal of the burning of Rose Allin's hand',[24] Bunyan never left any evidence of

---

21   Achinstein, *Literature and Dissent*, p. 18.
22   Ibid., p. 18.
23   John N. King, *Foxe's 'Book of Martyrs' and Early Modern Print Culture* (Cambridge: Cambridge University Press, 2006), p. 150.
24   Ibid., p. 167.

Behold here how the Slothful are a Sign
Hung up, cause holy ways they did decline.
See here too how the Child doth play the Man,
And weak grow strong, when *Great-Heart* leads the
(Van.

Figs. 7a and 7b (above and right): Illustrations of Christiana's pilgrimage from *The Pilgrim's Progress, the Second Part* (London: printed for Nathaniel Ponder at the Peacock in the Poultry, near the Church, 1684)

Tho' *Doubting* Castle be demolished,
And the Giant *Despair* hath loſt his head
Sin can rebuild the Caſtle, mak't remain,
And make *Despair* the Giant live again.

Deſ

his participation in the illustrating of his allegory. While '[John] Day collaborated with Foxe in planning the illustrations for his massive ecclesiastical history',[25] it is uncertain whether Ponder and the illustrators he commissioned worked with Bunyan at all. As King remarks with respect to Foxe's time, 'printers, rather than authors, maintained control over illustration'.[26] This was still true in Bunyan's time, as evidenced by Ponder's advertisement to the fifth edition of The Pilgrim's Progress.

The Question of Authorial Involvement

Nothing is known of Bunyan's very first illustrator (or, perhaps, illustrators) in so far as the original set of plates commissioned by Ponder has remained anonymous – and no longer exists as such. Yet, since it was produced when Bunyan was still alive, the question of its origin should involve the author himself. Until new material evidence is uncovered, the question of Bunyan's involvement in the commissioning of the thirteen engravings provided by Ponder from the fifth London edition onward, as well as the two new engravings added to the first edition of Part 2, can only remain conjecture (Figs. 7a and 7b). Ponder had claimed in his advertisement to have endeavoured to satisfy the public's desire for pictures in providing illustrations for the work. No such advertisement, however, appeared in the first editions of Part 2, which were also published by Ponder. It seems that, four years later, illustrations had simply become part of Bunyan's text, or at least part of the publishing of that text.

It is not known whether Bunyan had a say in the illustrating of his allegory. The functioning of the book market in his time was such that authorial involvement in post-publication matters seems unlikely. It was the publisher (or 'undertaker', in Adrian Johns's terms[27]) who entered a book into the Register Book of Copies of the Stationers' Company, thus becoming its sole 'proprietor' or 'copy-owner'. However, Bunyan's later additions to the original text, his frequent business relationships with Ponder, as well as the religious sympathies of the two men, could lend support to the view that Ponder involved Bunyan in, if not the choice

---

25   Ibid., p. 167.
26   Ibid., p. 166.
27   Adrian Johns, The Nature of the Book: Print and Knowledge in the Making (Chicago: University of Chicago Press, 1998), p. xix.

of illustrator(s), if not even perhaps the selection of textual moments to be illustrated (and certainly not the number of illustrations to provide), then perhaps at least in what we could call the marginal gloss of these illustrations. Several distinguished Bunyan scholars have indeed found the spirit and style of the quatrains accompanying the early engravings in English editions of the work sufficiently Bunyanesque to claim that Bunyan was their author. In his analysis of John Flaxman's drawings for *The Pilgrim's Progress*, for instance, G. E. Bentley, Junior, reports that:

> Under each of the thirteen plates were four lines of yeomanlike verse, presumably by Bunyan, and these designs, or the verses they apparently illustrated, were the inspiration of many of the plates in succeeding editions. Indeed, in editions of 1688 and later which were illustrated with woodcuts set into the type-set text, the quatrains became, as it were, part of the text, and some editions lost the woodcuts but preserved the verses. Thus the early designs had a reciprocal effect on the text through the quotations, and doubtless some later artists illustrated the quatrains without knowing that they had been originally created to elucidate the first designs. These verses had a powerful effect upon controlling the designs to *Pilgrim's Progress*, for they seemed to give Bunyan's authority to the subjects. Most of the hundreds of later editions of *Pilgrim's Progress* were illustrated, and for a century many editions had some of their designs derived from this first illustrated edition of 1680.[28]

First of all, Bentley posits Bunyan's possible authorial responsibility in writing these lines – an argument taken up and expanded upon by Roger Pooley in the Spring 2000 issue of *The Recorder* (the official newsletter of the International John Bunyan Society), in which he raises the questions of authorial and editorial intention in writing and publishing the verses. These (as Bentley notes as well, and as scrutiny of the corpus of illustrated editions of the work reveals) had indeed appeared in several editions of *The Pilgrim's Progress* without the original engravings, and sometimes even as footnotes to the text or, still, as part of the metatext.[29]

---

28   G. E. Bentley, Junior, 'Flaxman's Drawings for *Pilgrim's Progress*', in *Woman in the Eighteenth Century and Other Essays*, ed. Paul Fritz and Richard Morton (Toronto: Samuel Stevens Hakkert & Co, 1976), p. 247.
29   According to Brown in 'Editions, Versions, Illustrations', p. 441, 'these

Secondly, Bentley raises the question of authorial creation: did Bunyan (or another writer) compose the quatrains from the text, deciding (or being told by Ponder) what textual moments to select for an illustrator, or did he (or anyone else) write them from existing images, thereby providing textual illustrations for iconographic ones?

A third question relates to the lasting influence of these early quatrains, not only on the development of the iconographic tradition they and their accompanying images had initiated, but also on the editing and publishing of Bunyan's text. Bentley goes as far as to claim that the verses 'controlled' the designs to *The Pilgrim's Progress* by '[giving] Bunyan's authority to the subjects', a point which seems to be confirmed by the perennial appeal of the early illustrated scenes, not only in the eyes of Bunyan's publishers and readers, but also in those of his literary critics. It is indeed quite remarkable that the textual moments most often dealt with by literary critics are also those that were initially and continually illustrated by Bunyan's iconographic interpreters.

Dissenting Images?

Another issue raised by these considerations is that of the Dissenting dimension of these early images and verses, both in the religious meaning of the term and in a more conceptual one. From a religious point of view, accepting the idea that Bunyan wrote the quatrains would certainly mean that he agreed – or at least did not *disagree* – with the iconographic treatment of his text presented in the early engravings, and thus with the interpretation of his view of the Christian life on earth offered by his illustrators. The very form and style of the verses accompanying the early engravings recall the various celebratory and commemorative songs punctuating the narratives of Parts 1 and 2.

Examining hymn writing and singing as they were generally practiced in seventeenth-century literature, Achinstein underlines their importance in Nonconformist poetics and worship. The hymn, she writes, 'was a vehicle for expressing links between divine and human action and for

lines [are] evidently from Bunyan's pen'. According to Roger Pooley in 'The earliest illustrations of *The Pilgrim's Progress*: Notes and Queries', *The Recorder* 6 (Spring 2000), [11]: 'The engravings were added in Bunyan's lifetime, indeed before he produced the Second Part. He must have known about them. Did he have any say in them? And, in particular, did he write the verses?'

justifying politics by providence'.[30] Pointing out 'the radical roots of this genre', she stresses 'the social function of the hymn for Dissenters across the early modern period'[31] and re-evaluates 'the purpose of hymn singing in a broader culture of persecution, its role in building community and securing religious commitment in forms of worship and expression'.[32] If taken one step further, Achinstein's argument that '[s]ong is an especially powerful artistic medium', and that '[t]he poetics of hymn may be taken not solely in theological terms, but in terms of a mode of labor and action',[33] would essentially validate the idea behind authorial intention. The pilgrim's songs, as well as in the captions for the original illustrations, may be seen as modes of authorial intervention, and further means on the part of Bunyan to reach and instruct his intended audience.

Combined with the maxim that pictures are worth a thousand words, these ideas acknowledge the impact of the early illustrations of *The Pilgrim's Progress* on Bunyan's original readers. Made of an engraved image followed by related verses reading literally like hymns (and functioning to some extent like emblems), these illustrations were no doubt forceful and eloquent for a Nonconformist audience used to employing hymns to perform 'acts of recitation, commemoration, and ritual'.[34] As Achinstein observes,

> [t]he Baptist John Bunyan in *Pilgrim's Progress* shows how hymn singing was a powerful mode of utterance, as his characters often make song to express faith in times of duress; to celebrate their deliverance; or to signify resistance to often painful physical force. Bunyan reacted to the rise of hymn singing in his own day, and between the publication of the first part of *Pilgrim's Progress* in 1678 and the second part, in 1684, seems to have accepted hymns as a distinct genre. [. . .] This transformation mirrors the acceptance of hymns among some Baptist worshipers. Bunyan advocated hymn singing in his Bedford Congregation, and he illustrates the singing of a hymn in the celebration of the downfall of the Giant Despair.[35]

30   Achinstein, *Literature and Dissent*, p. 210.
31   Ibid., p. 210.
32   Ibid., p. 211.
33   Ibid., p. 212.
34   Ibid., p. 212. 'Song and sound', Achinstein reminds us on p. 225, '[were both] vocal opportunities to express faith and move listeners to sympathy'.
35   Ibid., pp. 225–6.

More directly in line with the subject of illustration is the idea that '[t]he human labor involved in creating the hymn was always to be secondary to its relation to the divine, and to a social economy'. 'These relational qualities', Achinstein writes, 'make for a theory of originality, composition, authorship and aesthetic form that runs opposite to many modern assumptions about literary value and ownership'.[36] Strikingly, what the few scholars who have dealt with the early illustrations of *The Pilgrim's Progress* have noted about them is what they have termed their 'crudeness' or 'rudeness' – in other words, their lack of artistic merit and aesthetic value – as well as the repetitive and therefore 'dull' nature of their copies, imitations and variations in seventeenth-, eighteenth- and early nineteenth-century illustrated editions of the work.[37]

What they have failed to consider, however, is the reason behind such 'crudeness' and 'dullness'. In fact, the functioning of the book market at the time (when copying and borrowing was still common practice in the production of images), the astonishing success of *The Pilgrim's Progress* (which required reprints and new editions in quick succession), and the relatively low status of book illustration, as well as the political agenda of the early illustrations, all account for their anonymous, 'rude' and 'repetitive' nature. Their function was certainly deemed more important than their 'originality, composition, authorship and aesthetic form'. For, as Achinstein argues, '[b]y their writing and singing hymns, Dissenters performed acts of opposition to the official state church'. And 'on the aesthetic front, the hymn is involved in a counter-tradition of antiproprietary aesthetics, contributing to a stream in the current of English literature whose values were not those of originality or uniqueness, but of accessibility, commonality, and spontaneity'.[38]

In spite of the uncertain collaboration between Ponder and Bunyan in producing the early engraved images for *The Pilgrim's Progress* and their accompanying verses, we may claim that these illustrations, like hymns, were 'one means of the production and dissemination of Dissenting experience',[39] and that both 'rested upon a material base of

---

36   Ibid., p. 212.
37   See, in particular, F. M. Harrison, *Some Illustrators of 'The Pilgrim's Progress'* (Part one): John Bunyan (London: The Bibliographical Society, 1936).
38   Achinstein, *Literature and Dissent*, p. 213.
39   Ibid., p. 226.

book publishers, printers, and sellers who comprised an oppositional sphere of cultural activity'.[40]

As Achinstein observes, '[h]ymn collections often ran into several editions, revealing the lucrative side of the enterprise' – a comment that can certainly be applied to the illustrated editions of popular works like *The Pilgrim's Progress*.

'A marked feature of nonconformist writing', Isabel Rivers notes in her exploration of the relationship between religion and ethics in England from 1660 to 1780, 'is an interest in different classes of reader with gradations both social and spiritual, in the characteristics and needs of different members of the audience, in the different stages of Christian experience which require different kinds of instruction and different methods of awakening, exhortation, and encouragement'.[41] As productions reminiscent of the hymn and emblem traditions, and as channels through which Bunyan's allegory could be retold – and therefore doubly imprinted on his readers' minds – the illustrations of *The Pilgrim's Progress* contributed *with* the text to giving their viewers and readers a salutary sense of community in times of social and political exclusion and persecution.[42]

Conclusion

At the time of the writing and publishing of *The Pilgrim's Progress*, the printing press was still used as an agent of conversion and dissemination of ideas, and made the most of by Dissenting writers and publishers. Throughout the troubled times of the Civil War and the Restoration years, it was therefore a key mode not only of expression, but also of action. Considering that for most readers of the seventeenth, eighteenth and nineteenth centuries, *The Pilgrim's Progress* was both the text by Bunyan *and* the images it had inspired, the iconographic tradition born of Bunyan's allegory invites us to re-think the links between a

40   Ibid., p. 237.

41   Isabel Rivers, *Reason, Grace, and Sentiment: Whichcote to Wesley: A Study of the Language of Religion and Ethics in England 1660–1780*, 2 vols. (Cambridge: Cambridge University Press, 1991), I, pp. 117–18.

42   As Achinstein explains, 'Dissenters to be sure elicited sympathy by casting their experiences in a heroic light, relying upon known habits of interpreting suffering after the model of Christ. Their printing and disseminating such models was recognized as a primary mode of survival' (*Literature and Dissent*, p. 19).

text and its illustrations, or between literature and its iconographic representations.

It would be illusory to claim that the work of a Dissenting writer inspired similar-minded illustrators and produced illustrations which supported the views of its author and assisted him in his self-appointed evangelical mission. Moreover, lack of extant evidence regarding the identity and religious creeds of the early illustrators of the work does not allow us to draw definitive conclusions as to their intentions. Yet the effect of their creations on Bunyan's contemporary and later readers has certainly been underestimated.

A seventeenth-century religious allegory written by a Nonconformist preacher of humble origins, *The Pilgrim's Progress* continues to be published in many forms and interpreted in a wide variety of media – iconographic, but also theatrical and cinematographic. It has been adapted through time, via its illustrations, to various groups of readers and to multiple audiences around the globe.[43] It has travelled worldwide through translations, in particular in the nineteenth century in the hands of missionaries,[44] and has long been considered an established classic of English literature. Various eras, countries and cultures have adopted *The Pilgrim's Progress* as a religious treatise, an entertaining allegory, a tale of far-away, or a literary classic (or a combination of all these). The fact that they have also adopted and adapted the original illustrations to their target publics proves that the former were not mere adornments or embellishments. Rather, they played a significant part in the reception of both the text they accompanied and the book that circulated them jointly.

Whether Bunyan's illustrators expressed his Nonconformist views and ideals, or whether they expressed their own, or replicated previous illustrators' renderings of these views and ideals, they produced forms of expression that are worth examining, not just in themselves, but in their relationship to the text and the contexts from which they originated. As Richard Baxter once wrote, 'Preachers may be silenced or banished, when Books may be at hand'[45] – and even more so, perhaps, when those books are illustrated. To be sure, the rapid succession of

43   See Nathalie Collé-Bak, 'Spreading the Written Word'.
44   See Isabel Hofmeyr, *The Portable Bunyan: A Transnational History of* The Pilgrim's Progress (Princeton: Princeton University Press, 2004).
45   Richard Baxter, *The Practical Works*, 4 vols. (London: George Virtue, 1838), I, chapter 2, p. 57.

editions with 'new additions never made before' derided by Gay in his play tells us much more than simply the success story of a writer of lowly origin.

Printing for the Author in the Long Eighteenth Century

J. A. DOWNIE

NOT SO VERY LONG AGO, critics and historians were maintaining with increasing confidence that the system of patronage which had operated time out of mind was superseded in the later seventeenth century by a new relationship between author and publisher. It is likely that the publication in 1989 of the English translation of Jürgen Habermas's hugely influential *The Structural Transformation of the Public Sphere* (first published in German in 1962) contributed to this new-found confidence. Certainly, the awesome assurance with which Habermas articulated the thesis that a 'bourgeois public sphere' first emerged in Britain 'at the turn of the eighteenth century' can scarcely be overstated:

> The court aristocracy of the seventeenth century was not really a reading public. To be sure, it kept men of letters as it kept servants, but literary production based on patronage was more a matter of a kind of conspicuous consumption than of serious reading by an interested public. The latter arose only in the first decades of the eighteenth century, after the publisher replaced the patron as the author's commissioner and organized the commercial distribution of literary works.[1]

For a number of reasons, however, the notion that the system of patronage was superseded between 1680 and 1750 has fallen under increasingly intense scrutiny in recent years. Attention has been drawn to certain inadequacies in the thesis that the rise of the professional writer was

1 J. Habermas, *The Structural Transformation of the Public Sphere: An Inquiry into a Category of Bourgeois Society*, trans. T. Burger with the assistance of Frederick Lawrence (Cambridge: Polity Press, 1989), p. 38. Habermas tends to support his thesis about 'the model case of British development' by citing single, out-of-date secondary sources to support what must be regarded as huge generalisations, in this case Arnold Hauser's *The Social History of Art* (London: Routledge and Kegan Paul, 1951).

facilitated by the expiry of the Printing or Licensing Act in 1695 (13 & 14 Car 2, c. 33),[2] followed by the passing of the first 'Copyright' Act in 1709 (8 Anne, c. 8).[3] While it is true that, after 1695, writings were no longer subject to pre-printing censorship, it is important to stress that 'it is nonsense to suppose that England suddenly acquired a free press in anything like the sense in which the concept was understood in the liberal democracies of the nineteenth and twentieth centuries'.[4] Authors, printers and publishers were still liable to be prosecuted for their involvement in the production of seditious libel, and truth was no defence. Prosecutions for seditious libel continued intermittently as the eighteenth century ran its course,[5] most famously in the case of John Wilkes and *North Briton* no. 45. However, the government reaction in the 1790s to radical publications sympathetic to developments consequent upon the French Revolution – the proscription of Paine's *Rights of Man* and the treason trials in particular – was so severe that contemporaries referred to it as Pitt's Terror.[6] Given these considerations, the thesis that the 'elimination of the institution of censorship' led to the publisher replacing the patron 'as the author's commissioner' is difficult to accept, at any rate in its undiluted form.[7]

On the contrary, when the Stationers' Company's privileges were removed along with the removal of restrictions on publishing, the government no longer had at its disposal an effective mechanism for preventing the 'piracy' or unauthorised printing, publication, and sale of books. As *The Case of the Booksellers['] Right to their Copies, or Sole Power of Printing their Respective Books, represented to the Parliament* explained:

2   An Act for preventing the frequent Abuses in printing seditious, treasonable, and unlicensed Books and Pamphlets, and for regulating of Printing and Printing Presses.

3   An Act for the Encouragement of Learning by vesting the Copies of printed Books in the Authors or Purchasers of such Copies, during the Times therein mentioned.

4   John Feather, 'The English Book Trade and the Law 1695–1799', *Publishing History* 12 (1982), 52.

5   On this point, see Donald Thomas, *A Long Time Burning: The History of Literary Censorship in England* (London: Routledge and Kegan Paul, 1969).

6   See Clive Emsley, 'An Aspect of Pitt's "Terror": Prosecutions for Sedition during the 1790s', *Social History* 6 (1981), 155–84. Cf. John Barrell, *The Spirit of Despotism: Invasions of Privacy in the 1790s* (Oxford: Oxford University Press, 2006), p. 4, n. 5.

7   Habermas, *Structural Transformation*, pp. 58, 38.

'UPON presumption that every one of Us, to whom an Author conveys
a Copy, or, by whom a Book is first Printed, hath the sole Power of
Printing that Book for ever after; We have always esteemed that Right a
Just and Legal Property, and have therefore given great Sums of Money
for Copies'.[8] Prior to the provisions of the Copyright Act coming into
force on 10 April 1710, therefore, the probable effect of the end of the
licensing system on author–publisher relations would have been that
booksellers would have been more, rather than less, reluctant to give
'great Sums of Money for Copies', for the simple reason that, with nothing to prevent their being reprinted by pirates as soon as they were published, there was little incentive for them to take the risk of buying
'copies' in the first place. And even if it can be argued that, with the
passing of the Copyright Act, the rights of the author were legally recognised for the first time, there was little in the provisions overall to
suggest that it ushered in an era in which there was a transformation in
author–publisher relations.

The assumption that this took place is based on a belief that, if
not immediately after 1695, then certainly after the provisions of the
Copyright Act came into force, most titles were published as a consequence of booksellers opting to buy the 'copies' or copyrights of new
books from aspiring authors. Thus John Brewer refers to 'the remarkable
transformation in British publishing that occurred between the late seventeenth and late eighteenth centuries', according to which:

> The first step to becoming an author was to find a publisher, an in-
> timidating task best accomplished in person. Authors sought out
> publishers in the numerous booksellers' shops and offices that hud-
> dled in the shadow of St. Paul's Cathedral and they took their manu-
> scripts to the Chapter Coffee House in Paternoster Row, where many
> booksellers and printers carried on their business.[9]

---

8   *The Case of the Booksellers['] Right to their Copies, or Sole Power of Printing
their Respective Books, represented to the Parliament* (London: no publisher, no
date), no page number.

9   John Brewer, *The Pleasures of the Imagination: English Culture in the Eighteenth
Century* (London: HarperCollins, 1997), pp. 125, 154. Cf. Margaret J. M. Ezell,
Social Authorship and the Advent of Print (Baltimore and London: The Johns
Hopkins University Press, 1999), p. 91: 'Once our author, amateur or struggling
hack, having traveled to London, secured a printer or bookseller and sold his or
her rights in the book-length volume, the real work of print production would
begin.'

As a general survey of its subject, *The Pleasures of the Imagination: English Culture in the Eighteenth Century* is possibly not the place to go for definitive information about the book trade, but Brewer's account is misleading in several respects. Not only is it potentially confusing in its failure to distinguish between the different functions of bookseller, printer and publisher in the eighteenth century,[10] but it also gives the impression that the first task of the aspiring author was to persuade a London 'publisher' to take the financial risk associated with publishing a book. While this remains a major obstacle facing today's would-be author,[11] in eighteenth-century England the book trade operated very differently. If authors really wanted to see their work in print, then the best way for them to achieve their objective, even after the passing of the Copyright Act, would have been to publish at his or her own risk. And authors no longer had to travel to London to do this, because one of the most remarkable transformations in publishing which came about as a direct consequence of the expiry of the Printing Act was the growth of provincial publishing. By the terms of the Act, printing in England had been restricted to London, Oxford, Cambridge and the archiepiscopal see of York. By the end of the eighteenth century, however, examples of printing 'for the author' in England can be found at Bath, Birmingham, Bolton, Bristol, Canterbury, Chelmsford, Deptford, Evesham, Exeter, Farnham, Frome, Harborough, Ipswich, Leeds, Liverpool, Manchester, Market Harborough, Newark, Newcastle upon Tyne, Norwich, Nottingham, Reading, Sheffield, Shrewsbury, Southampton, Southwark, Stamford, Trowbridge, Uxbridge and Wakefield.[12]

---

10   Copyright-holding booksellers should be distinguished from 'what the eighteenth century called "a publisher", or one who distributes books and pamphlets without having any other responsibility – he does not own the copyright or employ a printer, or even know the author' (D. Foxon, *Pope and the Early Eighteenth-Century Book Trade*, rev. and ed. J. McLaverty [Oxford: Clarendon Press, 1991], p. 2). For the standard account of these 'trade publishers', see M. Treadwell, 'London Trade Publishers 1675–1750', *The Library*, sixth series, 4 (1982), 99–134.

11   It can of course be argued that, with the advent of the World Wide Web, this is no longer the case.

12   In addition to printing-presses operating in provincial towns throughout England, many books were printed in Dublin, Edinburgh and Glasgow, as well as in several towns and cities across Scotland. By the end of the eighteenth century, there were also instances of printing for the author in no fewer than sixteen locations in the USA. These data are derived from the English Short Title Catalogue (ESTC), first by searching for the phrase, 'printed for the author', and then by

Authors who pay for their work to be published today, even given self-publishing's new-found e-publishing parameters, run the risk of being seen to be continuing in the tradition of vanity publishing. In the eighteenth century it was not so straightforward. In the conclusion to *The Nature of the Book*, Adrian Johns invites us to

> consider the following account of the making of an author, and ask yourself whether he was living in 1620 or 1920. The man concerned was an aspirant young philosopher recently returned from military service in a cataclysmic war. Clutching the manuscript of a treatise that he was convinced would transform the enterprise of philosophy itself, he traversed the world of print looking for a publisher. One entrepreneur offered to produce the book if the writer himself would pay for the paper and printing. He refused, saying that such a process would be 'indecent' and would signal disrespect for the work and its would-be author.[13]

The author concerned was Ludwig Wittgenstein, and for several further pages Johns continues to relate the circumstances attending the original publication of the *Tractatus Logico-Philosophicus*. What I find especially interesting about Johns's account, however, is his enumeration of the options open to the would-be author in the early twentieth century, and his explanation of the reasons why Wittgenstein refused to pay for the privilege of seeing his work in print.

Wittgenstein's experience, Johns writes, 'could well have been Descartes's, Galileo's, Spinoza's, or Flamsteed's, and it could have befallen any would-be learned author of the sixteenth, seventeenth, or eighteenth century'.[14] I think the reference to the 'would-be learned author' is particularly apt. Writing specifically about the eighteenth century in *The Enlightenment and the Book*, Richard B. Sher refers to 'the stigma of self-publication'.[15] But, as Keith Maslen pointed out forty years ago in an attempt to 'explain the frequent attempts by eighteenth-century authors, noticeably after 1715, to publish on their own account', 'many

---

refining the search to the publication years 1798 and 1799.

13   Johns, *Nature of the Book*, p. 633.
14   Ibid., p. 635.
15   Richard B. Sher, *The Enlightenment and the Book: Scottish Authors and Their Publishers in Eighteenth-Century Britain, Ireland, and America* (Chicago and London: University of Chicago Press, 2006), p. 236.

deserving works of scholarship saw the light in the earlier part of the eighteenth century mainly because their authors were willing and able to pay for their production'.[16] I suspect that, in the eighteenth century, it was not only learned authors who paid for the privilege of seeing their works in print. In his 1976 Lyell lectures, David Foxon explained that: 'There is abundant evidence in the printers' ledgers of an author's controversial works being printed either at his own expense or by the order of his usual bookseller but issued through a publisher.'[17] As an example, Foxon cited the interesting example of the first edition of *The Dunciad*. 'What does seem very likely', he argued, 'is that Pope (like many authors of controversial pamphlets) paid the printing costs, and recovered them, together with the profits, from the pamphlet-sellers'.[18] Hence, presumably, the numerous imprints of controversial pamphlets reading 'Printed for the Author, and sold by the Pamphlet-Sellers', or 'Printed for the Author, and sold at the Pamphlet Shops of London and Westminster'.

But who or what were these 'pamphlet-sellers'? As the 'best definition of a publisher' of which he was aware, Foxon quoted from *The Parents and Guardians Directory* (1761): 'The Publisher advertises Pamphlets, enters them at the Stamp-office, folds, stitches them and publishes them for such gentlemen as print them at their own expence, and for the booksellers who do not chuse to set their names to them.'[19] As Foxon explained, the 'fullest form of an imprint' carried the place of publication, the name of the printer, the copyright-holding bookseller for whom it was printed, and the publisher who actually distributed or sold the work, e.g. 'London: printed by X (the printer), for Y (the bookseller who

---

16   Keith Maslen, 'Printing for the Author: From the Bowyer Printing Ledgers, 1710–1775', *The Library*, fifth series, 27 (1972), 302.

17   Foxon, *Pope and the Early Eighteenth-Century Book Trade*, ed. McLaverty, p. 4.

18   Ibid., p. 110. Interestingly, Pope sold the copyright of *The Dunciad Variorum* – the only copyright he sold once he was financially independent as a consequence of his translations of Homer – not to a bookseller, but to the earls of Oxford, Bathurst and Burlington as a cautionary measure in case of a libel action. As Foxon observes: 'The 1709/10 [Copyright] Act is supposed to have brought [about] a new alliance of author and bookseller, but from the 1720s Pope was using it to strengthen his own position and lessen his dependence on the book trade' (p. 237).

19   J. Collier, *The Parents and Guardians Directory* (1761), p. 233, quoted in Foxon, *Pope and the Early Eighteenth-Century Book Trade*, ed. McLaverty, p. 5.

owned the copyright), and sold by Z'.[20] But if political pamphlets, particularly those most likely to be prosecuted by the government for seditious libel, carried an imprint at all, it was merely 'London: printed and sold by Z', or even 'Printed and sold by the Booksellers'. And as Foxon observed, 'any work as unspecific as "London: printed in the year 1715" must be suspected of being surreptitious or printed for private circulation'.[21] The huge polemical output of Daniel Defoe is a case in point. The vast majority of his pamphlets – particularly early on his writing career – simply stated that they were 'Printed in the Year X'.[22] And this was precisely the formula followed at the very end of the century by Vicesimus Knox when he published *The Spirit of Despotism* anonymously in 1795.

It seems to me to be an important consideration that, if not published 'for a Faction in the Name of the Community' (as James Ralph memorably put it), a significant proportion of new works issuing from the presses both in London and in the provinces were probably printed not for a copyright-holding bookseller or publisher, but silently 'printed for the author'.[23] This obtained even after the Copyright Act became law. As Defoe explained to Lord Treasurer Oxford on 31 October 1713 in seeking to account for the proliferation of Whig propaganda: 'No printer will now print at his Own Charge, which is the Reason The world is Over-run with their Pamphlets, which they disperse privately Two or Three Editions at a Time, and No Man stirs a hand to Oppose Them because They Must do it at Their Own hazard and Expence.'[24] Thus while James Raven is correct to point out that authors 'faced great risk if they rejected the usually meagre outright sale of the manuscript',[25] apparently it was not only a risk that many were willing to take but, as in the case of Brewer's assumption about how one became an author in

20   Ibid., p. 2.
21   Ibid.
22   The simplest way to appreciate this is to consult those published between 1700 and 1703 in *A Critical Bibliography of Daniel Defoe*, ed. P. N. Furbank and W. R. Owens (London: Pickering & Chatto, 1998), pp. 18–43.
23   J. Ralph, *The Case of Authors by Profession or Trade, Stated. With Regard to Booksellers, the Stage, and the Public. No Matter by Whom* (London: R. Griffiths, 1758), p. 19.
24   *The Letters of Daniel Defoe*, ed. G. Harris Healey (Oxford: Clarendon Press, 1955), p. 424.
25   James Raven, 'Publishing and Bookselling 1660–1780', in *The Cambridge History of English Literature, 1660–1780*, ed. J. Richetti (Cambridge: Cambridge University Press, 2005), p. 33.

the eighteenth century, it seems to relate specifically to those who were writing for money. And even if this were the case, there were a number of other options open to those who were unable or unwilling simply to pay for their writings to be published. Subscription publishing became so popular in the early eighteenth century, more particularly after Pope's spectacular success with his translations of Homer, that, as Charles Ford explained to Swift in 1733: 'All books are printed here [i.e. London] now by subscription'.[26] While this was undoubtedly an exaggeration, subscription schemes remained an option both for authors who wished to make as much money as possible out of their works, or for authors who were not in a position to subsidise publication of their works entirely out of their own pockets.

Frances Burney's final resolution to publish her third novel, *Camilla*, by subscription in 1796 provides a particularly interesting example of the first option at work. The decision had not been straightforward because Burney patently had misgivings about the propriety of resorting to this form of publishing. What her correspondence makes clear is that the deciding factor was the prospect of making a larger amount of money than she was likely to be offered if she were simply to sell the copyright to her bookseller. As she wrote to her brother on 10 June 1795: 'As in some points it is very disagreeable to us both to take such a measure – And as in all points, it is a thing to be done but ONCE in a Life, we wish to do it to MOST advantage.'[27]

There are numerous examples of authors, particularly women, resorting to subscription publishing not as a means of squeezing as much profit as possible out of the enterprise, but simply in order to generate whatever income they could. As Susan Staves points out, Mary Davys's novel, *The Reform'd Coquet* (1724), and Mary Barber's *Poems on Several Occasions* (1734) were 'partially supported by local subscribers who under-wrote the publication of their books'.[28] In this sense, as Thomas Lockwood has stridently argued, subscription publishing can be seen as

26   *The Correspondence of Jonathan Swift, D.D.*, ed. David Woolley, 4 vols. (Frankfort am Main: Peter Lang, 1999–2007), III, p. 698.

27   *The Journals and Letters of Fanny Burney (Madame D'Arblay)*, ed. J. Hemlow, 10 vols. (Oxford: Clarendon Press, 1972–), III, p. 111, quoted in Emma E. Pink, 'Frances Burney's *Camilla*: "To Print my Grand Work . . . by Subscription" ', *Eighteenth-Century Studies* 40 (2006), 58.

28   Susan Staves, *A Literary History of Women's Writing in Britain, 1660–1789* (Cambridge: Cambridge University Press, 2006), p. 225.

an intensely nostalgic replication of personal patronage within a
publishing system long since operating on market motives – a com-
mercialization of patronage, or even a democratization of it, but in
the sense only of a commercially expanded opportunity for lots of
people to play cheaply at being patrons as of old.[29]

To return to Adrian Johns's account of Wittgenstein's attempt to get the
Tractatus Logico-Philosophicus published, it is revealing that the 'entre-
preneur' to whom he refers (who offered to 'produce' – i.e. publish? – the
book provided Wittgenstein was prepared to pay the printing costs) appears strikingly similar to those publishers at the turn of the nineteenth
century who agreed to arrange for the printing and publishing of books
'on commission'. This arrangement is explained with exceptional clarity in a letter from the House of Longman dated 1816: 'The Publisher
gets the W[or]k Printed at the trade price, purchases the Paper at the
best market, superintends the general interests of the W[or]k & takes
upon himself the risk of Bad Debts for which he charges a commission
of 10 per cent on the Sales.'[30] Unfortunately, documentary evidence
of such arrangements is scanty. It is for this reason, perhaps, that James
Raven is sceptical about the incidence of '[c]ommission agreements
whereby the publisher put up the capital for printing an edition, on the
understanding that the author would bear any loss', maintaining that
such arrangements 'seem to have been very rare'.[31] As comparatively
few publishers' contracts have survived, we should be careful about
jumping to any conclusions, however, let alone simply assuming that
authors who published 'on commission' did so because they were unable
to find a bookseller prepared to purchase the copyright.

This line of reasoning applies particularly to Jane Austen. Even
though she made a healthy profit by publishing 'for herself' (as she called
it), scholars still seem reluctant to accept that it was a shrewd business
move, and not a desperate attempt on her part to see her novels in print.
Thus Anthony Mandal asserts that commission agreements usually arose
'from a publisher's uncertainty regarding the success of a venture, because it ensured that the author bore all the costs of producing the work

---

29   Thomas Lockwood, 'Subscription Hunters and their Prey', *Studies in the
Literary Imagination* 34 (2001), 32.
30   Quoted in Jan Fergus, *Jane Austen: A Literary Life* (London: Longman,
1992), p. 16.
31   Raven, 'Publishing and Bookselling 1660–1780', p. 34.

(printing, paper, advertising)'. He argues that, having bought the copyright of what was by far Austen's most commercially successful novel, *Pride and Prejudice*, for £110, the publisher Thomas Egerton published her next novel, *Mansfield Park*, 'on commission, and produced it less speedily but more cheaply than *Pride and Prejudice*, [which was] possibly indicative of a less concerted commitment' on his part.[32] But it was almost certainly more complicated than that. Egerton had published *Sense and Sensibility* – the first of Austen's novels to appear in print – 'on commission' in November 1811. The entire first edition sold out. By publishing 'for myself' – which is what she called the process when writing to her sister, Cassandra, about trying to get *Emma* published[33] – Austen not only retained the copyright of *Sense and Sensibility*, she also retained considerable control over the way her novel appeared in print.

There is no documentary evidence to suggest that Austen published *Sense and Sensibility* 'for herself' because she was unable to find a publisher willing to take the risk. Given that she chose to publish all her novels in this way except *Pride and Prejudice*, it seems reasonable to consider the reasons why she elected to do so. Although, according to the editor of the *Quarterly Review*, *Pride and Prejudice* was 'wretchedly printed, and so pointed as to be almost unintelligible',[34] the principal consideration was almost certainly financial. Austen had learned from experience that copyrights were cheap, having sold the rights to what would eventually be posthumously published as *Northanger Abbey* to the firm of Benjamin Crosby & Co. for the princely sum of £10 in 1803. This was not an unreasonable amount, especially for the work of an unknown novelist. The Minerva Press paid its authors around £5 a volume, and *Northanger Abbey*, as it was eventually published, was a work of two volumes. By publishing *Sense and Sensibility* 'on commission', therefore, Austen made a profit of £140 rather than the £15 which is

32   Anthony Mandal, *Jane Austen and the Popular Novel: The Determined Author* (Basingstoke: Palgrave, 2007), p. 80, 101.

33   See *Jane Austen's Letters*, collected and edited by Deirdre Le Faye, third edition (Oxford and New York: Oxford University Press, 1995), p. 291: 'Mr Murray's Letter is come; he is a Rogue of course, but a civil one. He offers £450– but wants to have the Copyright of M[ansfield]P[ark]. & S[ense]&S[ensibility] included. It will end in my publishing for myself I dare say.'

34   Quoted in Samuel Smiles, *A Publisher and His Friends: Memoir and Correspondence of the Late John Murray, with an Account of the Origin and Progress of the House*, 2 vols. (London: John Murray, 1891), I, p. 282.

likely to have been the most she would have received from a publisher had she sold the copyright of the three volumes.

That, in the light of the commercial success of *Sense and Sensibility*, Egerton offered to buy the copyright of Austen's next novel, *Pride and Prejudice*, is therefore perfectly understandable. 'P. & P. is sold,' Austen wrote to Martha Lloyd on 29 November 1812. 'Egerton gives £110 for it. – I would rather have had £150, but we could not both be pleased, & I am not at all surprised that he should not chuse to hazard so much.'[35] In that the risk of underwriting the cost of the novel's publication had to be taken by either the author or the publisher, Austen's choice of verb seems particularly apposite. Given the success of *Sense and Sensibility*, surely the question should be not why Egerton chose to buy the copyright of *Pride and Prejudice*, but why Austen chose to sell it, because she would have known that she would almost certainly have made more money out of publishing it at her own risk. And this, in the event, proved to be the case.

This is potentially of considerable significance because Austen chose to publish her subsequent novels on commission rather than selling the copyright. In other words, it was Austen's selling the copyright of *Pride and Prejudice* that was out of the ordinary, not her decision to publish *Mansfield Park* at her own risk, as she had done in the case of *Sense and Sensibility*, and persuasive biographical reasons can be adduced for her taking this decision. 'Its' [*sic*] being sold will I hope be a great saving of Trouble to Henry', her letter of 29 November 1812 continues, '& therefore must be welcome to me.'[36] Austen's rider suggests that high on the list of considerations which led to her selling the copyright of what proved to be the most popular – and therefore best-selling – of all of her novels was the inconvenience it caused her brother, Henry, who acted as her literary agent in negotiations with publishers, and whose wife was lying terminally ill at the time. If, as is almost certainly the case, Austen disappointed Egerton by reverting to her chosen method of publishing at her own risk rather than selling him the copyright of *Mansfield Park*, then it offers a different perspective on his 'commitment' to the novel. The publishing history of Austen's novels suggests that we should be cautious before we jump to conclusions either about her business acumen in electing to publish 'on commission', or about her publisher's assessment of the likely commercial appeal of *Mansfield Park*.

*

35 *Jane Austen's Letters*, ed. Le Faye, p. 197.
36 Ibid.

Around fifty years earlier, when Laurence Sterne tried to sell the copy-right of the first volume of 'the Life & Opinions of Tristram Shandy' to Robert Dodsley for £50, Dodsley explained: 'That it was too much to risk on a single Vol. – which, if it happen'd not to sell, w^d. be hard upon [his] Brother', the copyright-holding bookseller, James Dodsley. Sterne's response was to 'propose therefore to print a lean Edition in 2 small Vols, of the Size of Rasselas, & on the same paper and Type, – at my own Expence merely to feel the Pulse of the World – & that I may know what Price to set upon the Remaining Volumes, from the recep-tion of these'.[37] As everybody knows, *The Life and Opinions of Tristram Shandy, Gentleman* proved to be a huge popular and commercial success. Six months later, Sterne was to write that, in London, 'Tristram is the fashion'.[38] He eventually sold the copyright of the first two volumes to Dodsley's brother, James, in March 1760 for £250, and the two subse-quent volumes for £380.

While things turned out well for Sterne in the end, Dodsley's corre-spondence suggests that his predicament was hardly unusual, let alone unique, and that if authors wished to see their works in print, it was rather more complicated than the relatively straightforward task of find-ing a publisher (or bookseller) willing to buy the copyright. If booksell-ers were not necessarily willing to take the risk of buying the copyright of works by little-known authors, they were not always prepared to go to the trouble of publishing them 'for the author' either. 'I wish you had told me directly whether you are willing to purchase the Copy of the Poem I sent you, upon any Terms, or not,' John Brown of Carlisle wrote to Dodsley in September 1743. 'If you are, I desire you will let me know what you can give: If you are not, pray inform me particularly upon what Terms you will print, and sell it, upon The Author's Account.'[39] The blind Scottish clergyman and poet, Thomas Blacklock, wrote to Dodsley from Dumfries in similar terms in 1760 to ask his advice about what he called 'the most desperate of all employments, that of publish-ing Sermons'. In doing so, he offers a particularly striking representa-tion of the choices facing an author in the middle of the century. 'I beg to know therefore, how far you think such a scheme practicable,'

37   *The Correspondence of Robert Dodsley 1733–1764*, ed. James E. Tierney (Cambridge: Cambridge University Press, 1988), p. 421.
38   *Letters of Laurence Sterne*, ed. Lewis Perry Curtis (Oxford: Clarendon Press, 1935), p. 102.
39   *Correspondence of Robert Dodsley*, ed. Tierney, pp. 70–1.

Blacklock enquired, 'whether it can be done by subscription, whey^r any Bookseller will take the Copy, or whey^r I may prudently run the risk myself.'[40]

Blacklock's case is of particular interest not only because he enjoyed an extended relationship with the Dodsley brothers, but because they went to considerable lengths to promote his *Poems on Several Occasions*. When first published in Glasgow in 1746, *Poems on Several Occasions* was a slim volume which, according to the title page, was 'Printed for the AUTHOR; and sold by the Book-sellers in Town and Country'. A second edition, published in Edinburgh in 1754, was printed by Hamilton, Balfour, and Neill, but, as Richard B. Sher points out, it was also 'self-published, and in a most unusual manner'.[41] Sher cites a letter in which David Hume describes an arrangement by which he and others agreed to 'take copies' from Blacklock and 'distribute them among their acquaintance'.[42] This complicates the way in which arrangements between authors and booksellers or publishers might be viewed. The 1754 edition of Blacklock's *Poems* cost three shillings. It made him one hundred guineas. The edition was indeed 'printed for the author', but there was apparently a strong element of subscription publishing involved also, so that the arrangement was in fact a sort of hybrid. The volume of Blacklock's *Poems*, once printed, was not simply left to take its chances as far as sales were concerned. Instead, multiple copies were (presumably) bought up by his friends and 'distributed' (given away?) 'among their own acquaintance'.

Interestingly, the 1754 edition was introduced by a hand purporting to be other than Blacklock's own. Immediately following the title page, signed 'G. G-----N', and dated 'DUMFRIES, *Dec.* 15. 1753', is the following:

To the PUBLISHER.

SIR,

SINCE my arrival from the country, I have been informed, that Mr. BLACKLOCK proposes to send a new edition of his poetical performances into the world, without either preface or introduction. I am ignorant what motives may influence him to this; except, perhaps, the great difficulty which a man finds in speaking with propriety of himself

40   Ibid., p. 436.
41   Sher, *Enlightenment and the Book*, p. 224.
42   *The Letters of David Hume*, ed. J. Y. T. Greig, 2 vols. (Oxford: Oxford University Press, 1932), I, p. 184.

and his own productions. However, I cannot forbear thinking, that
the singularity of Mr. BLACKLOCK's circumstances will, not only render
a short account of him and his performances acceptable to the curious
reader, but recommend his talents more to public observation.[43]

'G. G-----N' then proceeds to offer an extended account of Blacklock's
life and 'poetical performances', but his introduction raises other questions, particularly in the context of Hume's insinuation that the idea for
a second, Edinburgh edition of *Poems on Several Occasions* had originated
with Blacklock's friends, and was intended to make a profit for the poet.[44]
    When, also in 1754, the Dodsleys published *An Account of the Life,
Character, and Poems of Mr. Blacklock*, by the Oxford Professor of Poetry,
Joseph Spence, Hume wrote 'under Cover to [Dodsley] a Letter to M[r]
Spence'. 'All the Contents of it regard M[r] Blacklocke', Hume explained,
'and are equally your Concern, as M[r] Spence's & that of every Lover of
Ingenuity.'[45] 'Your scheme of publishing his poems by subscription, I
hope will turn to account,' he told Spence. 'I think it impossible he
[Blacklock] could want, were his case more generally known.'[46] When
the Dodsleys published a London edition of *Poems on Several Occasions* in
1756 'For the Author', Spence's *Account* was prefixed in much the same
way as 'G. G-----N''s introduction had been pre-fixed to the Edinburgh
edition. The impressive list of subscribers printed in the so-called
'SECOND EDITION' of Blacklock's *Poems* was headed up by the Duke and
Duchess of Beaufort, the Duke of Dorset, the Duke of Manchester, the
Duke and Duchess of Newcastle, the Marquis of Rockingham, no fewer
than twelve earls, numerous lords, the Archbishop of Canterbury, and
a handful of bishops. Several put their names down for multiple copies,
while over two hundred – getting on for half of the total number – sub-
scribed for the 'Large Paper' edition.
    Although, later on in their association, Blacklock may have

43 Thomas Blacklock, *Poems on Several Occasions* (Edinburgh: Printed by
Hamilton, Balfour and Neill, 1754), no page number.
44 In an undated, unaddressed letter, Hume writes: 'The Preface you sent me
is really very well wrote; & it was not easily possible to do it better. However I
have us'd the Freedom of making some small Alterations: I wish it were in my
Power to do you any more material Service: & I shall lay hold of every such Opportunity with Pleasure.' J. Y. T. Greig conjectures that it is 'almost certain' that
Blacklock is the addressee of this letter (*Letters of Hume*, I, p. 183).
45 Ibid., p. 175.
46 Ibid., p. 203.

complained about Dodsley's tardiness in replying to his letters, the blind poet was patently an object of interest as far as the influential and prestigious editor of the six-volume *Collection of Poems by Several Hands* was concerned. Blacklock's *Poems*, albeit originally 'Printed for the AUTHOR; and sold by the Book-sellers in Town and Country', was taken up by the gentry of Dumfriesshire and Galloway, and finally by the nobility and gentry of Great Britain. In his turn, Blacklock played a part in promoting Robert Burns's *Poems, Chiefly in the Scottish Dialect*, both as a subscriber, and subsequently by suggesting that Burns might follow the example of his own *Poems on Several Occasions* by publishing an expanded second edition which might have 'a more universal circulation than any thing of the kind which has been published within [his] memory'.[47] As Sher observes, Burns explained 'that Blacklock's letter "overthrew all my schemes" of emigration "by rousing my poetic ambition" '.[48]

In the second half of the eighteenth century, as *The Enlightenment and the Book* reveals, a number of Scottish authors elected to retain the copyright of their works and take the risk of publishing for themselves. Different factors operated in different cases, but if, as was usually the case, the decision was based on individual authors' assessments of how the greatest financial benefit might be gained from their labours, it is evident that it was by no means a straightforward choice whether to retain or to sell the copyright. Perhaps Boswell's *Life of Johnson* provides the most celebrated example of an author's uncertainty as to what would be the best course of action to follow. Sher draws attention to 'the drama' of this particular 'self-published best seller' as a means of illustrating the 'high degree of anxiety that authors sometimes experience over the terms of publication',[49] and it is edifying to observe, through his extant correspondence, the way in which Boswell's confidence ebbed and flowed. 'I have printed twenty sheets of my Magnum Opus,' Boswell wrote to Bennet Langton on 9 April 1790. 'It will be the most entertaining Book that appeared.' 'Only think of what an offer I have for it – *A Cool Thousand*,' he gleefully continued. 'But I am advised to retain the property myself.'[50]

47   Quoted in Sher, *Enlightenment and the Book*, p. 231.
48   Ibid.
49   Ibid., p. 220.
50   *The Correspondence and Other Papers of James Boswell Relating to the Making of the Life of Johnson*, ed. M. Waingrow, The Yale Edition of The Private Papers of James Boswell, second edition, corrected and enlarged (Edinburgh, New Haven and London: Edinburgh University Press and Yale University Press, 2001), p. 244.

In reality, as subsequent correspondence between Boswell and the great Shakespearean scholar Edmund Malone makes apparent, the nature of the offer of £1,000 for the copyright of the *Life of Johnson* from the bookseller, George Robinson, was less clear-cut than Boswell's initial enthusiasm warranted. Moreover, Boswell was in financial difficulties. In these circumstances, he repeatedly weighed the pros and cons of publishing for himself rather than selling the copyright to a bookseller. 'I am in a distressing perplexity how to decide as to the property of my Book,' he wrote to Malone on 25 February 1791. 'You must know that I am *certainly* informed that a certain person who delights in mischief has been *depreciating* it, so that I fear the sale of it may be very dubious [. . .] I believe in my present frame I should accept even of £500, for I suspect that were I now to talk to Robinson I should find him not disposed to give £1000. Did he absolutely *offer* it, or did he only express himself so as that you *concluded* he would give it?'[51] 'I really forget what words he used, when he talked to me about your book', Malone replied, 'but the import, I think, was, that he was willing to give 1000£ for the copy. As it was then to be in one volume, I conceive he could not now offer for two less than 1000£.'[52] After several further bouts of indecision, and regardless of his pressing financial circumstances, Boswell finally decided to retain the copyright of the *Life of Johnson*. 'I am quite resolved now to keep the property of my *Magnum Opus*', he informed Malone on 9 March 1791, 'and I flatter myself I shall not repent it.'[53] It proved to be the right decision. 'My *Magnum Opus* sells wonderfully,' he wrote on 22 August. '1200 are now gone and we hope the whole 1700 may be gone before Christmas.'[54]

As there were in fact a number of publishing options available to an author in the eighteenth century, I should like to conclude by offering some general remarks about the actual incidence of 'printing for the author' in the period. Interesting data can be derived from the ESTC. Searching the database for the exact phrase, 'printed for the author', refining the search by restricting it to the 'Publisher' field, further refining the search by publication year, and finally adding up the results for each year of the eighteenth century, indicates that up to 11,163 examples of printing for the author from the period 1701–1800 have survived.[55] Although the vast

51   Ibid., p. 298.
52   Ibid., p. 301.
53   Ibid., p. 302.
54   Ibid., p. lxvii.
55   This was the total at the end of 2011. I have deliberately written 'up to'

majority of these titles were published in London, an increasing number
were published not only in the provinces, but in Scotland and America,
particularly towards the end of the century.[56] It must also be emphasised
that these totals include multiple editions of some titles, and of course
the number of titles not so indicated which nonetheless were paid for by
authors (such as their controversial works) remains an unknown quantity.

These cautions notwithstanding, some noteworthy observations can
be made about the raw data. First, and perhaps most interesting given
claims that the end of pre-printing censorship in 1695 led to a change
in author–publisher relations and the rise of the professional author, is
that, with the single exception of a slight dip in the 1720s, the number
of titles 'printed for the author' seems to have increased from decade to
decade throughout the century:

Years	Number of volumes 'printed for the author'
1701–10	357
1711–20	538
1721–30	506
1731–40	680
1741–50	812
1751–60	943
1761–70	1309
1771–80	1512
1781–90	1984
1791–1800	2522

11,163 because a few of these titles do not actually employ the phrase 'printed
for the author' – one of the vagaries of using wordsearch facilities. The total
number is of course likely to increase.

56 In 1701, all but one of the extant examples of titles 'printed for the author'
were printed in London. By the end of the century the situation was decidedly
different. Around 50 per cent of the more than 200 titles 'printed for the author'
in 1799 were printed in London: 35 were printed in eighteen towns across the
United States of America, including Baltimore, Boston, and Philadelphia as
well as many much smaller settlements; 20 were printed in Scotland, not only
in Edinburgh and Glasgow but also in Ayr, Louth, Montrose and Paisley; and
8 were printed in Dublin. The remainder were published in the following locations: Bath, Birmingham, Bolton, Bristol, Canterbury, Chelmsford, Deptford,
Evesham, Farnham, Harborough, Ipswich, Leeds, Liverpool, Manchester, Market Harborough, Newark, Newcastle upon Tyne, Norwich, Nottingham, Reading, Sheffield, Southwark, Stamford, Trowbridge, Uxbridge, and Wakefield.

While this upward trend might be readily interpreted as a reflection of the overall growth in printing in England which took place over the period, particularly in the last three decades of the eighteenth century, at the very least it complicates the thesis that, after 1695, 'the publisher replaced the patron as the author's commissioner'.[57] In a number of cases, over and above the examples of Austen and Boswell offered earlier on in this essay, it is evident that authors were prepared to take the risk of publishing for themselves rather than attempting to sell the copyright to a bookseller. This applies to the later as well as to the early years of the century, when writers such as the maverick John Dunton (who, in his *Life and Errors* of 1705, exposed the sharp practices of those involved in the book trade, and who has attracted considerable attention in recent years as the shady mastermind behind *The Athenian Mercury*), the eccentric Quaker apostate Francis Bugg and the poet Elkanah Settle apparently chose to publish their numerous writings entirely on their own account.

Poems, plays and novels made up only a tiny proportion of the thousands of works which indicated on their title pages that they were printed for the author. By far the greatest number of publications 'printed for the author' in 1701 were on religious subjects, defined as broadly as possible, including, but by no means restricted to, sermons. There were, in addition, musical scores, various titles on medical topics, including quack remedies, a couple of plays and a couple of poems, and assorted publications on arithmetic, book-keeping, navigation, English grammar, foreign language dictionaries, Latin and, of course, politics. By contrast, although religion, including sermons, continued to make up a significant proportion of the titles listed in the ESTC for the year 1799 as printed for the author, over half might reasonably be described as miscellaneous publications of one kind or another.

In 1799, there were also thirty-six titles which indicated that they consisted of verse of various kinds. As the example of Blacklock's *Poems* suggests, it is scarcely surprising that many collections of poetry saw the light of day principally because their authors paid for their production. As William St. Clair points out in *The Reading Nation in the Romantic Period*, at the turn of the nineteenth century 'almost all first volumes of poetry were published at the author's expense'.[58] This certainly applied in

57   Habermas, *Structural Transformation*, p. 38.

58   William St. Clair, *The Reading Nation in the Romantic Period* (Cambridge: Cambridge University Press, 2004), p. 611 n. 192. In connection with James Hogg's collection of poems, *The Mountain Bard* (1807), St. Clair quotes the pub-

the case of Shelley. *Queen Mab* was privately printed and not sold, while several of Shelley's other works were published 'on commission'. Byron's *Poems on Various Occasions* (1807) was also printed for private circulation, although St. Clair speculates that both his *Hours of Idleness* (1807) and Keats's *Poems* (1817) were probably published 'on commission'.[59]

According to the ESTC, there were ten instances of prose fiction printed for the author in 1799. Since the publication in 2000 of *The English Novel, 1770–1829: A Bibliographical Survey of Prose Fiction Published in the British Isles*, it has been possible to offer a clear picture of the number of novels printed for the author in the period:

Years	Number of volumes 'printed for the author'
1770–79	16
1780–89	29
1790–99	50
1800–1809	35
1810–19	34
1820–29	17

Source: *The English Novel 1770–1829: A Bibliographical Survey of Prose Fiction Published in the British Isles*, ed. P. Garside, J. Raven and R. Schöwerling, 2 vols. (Oxford: Oxford University Press, 2000), I, p. 91, n. 221; II, p. 81.

Statistically, the amount of fiction published for the author may be negligible – rising from 5 per cent of titles in the 1770s to 7 per cent in the 1780s and 1790s, before declining to 5 per cent once more between 1800 and 1809[60] – but it nonetheless suggests that some novelists were prepared to pay for their novels to be published rather than sell the copyright for perhaps £5 a volume. This seems to be borne out by

lisher's warning to Walter Scott, who was assisting Hogg, that 'nobody's poetry would sell'. Constable, however, agreed to publish the volume if two hundred subscribers could be found. Hogg found five hundred subscribers, making almost £300 from his collection (ibid., p. 609).

59   Ibid., pp. 585–6, p. 611. St. Clair suggests, in connection with the publication of *Endymion* (1818), that: 'Losses on one book [were] to be offset against profit on others' (ibid.).

60   *The English Novel 1770–1829: A Bibliographical Survey of Prose Fiction Published in the British Isles*, ed. Peter Garside, James Raven and Rainer Schöwerling, 2 vols. (Oxford: Oxford University Press, 2000), I, p. 91.

the incidence of imprints at the turn of the nineteenth century which read: 'London: Printed for the author at the Minerva-Press, and sold by William Lane, Leadenhall-Street', followed by the year of publication.[61] We also know that, prior to 1770, a number of best-selling novels were printed for the author, such as Samuel Richardson's *Clarissa* (1747–8) and *Sir Charles Grandison* (1753–4), the anonymous *History of Charlotte Summers, the Fortunate Parish Girl* (1750), Tobias Smollett's *Peregrine Pickle* (1751), and the first (Dublin) edition of Henry Brooke's *The Fool of Quality* (1765). 'As in the case of subscription publishing', Peter Garside observes, 'as a means of publication "by the author" is much less evident later in the period'.[62]

Whether, by 1830, the publishing system had indeed changed as a consequence of a transformation in author–publisher relations so that the 'normal' way for books to find their way into print was for publishers to buy the copyright from the author and take the risk of publication, it certainly seems to be the case that the incidence of both subscription publishing and printing for the author was by then in decline. (Interestingly, the 1820s was also the decade in which serial publication began in earnest.[63]) As the resources of the ESTC end in 1800, however, there are as yet no data to endorse such a conclusion.

61   The ESTC also records a publication entitled *The Authentic and Interesting History of Miss Moreton, and the Faithful Cottager. In Two Volumes* (1799) which was not only 'printed for, and sold by the author, no. 13, Deansgate', Manchester, but also printed for the author in Nottingham. Interestingly, the imprints of subsequent editions published in Birmingham and Norwich were not designated as 'printed for the author'. Perhaps by then 'Miss Moreton' had sold the copyright.

62   *The English Novel 1770–1829*, ed. Garside, Raven and Schöwerling, II, p. 81.

63   Mandal, *Jane Austen and the Popular Novel*, p. 215.

Robert Burns's Interleaved Scots Musical Museum: A Case-Study in the Vagaries of Editors and Owners

GERARD CARRUTHERS

As MUCH AS ANY SCHOLAR could wish, the authorship of Robert Burns (1759–96) presents problems in textual editing and book history: uncertain attributions, bibliographical conundrums, egregious editorial interference and lost manuscripts to say nothing of a large dose of fraudulence and forgery. Providing a complete edition of Burns's works across poetry, prose and song, to consistently high standards of editorial practice and archival retrieval, has only recently begun, more than 250 years after the writer's birth.[1] That editorial project is examining materials that have remained surprisingly occlusive, manuscripts and books that would (one cannot help feeling) have been pored over by generation after generation of scholars if they had pertained to Burns's Romantic near contemporaries, for instance, Wordsworth or Coleridge.[2] One of the most important association print copies of Burns presents an instructive case here. It highlights the fragile and complex transmission of the Burns canon as well as the vexed cultural politics which have attached to Scotland's national bard – all the more so since his death. This is a four-volume interleaved set of *The Scots Musical Museum* (1787–92) in which Burns provided additional material to the original publication and that eventually he gifted to Captain Robert Riddell (1755–94).

I am grateful to the University of Glasgow for granting me a sabbatical period during 2011–12, in which time this essay was completed, and to the Department of English, especially Professor Caroline McCracken Flesher, at the University of Wyoming, for accommodating me with research facilities during that period. Thanks too to Nigel Leask, Norman Paton, Murray Pittock and Jeremy Smith who read and commented on an earlier version of this essay.

1   The Oxford University Press edition of the *Works of Robert Burns* is now underway and to be published from 2014 (general editor, Gerard Carruthers).
2   In spite of what I am arguing, however, it might be mentioned that, surprisingly, William Wordsworth's Commonplace Book has never been properly edited.

From 1787 Robert Burns began collecting song material to contribute to James Johnson's *Scots Musical Museum*. Already enjoying his first flush of fame as a poet, Burns now embarked on a project that would become one of the main channels to his achievement as a song writer, indeed Scotland's greatest one. Received wisdom has it that he contributed around 150 of his own compositions to the *Museum* (these six volumes appearing between 1787 and 1803) as well as collecting, sometimes 'repairing', at least another fifty texts for the publication, becoming 'de facto editor'.[3] In the course of his song labours, at some point probably in late 1792, Burns had made up for himself an interleaved set of the first four volumes of the *Museum*.[4] In these he provided additional songs and annotative material but, before long, Burns made a present of this interleaved set to his close friend, Robert Riddell, an encouraging mentor to the poet in his early years (from 1788) in Dumfriesshire. In this context it might also be mentioned that another very important association copy, the 'Geddes Burns', an 'Edinburgh' edition of Burns's *Poems, Chiefly in the Scottish Dialect* (1787) contains holograph insertions of thirteen new texts, several of them inspired by Riddell.[5] The new works in the 'Geddes

3   Robert Crawford, *The Bard: Robert Burns, a Biography* (London: Jonathan Cape, 2009), p. 278. Donald Low's very useful two-volume edition, *The Scots Musical Museum 1787–1803* (Portland, Oregon: Amadeus Press, 1991), does no modern recalculation of the input of Burns, or, indeed, of that of Stephen Clarke, the musical editor of the *Museum*. The precise extent of the hand of Burns in both words and music remains in need of sharp reappraisal, and will be investigated more thoroughly than before by Murray Pittock in his edition of the *Scots Musical Museum* for the new Oxford University Press edition of Burns.
4   Robert Burns informs James Johnson in a letter dated October 1792(?) that he has instructed the bookseller, Peter Hill to make up for him an interleaved version of the *Museum*. See *The Letters of Robert Burns*, 2 vols., second edition, ed. J. De Lancey Ferguson and G. Ross Roy (Oxford: Clarendon Press, 1985), II, pp. 156–7.
5   As well as the interleaved *Scots Musical Museum* and the 'Geddes Burns', there is also the 'Glenriddell Manuscripts', the largest single self-compilation of Burns holograph material. Burns poems and songs (vol. 1) and letters (vol. 2) in the 'Glenriddell MSS' were carefully compiled with a significant amount of fair-copy redrafting to be presented to Robert Riddell. The breach in the friendship of the pair referred to in this essay meant that Robert Riddell received only the first volume. The 'Glenriddell MSS', the 'Geddes Burns' and the interleaved *Scots Musical Museum*, taken together, show Riddell to be probably the single most important reader Burns ever had (from Burns's own perspective). This fact has been obscured not only by the rather calamitous history of the interleaved

Burns' make it clear that the area around Riddell's home, Friar's Carse, a veritable sanctuary for Burns in the late 1780s and early 1790s, had become a rich and expansive imaginative resource for the writer. For instance, we have the remarkable spectacle of the cradle-Presbyterian poet signing one of his texts in medieval persona as 'a Bedesman' (that is, a hermetic reciter of the Rosary), this name being used also by Riddell as a creative antiquarian pseudonym.[6] Additionally, the 'Geddes Burns' takes its name from its owner, from whom Burns borrowed the book, Bishop John Geddes (1735–99), the Catholic prelate who, like Riddell, was one of Burns's smaller group of intimates following the poet's retreat to Dumfriesshire in the aftermath of his period of lionisation in Edinburgh from November 1786 to March 1788. Both interleaved books demonstrate Burns, to some extent, entering into a more reflective period, a time of retreat and reassessment after the whirlwind of his sixteen-month urban sojourn in the Scottish capital, a change of pace he later expressed in a letter to John Geddes of 3 February 1789 as 'tuning my lyre on the banks of Nith'.[7] Burns, certainly, in his tours, first of all formally and feted when he visits the borders (twice in 1786 and 1787) and the highlands (in 1787), but later more casually in the course of Excise duties through the south-west of Scotland (from 1789 to the end of his life), is interested in the historic song culture of Scotland and so in a sense, gregariously, of its 'people'. What should also be pointed out, however, is that as Burns's artistic life from the Dumfriesshire period is much more inflected by his involvement in song rather than in poetry, and as he takes on this amplified lyrical turn, there is as much emphasis on his own personal life as on the life of the people.[8] As Carol McGuirk says of this period in Burns's biography, in a certain sense he 'went underground' in his public self-effacement, in his turn to both song-writing and his own

Museum but also by the equally casual treatment of the Glenriddell MSS, a collection which was likewise lost to public view during the nineteenth century until 'rediscovered' in 1913. See Robert Burns, *The Glenriddell Manuscripts*, introduced by Desmond Donaldson (Wakefield: EP Publishing, 1973).

6   Nigel Leask, *Robert Burns and Pastoral* (Oxford: Oxford University Press, 2010), p. 259.

7   *The Letters of Robert Burns*, I, p. 367.

8   Robert Crawford's recent interesting argument in *The Bard* (pp. 327–8) that 'Tam o' Shanter' (published 1791), one of Burns's most vibrant 'folk-tales', reflects in codified fashion Burns's problematic recognition of his own adultery also generally supports this view of an increasingly inward-looking writer.

interior life.[9] Burns's gift of the interleaved *Museum* to Robert Riddell is a very private gesture, surrendering, as it does, some of the most sensitive biographical material about Burns into the hands of another. It also contains additional notes by Riddell, probably encouraged by the poet in a rare and intimate act of Burnsian literary collaboration.

Burns's present of the interleaved set to Riddell clearly shows that he went back on an original intention to use it as the basis for a revised second edition of the *Museum*. In a letter to James Johnson, Burns refers to the volumes, writing that he will 'insert every anecdote I can learn, together with my own criticisms and remarks on the songs. A copy of this kind I will leave with you, the Editor, to publish at some after period, by way of making the Museum a book famous to the end of time, and you renowned for ever'.[10] The reasons for Burns's change of mind are not precisely clear, but he withdrew from his euphorically projected engagement with his public and instead used the interleaved *Museum* to construct an expressively lavish 'private edition', one of the richest exemplars in what elsewhere I have called Burns's 'reserved canon'.[11] The first person to make use of the interleaved *Museum* material in print was Robert Hartley Cromek (1770–1812), in his *Reliques of Robert Burns* (1808). Burns's first editor, James Currie (1756–1805), working in the immediate aftermath of the writer's death, is a controversial figure in the textual history of the poet, at the same time both suppressing text and making unwarranted additions to Burns's text, but also retrieving material that otherwise might have been lost for ever without his sensitive ministrations.[12] Following the publication of Currie's *The Works of Robert Burns* (1800), it was clear to many Burns aficionados that there were large gaps in this edition. The general criticism that has often been made of Currie is that he censored areas of political and sexual expression (though it should be pointed out that Burns had also prudently done the same during his lifetime). This is obvious enough. Interestingly, however, Cromek was able to add to the published canon and claimed in his *Reliques* that he was following in the editorial footsteps of James Currie where 'nothing is there inserted which

9   *Robert Burns, Selected Poems*, ed. Carol McGuirk (London: Penguin, 1993), p. 251.
10   *The Letters of Robert Burns*, II, pp. 156–7.
11   See Gerard Carruthers, 'Burns and Publishing', in *The Edinburgh Companion to Robert Burns*, ed. Gerard Carruthers (Edinburgh: Edinburgh University Press, 2009), pp. 6–19.
12   See the online edition, *The Correspondence of James Currie 1756–1805*, ed. G. Carruthers and K. G. Simpson at the University of Glasgow.

can render his works unworthy of the approbation of manly taste, or in-consistent with the delicacy of female virtue'.[13] Even so, Cromek suggest-ed that much more of a biographical and antiquarian job was necessary, that it was the intimate, material, physical life of the writer that remained to a large degree wanting following Currie. The curious phenomenon of the Burnsian pilgrimage, something evident even during Burns's life and which makes him arguably the first British writer to be consumed in seri-ously Romantic fashion, is in strong evidence as Cromek becomes near obsessive in his chase for new material:

> In this pursuit I have followed the steps of the poet, from the humble Cottage in Ayrshire in which he was born, to the House in which he died at Dumfries. – I have visited the farm of Mossgiel where he re-sided at the period of his first publication; I have traversed the scenes by the Ayr, the Lugar, and the Doon. Sacred haunts![14]

Not for nothing is Cromek's volume entitled *Reliques*. As well as letters by Burns's father William, Cromek publishes for the first time Burns's first *Commonplace Book*, seventy-two new letters, twenty-five new po-ems, twenty-four new songs and various 'fragments' untidily gathered from a variety of manuscript sources. Of most interest to our purposes, however, is a long section Cromek calls 'Strictures on Scottish Songs and Ballads, Ancient and Modern; with Anecdotes of their Authors'. Cromek 'advertises' it as follows:

> The chief part of the following Remarks on Scottish Songs and Ballads exist in the hand-writing of ROBERT BURNS, in an inter-leaved Copy, in 4 Volumes, Octavo, of 'Johnson's Scots Musical Museum.' They were written by the poet for CAPTAIN RIDDEL, of GLENRIDDEL, whose Autograph the Volumes bear. These volumes were left by MRS. [Maria] RIDDEL [Robert Riddell's sister-in-law], to her Niece, MISS ELIZA BAYLEY, of MANCHESTER, by whose kindness the Editor is enabled to give to the Public transcripts of this amusing and miscellaneous Collection.[15]

---

13   R. H. Cromek, *Reliques of Robert Burns, Consisting Chiefly of Letters, Po-ems, and Critical Observations on Scottish Songs* (London: Cadell and Davies, 1808), p. iv.
14   Ibid., p. v.
15   Ibid., p. 188.

After Cromek, the volumes remained uninspected by scholarly eyes for almost one hundred years until J. C. Dick was granted access in 1902. Following Maria Riddell's bequeathing of the interleaved *Museum* to her niece, there is some ambiguity over the whereabouts of the set. Whether or not there were subsequent owners before 'John Salkeld, bookseller, London, [who] sold them in 1871 to a book collector named A. F. Nichols, for £110' is not known.[16] Nichols' housekeeper, Miss Oakshott, inherited the volumes and auctioned them via Sotheby's (London) in 1903, a Mr Quaritch paying £610 for ownership. Quaritch sold the volumes on again (for an unknown sum) to George C. Thomas of Philadelphia. The Burns Monument Museum's acquisition in 1964 of the interleaved *Museum*, however, was from the Rabinowitz Library (a private collection) in the USA, the Trustees at Alloway paying £5,500 for the interleaved *Scots Musical Museum*, and so at last the set came into public hands in Scotland.[17]

Burns's friendship with the Riddells was breached in December 1793, after a mysterious incident which has come to be known as 'The Rape of the Sabine Women' (though this coinage only dates from the early twentieth century), where he apparently offended Maria Riddell, in particular.[18] What is clear is that Burns was extremely agitated about the depths of the animosity between himself and the Riddells, and in the following year in the wake of Robert Riddell's death the poet was concerned to retrieve from the family the first volume of the 'Glenriddell Manuscripts'. This showpiece, fair-hand holograph album contains some of the writer's most important poetic texts but, as James Mackay has observed, Burns's 'claim to this volume was doubtful. The book itself was Robert Riddell's property from the outset, decorated with the Glenriddell coat of arms. [. . .] Almost half the contents, in fact, were in a hand other than the poet's. [. . .] Nevertheless, Elinor Riddell [Robert Riddell's sister] apparently complied with the poet's

16   D. McNaught, 'Cromek Convicted', *Burns Chronicle* (1909), 116.

17   The Rabinowitz Library is presumably that which belonged to Aaron Rabinowitz (1884–1973), who was a book collector from New York. At some point it seems likely that Rabinowitz acquired the interleaved *Museum* from George C. Thomas of Philadelphia. For the Alloway acquisition of the set, see '£5,500 For A Burns Work' in *Burns Chronicle* (1965), 86–9.

18   For the most modern comprehensive account of the 'Sabine Women' incident, see James Mackay, *Burns: A Biography of Robert Burns* (Edinburgh: Mainstream, 1992), pp. 555–64.

wishes, for the volume was duly returned to Burns without demur'.[19] Following the rupture, Burns seems to have made no such claim on the interleaved *Museum* even though, as things turned out, it contained sensitive material apropos Burns's love life; from the perspective of the nineteenth century, the most important information of all. Cromek's usage of this material in 1808 was to initiate a controversy that was to last until the twenty-first century. Cromek's revelation of the name of Burns's early lover, 'Highland' Mary Campbell (?1766–86), who died in controversial circumstances, was based on a note that he claimed accompanied the song, 'The Highland Lassie O', in the interleaved *Museum* but the release of this information, clearly, was licensed by the Burns family, and probably also the Campbell family. At the time of the breach with the Riddells and in the aftermath of Robert Riddell's death in 1794, Burns would seem to have been unperturbed by the family's continuing ownership of the note, trusting, presumably, in a pledge of honourable silence (drafted by Burns, as we shall see below) on the part of the Riddells.

The holograph note forms part of the canonical version of Burns's life-story that he seriously intended to emigrate to the West Indies, a plan abandoned, perhaps, when news reached the poet of Mary's death in Greenock (the port from which he (or both) according to some commentaries, was (were) to sail). No one attested to seeing the note after Cromek, while the volume remained in private hands. To the astonishment and outrage of J. C. Dick, when he was given permission to examine the interleaved *Museum* in 1902, the note was absent and fifteen other annotations that Cromek had presented to the world in the 'Strictures on Scottish Songs and Ballads' of his *Reliques* were likewise labelled 'spurious' by Dick, either because they were altogether absent (blank pages rather than physically missing in all but one case) or had been egregiously supplemented by Cromek. Dick's conclusion in 1903 was that Cromek had been fraudulent with these fifteen annotations and until the 1920s, the consensus was that the Burns world had long been duped and was now awakened. Dick was joined by Duncan McNaught, the notoriously fierce editor of the *Burns Chronicle*, who published in that journal his 'Cromek Convicted' (1909), a review of Dick's *Notes on Scottish Song by Robert Burns* (1908) which also expanded on the view of Cromek's calumny. McNaught notes Cromek's collaboration with 'Honest' Allan Cunningham in the volume *Scottish Songs* (1810) 'with

19   Ibid., pp. 563–4.

many additional "inventions" of the same kind as those in the *Reliques*; but in Allan Cunningham, who contributed the bulk of that volume, like Patie Roger, "oot o' his ain head", he met his master in literary deception, and was most appropriately "hoist with his own petard"".[20]

Gullible (taken in by his collaborator, Cunningham, in the matter of the spuriously attributed texts in *Scottish Songs*) and not always methodical as an editor, Cromek was not, in fact, dishonest, as emerged in 1921–2. In May 1921, David Cuthbertson published parts of holograph manuscripts in Burns's hand in the *Kilmarnock Standard* from the Laing collection in Edinburgh University (this material had been deposited since the late 1870s), which Davidson Cook realised included some of the missing notes that Cromek had printed in *Reliques* and which Dick had (erroneously, then) assumed to be fabricated.[21] In an article in the *Burns Chronicle* for 1922, still under the editorship of McNaught, who was creditably keen to set the record straight, Cook claimed that the Laing manuscript evidence showed that Cromek in his 'Strictures on Scottish Songs' 'had drawn upon at least one other *unstated* source – this very Burns Manuscript of twelve folio pages which is one of the Laing MSS. now treasured in the Library of Edinburgh University'.[22] Using the Laing manuscripts, Cook reinstates eight of the 'missing' notes from the interleaved *Museum*, pertaining to the songs 'Waukin o' the Fauld', 'Mill, Mill, O', 'Bob o' Dumblane', 'Kirk wad lat me be', 'Jackie's Gray Breeks', 'The Posie', 'Highland Laddie' and 'Clout the Cauldron'. In the case of 'Saw ye my Peggy' and 'Fy, gar rub her o'er wi' strae' and 'Tweedside', Cook found that Cromek had supplemented the notes in the interleaved *Museum* with additional material from the Laing manuscript. Even by the sometimes looser standards of early nineteenth-century editing, this is eccentric practise; nonetheless, what emerged at this point was that Cromek had not been pretending to have words by Burns that he did not have. Cook also highlights the erroneousness of what Dick claims to be the clearest pointer to Cromek's fraud, his citation of Burns referring to the fifth volume of the *Scots Musical Museum*, which appeared after Burns's death. In the Laing manuscripts, Burns refers to

20   McNaught, 'Cromek Convicted', 117.

21   See the *Kilmarnock Standard* (14 May 1921), 8. The relevant portion of the Laing manuscripts in the University of Edinburgh Library is La II 210 9 ('Notes on Scottish Songs').

22   D. Cook, 'Annotations of Scottish Songs by Burns', *Burns Chronicle* (1922), 4.

the fifth volume in both the 'Highland Laddie' and 'Auld Lang Syne' notes. From this newly verified fact, Cook sensibly deduced that '[the Laing manuscript] was probably written towards the close of the Poet's life'.[23] There are also, however, as Cook notes, five still absent of Dick's 'spurious notes', which in the light of the Laing material are likely to be genuine, including the 'Highland Lassie' note. With the exception of this last note, the situation in 2011 stands at four missing notes (three very short ones and a 'longer' one, the latter, 'The Bonie Lass made the Bed to me' being only two sentences in length) that remain so far not retrieved.[24] The very brevity of these items points strongly towards their authenticity.

The Laing manuscripts were probably those used by Cromek; alternatively, given discrepancies between these and what Cromek actually published, he may have utilised an altogether different manuscript source. Burns had a habit of making multiple copies of poems, songs and letters and, especially if we were to give Cromek the benefit of the doubt as a better editor than he sometimes appears to be, a different manuscript with closely similar but not identical material to that found in the Laing collection could have been employed by Cromek. Of the thirty-three items in the Laing manuscript, Cromek 'ignores' eight items, either mere titles without songs attached (two); or texts, fragments or complete (five, two with notes); and one additional note. Though these two unattached song titles in Burns's hand, 'The Moudiewart' and 'Maggie Lauder' reappear as songs in full in Cromek's *Select Scotish* [sic] *Songs* (1810). Intriguingly, 'The Moudiewart' appears in the 1810 volume with Burns's note, 'This song is mine' (not in the Laing manuscript); circumstantial evidence perhaps, since nowhere can Cromek be proved ever to have fabricated the poet's words, that there was in existence, at one point at least, a third Burns holograph manuscript.[25] Even more interestingly, the note to 'Maggie Lauder' reads in its sureness of judgement and diction as though it may well be an authentic Burns text (for which neither the Laing nor the interleaved *Museum* provides holograph authority):

23   Ibid., p. 18.
24   Along with 'The Bonie Lass', the three missing short notes are to 'Polwart on the Green', 'The Shepherd's Complaint' and 'We ran and they ran'.
25   R. H. Cromek, *Select Scotish Songs; Ancient and Modern*, 2 vols. (London: Cadell & Davies, 1810), II, p. 171.

This old song, so pregnant with Scottish naivieté and energy, is much relished by all ranks, notwithstanding its broad wit and palpable allusions. – Its language is a precious model of imitation: sly, sprightly, and forcibly expressive. – Maggie's tongue wags out the nicknames of Rob the Piper with all the careless lightsomeness of unrestrained gaiety.[26]

Also, as the Laing manuscript shows, leaving aside many minor differences with Cromek's printed texts, there are six song-texts or notes that seem either to be composites of the Laing and interleaved *Museum* sources or somehow in other ways are substantially disordered or even garbled.[27] Here again, however, a credible hypothesis, is the existence of a 'third' manuscript, or collection of materials, being drawn upon by Cromek, which may (or may not) have disappeared for ever. Cromek's phrase, already quoted, 'the chief part of the following [. . .] exist in the handwriting of Robert Burns [. . .] in an interleaved copy of [the] *Scots Musical Museum*' leaves in place considerable ambiguity. Is it simply Burns's handwriting that forms 'the chief part' rather than the less frequent hand of Robert Riddell, or is it, as may well be the case, that Cromek is signalling also other manuscript material, which might be the Laing material or, instead, our hypothesised missing 'third' manuscript? If the 'Maggie Lauder' note is authentically Burns, and the foregoing logic seems to present a reasonable probability, then this represents an interesting editing problem: does such a note merely go into the appendix of a new edition of *The Scots Musical Museum*, or does it call for a version never before found in print that requires the song 'Maggie Lauder' as well as the note to be introduced according to Burns's original intention? Or, since Burns seems to have given up on the idea of his revised second edition of the *Museum* based on the interleaved set, must such material count as 'cancelled' matter? This is one of those instances in editorial work where there seems to be no definitive answer.

The present author and some colleagues recently examined the four volumes of the interleaved *Museum* to ascertain the current status of its manuscript material (not tampered with since at least the time of the Dick inspection in 1902).[28] Most of the four-volume set has interleaves,

---

26   Ibid., I, p. 93.
27   These pertain to 'Mill, Mill, O', 'Saw ye nae my Peggy?' 'Fy, gar rub her o'er wi' strae', 'The Lass o' Liviston', 'Dainty Davie', and 'Tweedside'.
28   I am grateful to the assistance of Pauline Mackay and Rachael Renfrew

some of which are blank but the majority of which are extensively annotated by Burns, with a much smaller collection of notes by Robert
Riddell. There is, however, an absence of interleaves on two occasions
in Volume I, on four occasions in Volume II, on seven occasions in
Volume III and on five occasions in Volume IV.[29] In Volume I, one of
the absences is an obviously removed item, a remnant of it containing
Robert Riddell's handwriting. This, most likely, was removed by Riddell
himself as material that became increasingly sensitive toward the end
of his life and as the 1790s became a more fearful time in Britain. It
pertains to an item, possibly a song in its own right, 'The Lucubrations
of Henry D–nd–ss in 1792'. Whatever this item was precisely, it is interesting that it lies between 'Oh ono chrio' and 'Low down in the Broom'.
A note remains for the former, which Cromek prints in his *Notes on
Scottish Song*, but he does not print 'The Lucubrations' material, im-
plying either that he too, as someone later did on removing the note,
shied away from its political sensitivity, or much more likely, it had
been removed already (probably, as already suggested, by Riddell). A
version of 'Low down in the broom', very different from the innocent

---

in inspecting the interleaved *Scots Musical Museum*, and also to Nat Edwards,
Caroline Glenn and Amy Miller for so kindly facilitating the research.

29   The interleaf anomalies in the interleaved *Museum* are as follows: Volume
I: missing between pp. 78 and 79; missing, cut out, with remnants in Robert
Riddell's hand, between pp. 90 and 91. Volume II: missing between pp. 103
and 104 (though as J. C. Dick observes, 'The leaf was probably spoiled and de-
stroyed, for the Note on this song was inserted by Burns on the following interleaf' [see *Notes on Scottish Song*, p. 72]); pp. 121 and 122 (where the 'Highland
Lassie' note is assumed to have been); missing between pp. 135 and 136; missing
between pp. 161 and 162. Volume III: missing between pp. 210 and 211; missing between pp. 232 and 233; there is a double blank interleaf between pp. 252
and 253; missing between pp. 288 and 289 (where is situated another 'Highland
Mary' song, 'My Mary, dear departed shade', perhaps lending credence to Mary
Campbell material, including the 'Highland Lassie' note, being removed from
the interleaved set by someone with a special interest); missing between pp. 290
and 291; missing between pp. 292 and 293; missing between pp. 304 and 305;
missing between pp. 308 and 309; Volume IV: missing between pp. 314 and 315;
missing between pp. 316 and 317 (clearly cut out); missing between pp. 320
and 321; missing between pp. 328 and 329; missing between pp. 368 and 369
(fragment remaining to show clearly it has been removed). What should be
stressed is that these physically missing interleaves pertain to songs *other than*
those retrieved via the Laing manuscript. The one presumed physically missing
interleaf to have been re-discovered is the 'Highland Lassie' note.

pastoral version that Burns produces for the *Scots Musical Museum*, is part of a sequence of reformist political pieces attacking Henry Dundas and William Pitt, written by Alexander Geddes (1737–1802). Was the removed material underneath the 'Lucubration of Henry Dundas' a version, Geddes's or someone's else's (even Burns's own, perhaps) of a politicised 'Low down in the Broom'? This area, requiring further investigation and beyond the scope of this essay, is another tantalising puzzle from the interleaved set. Burns notes Geddes elsewhere in the interleaved *Museum* but his presence elicits no additional comment from Cromek, though in the case of another political reformist, James 'Balloon' Tytler (1745–1804), like Geddes a man of wide cultural production, Cromek provides an extensive biographical note in 'Strictures on Scottish Songs and Ballads'. Cromek describes Tytler as being involved in 'the wild irrational plans of the British convention' (of 1792, when largely moderate reformers gathered in Edinburgh to discuss the aim of greater democratic participation).[30] Tytler and Geddes were equally and heroically outspoken in the cause of liberty during the 1790s, but the politically conservative Cromek does not really want to know about these individuals in any even neutrally sympathetic fashion, even though both are admired by Burns. Elsewhere, Cromek shows himself to be painfully ignorant of recent cultural history as he mistranscribes from the interleaved *Museum* the name 'Johnson', when it should be [Samuel] 'Thomson', a very significant Ulster-Scots poet who is the author of 'To the Rose Bud'.[31] Cromek was, indeed, a scattergun, careless and sometimes purblind editor, who missed or was incapable of taking the opportunity to transmit a satisfactory sense of the interleaved set to the world.

As mentioned already, of the mishandled, excised material from the interleaved *Museum*, the 'Highland Lassie' note has been the most controversial item. Cromek printed it as follows:

THIS was a composition of mine in very early life, before I was known at all in the world. My Highland Lassie was a warm-hearted, charming young creature as ever blessed a man with generous love. After a pretty long tract of the most ardent reciprocal attachment, we met by appointment, on the second Sunday of May, in a sequestered spot by the Banks of Ayr, where we spent the day in taking a fare[w]el[l],

---

30   Cromek, *Reliques*, p. 310.
31   Ibid., p. 298.

before she should embark for the West-Highlands, to arrange matters among her friends for our projected change of life. At the close of Autumn following she crossed the sea to meet me at Greenock, where she had scarce landed when she was seized by a malignant fever, which hurried my dear girl to the grave in a few days, before I could even hear of her illness.[32]

When the note is read in the original, however, it reads additionally, 'For the sake of this, & similar anecdotes, Mr Riddell will keep these volumes solely for his private perusal.' One might at first consider Cromek's reason for omitting this part of the text has to do with the sensitivities of people still alive; though Robert and Mary Burns were dead their immediate family members were not. However, as mentioned, Cromek interviewed the Burns family and probably also members of the Campbell family. The inference that the information was licensed in this way can be drawn, in part, from the fact that Gilbert Burns, the poet's brother, was in the early decades of the nineteenth century acting almost as a policeman towards his brother's memory, correcting Currie on fairly minor details of fact and not always happy as information about Burns's love life continued to trickle out. Gilbert's silence about the Mary Campbell revelation and the use of the note implies tacit agreement and even encouragement. Cromek's non-use of the Riddell pledge part of the note probably shows nothing more than his limited editorial view that this portion was not significant to the topic in hand.

It was assumed that the note remained missing until Robert Crawford in his 2009 biography of Burns mentioned the online facsimile version of the note which was owned by the Birthplace Museum.[33] A team from the University of Glasgow, led by myself, and with the assistance of a senior curator of the National Library of Scotland and the curator at the Birthplace Museum began an investigation into this curious fact. We inspected the note itself which was easily to be found (referenced in the most recent catalogue of BPM holdings) and in the temporary keeping of the National Library of Scotland while the Birthplace Museum was being redesigned. As size and chain-lines showed, the paper was identical to the other interleaves in the interleaved *Museum*, as was the ink

32   Ibid., pp. 237–8.
33   See the Scran database (which is part of the Royal Commission on the Ancient and Historical Monuments of Scotland): www.scran.ac.uk/database/record.php?usi=000-000-497-835-C.

and an interleaf at the song 'The Highland Lassie O', between pp. 121 and 122 of Volume II, is, indeed, physically missing. We were fairly convinced that the 'Highland Lassie' note had been very carefully removed from the interleaved *Museum,* and when we replaced it between the appropriate pages within the volume, it fitted perfectly; on closing the volume the note disappeared smoothly within the book's page edging, just as the other interleaves do. We published findings to this effect.[34] However, I am now open to the possibility that the note was not in the volume in the first place and was part of a batch of paper, one and the same with the used *Museum* interleaves, which was perhaps held alongside it when Burns and later Riddell owned it and which Cromek inspected, these leaves becoming later, however, completely separated from it. That said, weighing against this hypothesis is the fact that an interleaf is missing precisely at that place in the set. Probably the only way immediately to test whether the Highland Lassie note had ever been part of the set would be the complete unbinding of Volume II of the interleaved *Museum,* something that is unjustified in the wider interest of conservation.

The other area of investigation demanding attention was the note's history, and here some deduction was possible using the exhibition and holdings catalogues of the Birthplace Museum. Burns scholars such as James Kinsley (who produced the best twentieth-century edition of the poems and songs in 1968) and James McKay (who produced his major biography in 1992 and who worked very closely with the Birthplace Museum during a long stint from the 1980s as editor of the *Burns Chronicle*) explicitly lamented the note being missing. This is surprising as my team was able to determine that the 'Highland Lassie' note was on public display at the museum in Alloway between the years of 1961 and 1974 at least. Since, as mentioned above, the Birthplace Museum acquired the interleaved set only in 1964, this proves that the 'Highland Lassie' note was not obtained together with it. Further, it is likely that the Birthplace Museum included the note among material described, in its 1931 and 1933 catalogues, merely as 'Thirteen leaves containing lists & words of songs, also music and notes (probably in connection

34   Gerard Carruthers, Lindsay Levy, Helena Reilly, Julie Renfrew and Mark Wilson, 'Some Recent Discoveries in Robert Burns Studies', *Scottish Literary Review* 2.1 (2010), 143–58. My thanks to the members of this research team, as well as to Jean Nicolson mentioned elsewhere in this essay and also Mr Kenneth Dunn of the National Library of Scotland.

with the "Scots Musical Museum") in the holograph of Burns, James Johnston and others'.[35] A trail can be followed through the series of entries in the museum's updated catalogues, pertaining to 'music and notes . . . probably in connection with the "Scots Musical Museum"'. Most recently, in the early twenty-first-century catalogue, this entry in the museum's lists appears as:

> Sixteen pages of lists and words of songs, with music and notes, probably compiled in connexion with Scots Musical Museum. It is written in the hands of RB, James Johnson et al.[36]

These sixteen 'pages' are nine separate manuscript items (but equal eighteen pages, verso and recto but with two blank, or without holograph, and so equalling sixteen 'sides' of manuscript). If we hypothesise that the 'Highland Lassie' note (holograph on one side, blank on the other) was originally in this bundle of material that would equal eighteen 'pages', or seventeen of holograph. In the 1931 catalogue the same core item is described as already mentioned:

> Thirteen leaves containing lists & words of songs, also music and notes (probably in connection with the "Scots Musical Museum") in the holograph of Burns, James Johnston and others.

In the 1933 catalogue we find a longstanding item reiterated:

> List of songs in the Holograph of James Johnson and of Robert Burns, compiled probably in connection with the "Scots Musical Museum": 4pp, quarto.[37]

We also find the 'Thirteen Leaves . . .' item from 1931 identical with the 1933 catalogue entry. By 1936, however, these two items have been conflated to become

---

35   *The Burns Cottage Alloway: Catalogue of Manuscripts, Relics, Paintings and Other Exhibits in the Cottage and Museum with Historical Note* (Ayr Advertiser: Ayr, 1931 and 1933), item 529.

36   See the list compiled for the Birthplace Museum's material deposited in the National Library of Scotland (but where some material is retained at Alloway and so also listed for purposes of identity of interim location), *Muniments of the Burns Cottage Museum* (Acc 9381), item 361 [NLS: 6270].

37   *The Burns Cottage Alloway: Catalogue of Manuscripts* (1933), item 62.

Twenty pages of lists and words of songs, also music and notes (probably in connection with the "Scots Musical Museum"), in the holograph of Burns, James Johnson and others; folio and quarto.[38]

This would provide us with precisely seventeen pages of holograph (including three blank) and twenty 'sides' of page. Exactly the right figure
on the assumption that the 'Highland Lassie' note has been originally
among the 'music and notes . . . in connection with the "Scots Musical
Museum"'.

A table makes this clearer:

Current catalogue

Items	Pages	Holographs
9	18	16

1936 catalogue

Items	Pages	Holographs
10	20	17

Assuming the 'Highland Lassie' note were added to the current
catalogue:

With 'Highland Lassie'

Items	Pages	Holographs
10	20	17

Crucially we can deduce the ten items, twenty pages and seventeen folios of holograph of 1936 because the two lists (or two items) in
Robert Burns's hand (or four pages holograph) are extant today among
the 'Sixteen pages' item. This leaves seven items to be accounted for, of
today's nine; and of these we have five (holograph, verso and recto) and
two (one side holograph only) equaling twelve sides of holograph (or
sixteen when added to the four pages of holograph list).

The recent research of Jean Nicolson, a participant in the World
Burns Club discussion forum and one of the majority convinced the

---

38 *The Burns Cottage Alloway: Catalogue of Manuscripts* (1936), item 211.

note was genuine, takes us as close to an answer to when precisely the note was acquired. She unearthed in the Ayrshire Archives a receipt for the 1907 purchase by the Birthplace Museum from an antiquarian book dealer, William Brown, in Edinburgh, for £150 of an item which appears in the 1908 Birthplace Museum catalogue as:

> Odd leaves of Johnson, Scottish Musical Museum, with original holograph notes throughout by the poet.[39]

Amid the transaction records with Brown is a receipt that is tantalisingly close to revealing, most likely, the 'Highland Lassie' note. It records, '1 page of Johnson's Museum'. If only it were just a little more specific. Absolute certainty would be good, but these items most likely highlight the time when the Birthplace Museum acquired the 'Highland Lassie' note. The receipt, the absence of any other likely Birthplace Museum items with which it might have been parcelled up, and the figures above make it now the best hypothesis we have: that the Birthplace Museum acquired the note in 1907. There is considerable historical irony here, as it was precisely at this time that J. C. Dick was compiling his Cromek-denouncing *Notes on Scottish Song*. This publication appeared in the same year as the Birthplace Museum was, seemingly, though not with entire clarity, publicly cataloguing the item. However, generations of twentieth-century Burns scholars might, in a sense, hang their heads in shame since the note was certainly extant in 1961, and most likely the same can be said for 1931 as well as going further back to 1907.

What the story above tells us is a very familiar one to scholarly editors and students of book history: that manuscript (and print) materials can quite quickly become almost impossibly confusing and in need of a reconstruction that can often never be easily or fully completed. In the case of Robert Burns, we have the added complexities of a life and work bitterly contested, both in the collection of materials and in their interpretation. Burns himself was capricious, we might say, in the disposing of his work; collectors ardently and privately sought ownership of his manuscripts, so that long periods of scholarly vacuum were created. In the case of the interleaved *Scots Musical Museum*, as with other important Burns sources, some form of souvenir hunting, either nefariously carried out or after less caring owners came into possession of the volumes and casually allowed the dispersal of some parts, may well have

---

39 *The Burns Cottage Alloway: Catalogue of Manuscripts* (1908), item 150.

gone on. There is more confusion over the Laing manuscripts that complement the interleaved *Museum*, clearly for some time in the possession of the antiquarian David Laing (1793–1878), himself the son of an Edinburgh bookseller, suggestively enough. How did he acquire these materials and at what point? To these questions, currently, we do not know the answers. The foregoing essay also hypothesises the existence of a third manuscript (or at least a variant set of materials to the Laing manuscript) drawn upon by Cromek. If this third manuscript did ever exist, we do not know where it is now, and, at the risk of undermining my own argument, no one has ever heard of this manuscript, but this might not be entirely surprising given the very private mentalities of some collectors, to say nothing of the casual practises of Burns's earliest editors. We have glimpsed too a little of the market for Burns, most especially during the nineteenth century but this is something that avidly continues in the twenty-first century. If many factors conspire to make the job of long-suffering editors, bibliographers and even mere literary critics sometimes almost entirely unachievable, scholars themselves do not always show themselves in creditable light. Cromek, however much we attempt to lessen the appearance of his odd editorial practices, was partial and careless. Currie before him, however well-motivated (and he was in intention in attempting to edit a Burns for the world that would be most widely acceptable so as to accrue money for the poet's widow and children), delayed publication of many materials at one time in his possession. Some of these, probably, passed to Cromek and other editors later who dealt with these no more thoroughly; other materials were later sold in the private marketplace by Currie's family, with no real moral license, following his death. One of the effects of Currie's 'editing' was that the Burns corpus became more confused than it might have been with the (probably permanent) loss of some material altogether. Dick was a little premature in lambasting Cromek for sins that he did not commit, though had the latter been more careful in the first place this situation need not have arisen. With almost comic timing the Birthplace Museum acquired the 'Highland Lassie' note as Dick was sharpening his pencil against Cromek. In a chain of error, to put it charitably, Burns scholars through the entire twentieth century (including the present one) missed what was under their noses all the time until 2009. That excellent institution, the Birthplace Trust Museum, is now much more professionally curated than once it was. For most of its history, well-meaning amateurs working heroically but in overwhelmingly difficult and under-resourced circumstances simply could not keep track of what the Birthplace Museum had in its possession and did not know what to tell the scholarly and wider world about its holdings. The material legacy of Robert Burns must be better served in future and Burns scholars also need to be more sharply attentive where too many of them were not in the past. It is time, in the twenty-first century, for Burns Studies to turn over a new leaf.

Packaging, Design and Colour: From Fine-Printed to Small-Format Editions of Thomson's The Seasons, 1793–1802

SANDRO JUNG

LIKE NO OTHER TEXT in the eighteenth century, James Thomson's *The Seasons* demonstrates the socio-economic importance of what James Raven has discussed in terms of product design: booksellers realised that 'tailoring products to a particular clientele, experimenting in the design and packaging of products, and presenting these, as well as wider publishing activities, as fashionable' contributed materially to increased sales.[1] At the same time, following the lapse of perpetual copyright, which the pirated reprinting in Scotland of *The Seasons* had indirectly brought about, a market for the reprinting of works previously controlled by the monopolies of individual booksellers emerged. This proliferating market saw the publication of editions of Thomson's work, in various formats, for a socially diverse buying public.[2] Ranging from relatively cheap, small-format and serialised editions to high-end subscription ventures, the print capital of *The Seasons* was seen as a

Part of the research for this essay was made possible through the award of a fellowship in the Graphic Arts Department at Princeton University Library. Unless otherwise noted, all illustrations have been reproduced from editions in the author's possession.

1   James Raven, *The Business of Books: Booksellers and the English Book Trade* (New Haven: Yale University Press, 2007), p. 269.
2   The most up-to-date scholarly account of eighteenth-century editions of *The Seasons* is: Sandro Jung, 'Visual Readings, Print, and Illustrations of Thomson's *The Seasons*, 1730–1797', *Eighteenth-Century Life* 34.2 (2010), 23–64. See also, the author's *James Thomson's 'The Seasons', Print Culture, and Visual Interpretation, 1730–1842* (Bethlehem, Pennsylvania: Lehigh University Press, 2014). Ralph Cohen's largely art-historical, qualitative-evaluative account of the illustrations of Thomson's work, *The Art of Discrimination: Thomson's 'The Seasons' and the Language of Criticism* (London: Routledge, 1964), does not take into account the developments in eighteenth-century print culture.

testing ground for bookseller-publishers' experiments with marketing strategies, which after 1765 no longer restricted an edition's format to that used by Thomson's formerly exclusive copyright holder, Andrew Millar. The impetus to reprint popular works not only culminated in a large number of competing editions; it also resulted in the formation of a canon of British literature that was underpinned, primarily, by economic considerations regarding available copyright and demand, rather than the recognition of aesthetic merit as a criterion for inclusion in the canon of eighteenth-century literary worthies. Collaboration between booksellers, artists, designers and various trades catering to booksellers' demand for improved materials such as paper and type culminated, in the 1790s, in some of the most impressive ventures in book printing and a range of subscription projects.[3] Given the large number of eighteenth-century editions of *The Seasons*, Thomson's work (as one of the texts that was commodified most diversely in the period) is ideally suited to an examination of the ways in which bookseller-publishers found new ways of marketing their editions. The text in its multifarious editions and formats lends itself to an investigation of innovations – in terms of technologies and design – that booksellers drew upon for their publishing projects. Contextualising the strategies used by bookseller-publishers to advertise their new editions of *The Seasons* and paying particular attention to colour-printed editions of the poem, this essay will examine in which ways the producers of these volumes embedded their works within a market for fine-printed editions. It will focus on the study of colour printing as a means to enhance designs based on paintings; at the same time, it will reconsider the medium of the colour-printed plate not only as an indicator of the image's or edition's cultural status and significance, but as an indication of its publisher's desire to create a uniquely competitive edition.

While aristocratic patronage had supported the first subscription edition of Thomson's poem in 1730, in the last two decades of the century the increased number of newspapers advertising subscription ventures targeted a much broader group of middle- to upper-class consumers.

---

3   Some of these subscription projects did not materialise, but the proposals and publishing prospectuses describing these ventures are important ephemeral sources of information that enable historians of the book and scholars of literature to gain an understanding of the ways in which booksellers and editors sought to distinguish their editions from one another and devised particular marketing strategies to compete on the market for elite or scholarly editions.

This shift from aristocratic patronage to a more heterogeneous group of subscribers is evident in the subscription edition in folio format of the poetical works of Thomson that Andrew Foulis published in Glasgow in two volumes in 1784. One year earlier, Foulis had issued a separate printing of *The Seasons* in folio. Selling at £1 and printed on 'the finest demy writing paper',[4] the edition celebrated Thomson as a national, Scottish poet and the appended list of subscribers comprised both dignitaries of rank and eminent scholars, including Hugh Blair, then professor emeritus of Rhetoric and Belles-Lettres at Edinburgh University. The subscription proposal for the edition insisted that the format adopted would be based on the Foulis edition of Virgil's *Bucolics, Georgics* and *Aeneid*.[5] It targeted 'the lovers of learning and of the arts' and was dedicated to His Royal Highness George, Prince of Wales. As Printer to the University, Foulis undertook to align Thomson with the classical author with whom his work had most directly, intertextually, been associated. The proposal contextualises the edition in terms of its aspiration as a production of classic status. By the 1780s, Thomson's *The Seasons* had transformed into important cultural and national capital in the vernacular and fed a market which Benedict Anderson has contextualised as a material-economic hub facilitating literacy through print capitalism.[6] The first Scottish subscription edition, Foulis's folio volumes did not feature illustrations as other editions did at the time to differentiate them from what had been the paradigmatic standard of Andrew Millar's quarto edition and its four allegorical tableau plates by William Kent. In his cultural-patriotic ambition, Foulis distinguishes himself from all other contemporaneous bookseller-publishers of *The Seasons*. The edition's expensive paper, specially cast type and excellent printing quality singled his project out in that Thomson was presented to buyers of fine-printed books as a national, learned poet who deserved the same paratextual treatment that Virgil's works had previously received.

Following Foulis's edition, Thomson's works experienced the kind of careful marketing and branding that Alexander Pope had taken such care to seek for his own works. The paratextual packaging of *The*

4   Foulis's publishing proposal, University of Glasgow, 6 January 1783, fol. 1r (NLS shelfmark 6.692 [1]).
5   *Publii Virgilii Maronis Bucolica, Georgica, et Aeneis*, 2 vols. (Glasgow: printed by A. Foulis, 1778).
6   See Benedict Anderson, *Imagined Communities: Reflections on the Origin and Spread of Nationalism* (rev. edn, London: Verso, 1983).

Seasons by different editors (such as John Aikin, Percival Stockdale and Robert Heron) and bookseller-publishers would take place in the competitive arena of the marketplace for illustrated books. The print culture of the 1790s was characterised by close links between industrial branches for book and print making, and booksellers would vary existing marketing strategies and formats, as well as devise 'competitive packaging devices',[7] to appeal to buyers and sell their editions as desirable commodities distinct from and, above all, superior to other editions of the same work.

The most impressive edition of *The Seasons* – in terms of the range of ambitious engravings, the high-quality printing and paper used, and its declared objective of offering a new model of subscription publication aligned with Thomas Macklin's subscription Bible[8] – was issued by Peltro William Tomkins (1759–1840) in early 1798, although the title page of the edition gives 1797 as the year of publication.[9] His subscription project took six years to complete. Printed by Thomas Bensley (bap. 1759, d. 1835), one of the most accomplished printers of his day, it represented a gold standard of typographical design and was produced at a time when other booksellers projecting editions of *The Seasons* addressed their proposals 'To the Lovers of the Fine Arts'[10] and 'To the Lovers of Fine Printing',[11] thereby explicitly relating their own editions to a tradition of lucrative and artistically produced subscription ventures (such as Thomas Hanmer's edition of Shakespeare's works) dating back to the beginning of the century. Bensley used Whatman's superfine woven paper, achieving an effect of a well-printed and crisp page that many publishers of subscription editions but also of more affordable editions of *The Seasons* sought to emulate. Superlatives on the quality of the materials used and the typographical execution of the text

7   James Raven, 'The Book as Commodity', in *The Cambridge History of the Book in Britain, 1695–1830*, ed. Michael F. Suarez, S.J., and Michael L. Turner (Cambridge: Cambridge University Press, 2009), V, p. 86.

8   An advertisement in *Diary or Woodfall's Register*, 7 May 1792, stated that 'This Work shall be printed on the same Paper and Letter as Macklin's Bible; and will class, in every respect, with that work'.

9   Some of the plates are dated 1798.

10   *General Evening Post*, 11 October 1792. This advertisement is for Archibald Hamilton's edition. A four-page advertisement (a copy of which is held by St. Bride Library, London) was issued as well.

11   *World*, 25 November 1791. This advertisement is for John Murray's 1791 edition.

abound in the advertisements of subscription editions in the 1790s, but Tomkins's edition represents a standard of its own. Tomkins's venture was the most ambitious and exclusive British edition of *The Seasons* and was rivalled only by the non-illustrated, typographically innovative editions of 1794 that David Steuart, eleventh Earl of Buchan (1742–1829), commissioned Giambattista Bodoni (1740–1813) to produce in folio and quarto formats.[12] While Steuart, the author of *Essays on the Lives and Writings of Fletcher of Saltoun and the Poet Thomson* (1792), was keen to establish the reputation of Thomson as an eminent literary Scotsman and wished 'to do justice to the memory'[13] of his countryman by responding to Johnson's strictures in the *Lives of the English Poets*, Tomkins's edition capitalised on a short-lived demand, in the early 1790s, for fine-printed subscription works that was largely uninformed by Steuart's idealistic programme of cultural improvement. Unlike Bodoni's edition, Tomkins's was marketed widely.

In his engraved plates and vignettes, Tomkins demonstrated the high level of technical sophistication that engravers like himself were able to master. His technical skill as demonstrated in the edition contributed to the redefining of the status of the medium of the expensive print that Thomas Macklin equally considered essential for his scheme of a Poets' Gallery. His project aimed to assemble, from 1787 onwards, a collection of one hundred paintings, to be exhibited at Macklin's Pall Mall gallery, of the works of the poets of Great Britain. According to Macklin, engraved illustration for elite consumption, by the early 1790s, had become an 'elegant art':[14]

> Under the guidance of [William] WOOLLETT, Engraving, as compared with Painting, became a congenial, not a subordinate art, and assumed the air of a favoured companion [of painting], rather than an humble attendant. [. . .] Formed in the schools of BARTOLOZZI and

---

12   See Brian Hillyard, 'David Steuart and Giambattista Bodoni: On the Fringes of the British Book Trade', in *Worlds of Print: Diversity in the Book Trade*, ed. Catherine Armstrong and John Hinks (New Castle, Delaware: Oak Knoll, 2006), pp. 122–3.
13   David Steuart, earl of Buchan, *Essays on the Lives and Writings of Fletcher of Saltoun and the Poet Thomson: Biographical, Critical, and Political. With some Pieces of Thomson's never before published* (London: printed for J. Debrett, 1792), p. 253.
14   *Poetic Description of Choice and Valuable Prints, published by Mr. Macklin, at the Poets' Gallery, Fleet Street* (London: printed by T. Bensley, 1794), p. vii.

of Woollett, the abilities and industry of our countrymen have carried this branch of the Fine Arts to a degree of perfection which may boldly be said to stand unrivalled.[15]

In 1766 Woollett had engraved the first painterly reworking of a tale from *The Seasons* by Richard Wilson, thereby making a large-scale reproduction in the format of the furniture engraving available to upper-class buyers.[16] It took another twenty years, however, until a number of smaller, more affordable prints of scenes from Thomson's poem were offered for sale by printsellers such as Charles Taylor and John Boydell. While stipple engravings became quickly fashionable, other prints were produced as mezzotints and issued, at the cost of 2s., in hand-coloured versions. Woollett's works frequently consisted in elaborately engraved landscape paintings, rather than the portraits or genre pieces that would become fashionable in the print medium in the 1780s. The 1790s were a decade in which a large number of extraordinarily exquisite large-scale prints were published in London, which represented a 'degree of perfection' that could rival prints produced in France at that time. Macklin's Gallery was conceived as a major example of the excellence of English engraving. Macklin issued the prints derived from the paintings he specially commissioned for his gallery in numbers but also sold them individually in both monochrome and colour versions. Each number sold at £3 3s. plain or £7 7s. in colour, whereas a single print sold at £1 1s. plain or £2 2s. in colour.[17] Tomkins likewise sold the prints for his edition as part of the edition as well as separately. Breaking with the illustrative structure of William Kent's full-page plate-per-season format for Millar's subscription edition, Tomkins's edition – like other editions of the 1790s – adopted the combinatory format of full-page plate and vignette, in the process offering one of the most wide-ranging visual narratives of iconographic moments produced in the eighteenth century.

The subscription proposal for Tomkins's 'Magnificent Edition'[18] had offered an explanation of why Thomson's poem was ideally suited to pictorial treatment. The edition included illustrations in the form of twen-

---

15 Ibid., p. vii.
16 See Sandro Jung, 'Painterly "Readings" of *The Seasons*, 1766–1829', *Word & Image* 26.1 (2010), 68–82 (72–3). Woollett's furniture print measured 67 × 30.5 cm and sold at £7 5s.
17 *Poetic Description of Choice and Valuable Prints*, p. 1.
18 *Diary or Woodfall's Register*, 7 May 1792.

ty-one designs undertaken by William Hamilton, RA (1751–1801), on whose paintings the plates were based. Tomkins issued a 'Description of Pictures Illustrative of Thomson's Seasons, now exhibiting at Tomkins and Co.'s, No. 49, New Bond Street', a practice that had also been used for Fuseli's Milton Gallery and the Boydell Shakespeare Gallery.[19] Tomkins's 'Description' included listings of the paintings that William Hamilton had based on the accompanying textual passages from *The Seasons*, including, among others, 'The Invocation and Approach [of Spring]', 'The Happy Family', 'Celadon and Amelia', 'Lavinia and Her Mother', 'Palemon's First Sight of Lavinia' and a series of large-scale vignettes termed 'Miniatures'. The edition also included explanations of the engravings such as one identifying the shepherd in the vignette for *Winter*:

In the Headpiece to Winter is introduced the portrait of Richard Brown, known by the name of The *Good Old Shepherd*, born at Botley Pound, near Oxford, on Ladyday in the year 1686. He lived in a cottage at Chawley in Berkshire, much esteemed for his piety and morality; enjoyed a good state of health and a retentive memory; was married to three wives; died Oct., 1795, in the 110th year of his age; and on the 15th of the same month was buried at Cumner, Berks, leaving behind him four sons and one daughter; the eldest 78, the youngest turned of 50. He quitted this life with the utmost serenity of mind, and resignation to his Maker's will.

These descriptions not only provided a commentary on the illustrative material but they also highlighted the anthropocentric character of the visual narrative of Tomkins's edition. They represent one additional paratextual feature that distinguishes the edition from its competitors.

At the same time as Tomkins started circulating proposals for his edition in both pamphlet form and as short advertisements in a range of newspapers, John Murray (1737–93), whose business had already issued two octavo editions in 1778 and 1791, published a rival prospectus in which he announced his projected subscription volume featuring engraved plates of 'Original Pictures' painted for the purpose of the edition by Robert Smirke (1752–1845). Probably capitalising on Francesco Bartolozzi's (1727–1815) status as royal engraver, Tomkins succeeded

19   See Luisa Calè, *Fuseli's Milton Gallery: 'Turning Readers into Spectators'* (Oxford: Oxford University Press, 2007).

in obtaining Queen Charlotte's support for his edition, which he and Bartolozzi dedicated to her. The prestige of the dedication may have been one of the reasons why Murray's project proved abortive. Murray's four-page printed proposal implied that 'Sharp and Murray's Edition of Thomson's Seasons' aimed to outdo Tomkins in that it advertised its visual apparatus to consist of twenty-two, rather than Hamilton's twenty-one, illustrations. Like Tomkins's edition, Murray advertised his projected venture as 'A correct and splendid edition'. Evidence of Murray and William Sharp's commitment to their edition is provided by a range of unlettered proof impressions of three designs that Sharp was preparing in late 1792. The size of these intaglio engravings (28cm × 20cm) and the combinatory format of full-page plate and vignette above the 'Argument' that Thomson prefixed to each of his seasons indicates in which ways Murray sought to capitalise on recent developments in the design of illustrated books, especially the models and formats of illustration used in the decade's Shakespeare editions.[20]

Sharp's designs capture two scenes, one of which was to be engraved, after a painting by Thomas Stothard (1755–1834), 'The Lover's Dream', for another subscription edition issued in 1793 by Archibald Hamilton. This edition was dedicated to the Earl of Buchan and included notes on *The Seasons* by Percival Stockdale. Hamilton issued his 'correct, elegant, and cheap' edition in five numbers, each part selling at 2s. 6d, but a brief comparison of Tomkins's venture and Hamilton's will illustrate in which ways the publishers catered to different niche markets. Hamilton's edition included four full-page plates based on paintings by Thomas Stothard and Henry Singleton. Three of Singleton's designs (including 'Musidora', 'Palemon and Lavinia' and 'The Shepherd's Care') are complemented by Stothard's full-page plate ('The Lover's Dream') and eight vignettes, four large headpieces and four smaller tailpieces. While the plates offer visual interpretations of iconographic moments that were becoming fashionable in the early 1790s, the designs are far less complex and both compositionally and tonally less sophisticated than those provided by William Hamilton for Tomkins's edition. The vignettes in Hamilton's edition are the most ambitious vignettes illustrating *The Seasons* produced at the time and are second

---

20   Some of these proofs are held by the British Museum Print Room. On Shakespeare and illustrated Shakespeare editions in the 1790s, see Stuart Sillars, *The Illustrated Shakespeare, 1709–1875* (Cambridge and New York: Cambridge University Press, 2008), pp. 148–80.

only to Tomkins's in size. Focusing on rendering scenes typical of the seasons but not concerned with interpreting Thomson's interpolated tales, Stothard's vignettes represent farming and leisure activities within these landscapes. The specific depictions of human life and relationships in the plates are bound into the individual seasons and are framed by the vignettes (at the beginning and end of each season) which frequently embed human life into rural nature and a natural environment that inspires reflection.

Stothard's emphasis on natural setting in the vignettes for Archibald Hamilton's edition was not adopted by William Hamilton, whose work was translated into the medium of print by Tomkins and Bartolozzi. By the time that Stothard and Singleton started illustrating Thomson's poem, William Hamilton had already twice produced visual interpretations of passages and tales from *The Seasons*. He furnished four designs for full-page plates for John Murray's 1778 octavo edition and undertook allegorical interpretations of the seasons for a series of four stipple-engraved prints that the print-seller John Boydell, the owner of Boydell's Shakespeare Gallery, published in 1784.[21] His history paintings formed part of Boydell's programme 'to promote the British school of history painting and encourage a choice of serious subjects by native authors'.[22] Hamilton contributed a range of canvases to Macklin's Poets' Gallery in Pall Mall, although the three paintings for Macklin's Gallery associated with Thomson's poem were produced by Sir Joshua Reynolds (the conversation piece 'The Gleaners'), Thomas Gainsborough ('Lavinia') and John Opie ('Damon and Musidora').[23] Writing about paintings such as Reynolds' and Gainsborough's, Richard Altick has pointed out that 'the name of Lavinia and the references to Thomson's poem were merely hung onto studies of gleaners, either returning from the fields with

---

21   These allegorical, feminising renderings of 'The Four Seasons' were popular, as is indicated by a set of four ovals that G. B. Cipriani designed for Macklin. These ovals, selling at 4s. each or at 6s. in colour, were engraved by Bartolozzi. See *The Poets' Gallery, Fleet-Street. Catalogue of the sixth exhibition of pictures, painted for T. Macklin, by the artists of Britain; illustrative of the British poets and the Bible* (London: printed by T. Bensley, 1793), p. 71.

22   Paul Goldman, 'The History of Illustration and its Technologies', in *The Oxford Companion to the Book*, ed. Michael F. Suarez, S.J., and H. R. Woudhuysen (Oxford: Oxford University Press, 2010), I, p. 140.

23   See T. S. R. Boase, 'Macklin and Bowyer', *Journal of the Warburg and Courtauld Institutes* 26.1–2 (1963), 151.

Fig. 1: John Opie's 'Damon and Musidora' (based on an original oil painting now at Petworth House)

their day's harvest or resting and quietly ruminating'.[24] The most original interpretation of a tale from Thomson's poem for Macklin's Gallery was furnished by John Opie (1761–1807) who painted the two lovers Damon and Musidora (Fig. 1),[25] a painting that Macklin had engraved by Bartolozzi in 1796.

The practice of commissioning paintings for editions of *The Seasons* was not uncommon in the 1790s,[26] and three editions featured engraved versions of paintings (including Henry Singleton's oil canvas of Palemon and Lavinia of 1792) that had been produced to serve as designs for engraved prints. Some of these were exhibited at the Royal Academy as well. As late as 1800, Henry Fuseli produced a painting of the Celadon and Amelia episode in *Summer* (lines 1169–1222), which was engraved by Francis Legat and William Bromley for Francis J. Du Roveray's 1802 edition.[27] Hamilton had painted this, the most frequently illustrated tale from *The Seasons*, in 1793 (Plate I and Fig. 2). His flamboyant painting of the two ill-fated lovers Celadon and Amelia overtaken by a thunderstorm in the course of which Amelia is struck by lightning and transformed into a 'blacken'd corse' became one of the signature episodes by which Thomson's poem was identified. Hamilton engaged with the tale one more time for the frontispiece design he contributed to the 1817 miniature edition issued by Suttaby, Evans and Fox. In the early 1790s, he also produced a range of other, smaller paintings representing well-known iconographic moments from the poem, including a visualisation of Palemon's first encounter with the gleaner Lavinia. These paintings were translated into the medium of print by Bartolozzi and Tomkins and resulted in what T. S. R. Boase considers 'Hamilton's masterpiece',[28] the series of designs supplied for Tomkins's subscription edition. Boase notes that the 'artificial elegance [of Hamilton's paintings of iconographic moments from *The Seasons*] equal the more famous

---

24   Richard D. Altick, *Paintings from Books: Art and Literature in Britain, 1760–1900* (Columbus: The Ohio State University Press, 1985), p. 393.

25   *The Poets' Gallery, Fleet-Street. Catalogue of the sixth exhibition of pictures, painted for T. Macklin, by the artists of Britain; illustrative of the British poets and the Bible* (London: printed by T. Bensley, 1793), p. 32.

26   Altick, *Paintings from Books*, pp. 392–4. For a discussion of paintings offering visualisations of the Celadon and Amelia episode, see Jung, 'Painterly "Readings" of *The Seasons*'.

27   *The Collected English Letters of Henry Fuseli*, ed. David H. Weinglass (Millwood and London: Kraus International Publications, 1982), p. 242.

28   Boase, 'Macklin and Bowyer', p. 151.

Painted by H. Fuseli R.A.   Engraved by W. Bromley.

Fig. 2: Henry Fuseli's 'Celadon and Amelia', which appeared in *The Seasons* (London: printed for F. J. du Roveray, 1802)

series of prints of Wheatley's "Cries of London" (the painted versions of which were exhibited at the Royal Academy between 1792 and 1795) that were appearing almost contemporaneously'.[29] Above all, the ways in which Hamilton interpreted the scenes and interpolated episodes he illustrated provided paradigmatic, iconotextual readings of Thomson's poem that many later illustrators reworked in their own visual paratexts for editions of *The Seasons*.

In his projected edition, Tomkins sought to capitalise on Hamilton's association with high-cultural painting and, at times, the muscular style of Henry Fuseli's art. In the publishing proposal, Tomkins noted:

> It is a point on which Artists are unanimously agreed, that no other author furnishes more delightful subjects for the pencil than Thomson. In rural scenery he is unequalled: whatever can engage, whatever can soothe, whatever can elevate the soul, is always at his command. The beauties of nature he has traced with a minuteness which the artist can scarcely rival. But he has not merely described; he has peopled his fields, his groves, his cottages; and his pathetic narrations furnish the most interesting situations in which the pen or the pencil can exhibit human nature.[30]

Moving away from the sublime landscapes of Richard Wilson's *A Summer's Storm* (1760; the first painting ever to depict Celadon and Amelia) and *Solitude* (c.1762), Hamilton focused on depicting Thomson's 'pathetic narrations', moments of sublimity and suffering, as well as domestic interiors. He supplies a design of the Palemon and Lavinia episode, which is his second rendering of the tale, having illustrated the meeting of the two lovers for Murray's edition in 1778. While Murray's edition was advertised as the most ambitious edition of *The Seasons* at the time, it was printed on laid paper, rather than on the more expensive wove paper of Tomkins's edition. Comparing the two plates in terms of their production, Robert Essick notes that 'the plate [for Tomkins's project] is an elegant combination of line, stipple, and roulette work. [. . .] The smooth texture, high level of finish, and tonal subtlety of the plate bespeak the engraver's efforts to produce a book illustration of the most fashionable and refined type' (Fig. 3a and

29   Ibid.
30   *World*, 12 April 1792.

PALEMON & LAVINIA.

Hamilton Delin.   *Caldwall Sculp.*

Then throw that shameful pittance from thy hand,
But ill applied to such a rugged task :
The Fields, the Master, all, my Fair, are thine .

London 1.st April 1778. Publish'd as the Act directs by J. Murray N.º32 Fleetstreet .

Fig. 3a: William Hamilton's 'Palemon and Lavinia', engraved by Richard Corbould for *The Seasons: A new edition. Adorned with a set of engravings from original designs. To which is prefixed an essay on the plan and character of the poem*, by J. Aikin (London: printed for J. Murray, 1778)

AUTUMN.

Fig. 3b: William Hamilton, 'Palemon and Lavinia', engraved by Francesco Bartolozzi for *The Seasons by James Thomson* (London: printed for P.W. Tomkins, 1797)

Fig. 3b).[31] The earlier, more cheaply executed intaglio plates offer little tonal depth, but should be understood in the context of Murray's issuing an illustrated edition at a time when a mythopoeic visual interpretation of Thomson's text had been the only one since 1730.[32] While his 1778

31   Robert N. Essick, 'William Blake, William Hamilton, and the Materials of Graphic Meaning', *ELH: English Literary History* 52 (1985), 864.

32   William Zachs, *The First John Murray and the Late Eighteenth-Century London Book Trade* (Oxford: Oxford University Press, 1998), p. 60. Zachs cites a letter, dated 5 May 1792, from John Murray to John Elder in which Murray states that 'Mr [William] Sharp is the first Engraver in London & the two first Pictures for the work are in the Exhibition and much admired' (p. 60). Zachs relates Murray's statement to 'the sale of his 1792 edition of Thomson's Seasons', but the reference to Sharp's engraving work of paintings should surely be linked

edition was reprinted in the same year and in 1779, Murray issued an-other octavo edition, with new engravings based on designs by Conrad Martin Metz, in 1791; unlike the 1778 edition, the illustrations to the later edition did not revisit Thomson's interpolated episodes.

Tomkins's edition was clearly marketed as a luxury commodity item and collectible. It was a monument in the history of book-making and memorialised Thomson as a poet of national importance and in terms of a mythic-inspirational canon. While the seasonal deities crown his bust in the edition's frontispiece design, the bust is placed on a pedestal featuring in medals the likenesses of Thomson, Tomkins and Bartolozzi. As a collector's item, the edition transferred mediated versions of the paintings into the realm of the collector's study and a community of like-minded lovers of books. Depending on whether they framed prints illustrating texts or gathered them together in a portfolio, collectors promoted the consumption of these paper-based decorative objects within the privacy of their commodified homes, which were also, as Maxine Berg has argued, frequently hubs of luxury.[33] An increasingly popular collecting practice was that of Grangerising, the extra-illustra-tion of editions of *The Seasons* with suitable print material, at times resulting in extensive print collections and interleaved copies of edi-tions expanded into a number of volumes.[34] Thomson's poem not only inspired a large number of paintings and prints by such eminent artists as Angelica Kauffmann and Thomas Stothard (who had produced three sets of designs illustrating *The Seasons*) but also fed a material culture that featured visualisations of iconographic moments from the poem on a range of different media, including enamelled watch-cases which re-peatedly depicted the Palemon and Lavinia episode. Enamel and porce-lain medallions for application on furniture and designs for coffee pots and vases (such as William Duesbury's and Thomas Soare's Chelsea soft paste ware) by Kauffmann catered to the desire of the financial elite to be fashionably up-to-date.[35] New, luxurious materials such as coloured silk, specially coloured bindings and gilt ornamentation facilitated the

with the 'Sharp and Murray' edition which, in the event, did not materialise.

33   See Maxine Berg, *Luxury and Pleasure in Eighteenth-Century Britain* (Ox-ford: Oxford University Press, 2005).

34   An example of the latter practice is held by the Pierpont Morgan Library, New York. The four volumes (call number 142153–56) include 140 extra il-lustrations.

35   Examples of these are held by the Victoria and Albert Museum, London.

customising of individual copies of Tomkins's edition, and a range of differently dyed leathers used in book binding contributed to creating unique and personalised examples of the edition. The folio format provided an appropriate frame for the gallery of Hamilton's visualisations. The auratic status of the edition that advertisements emphasised was highlighted further with the publication of colour-printed plates of Hamilton's designs, which more closely than their monochrome variants invoked the painterly origin of the plates.

Elaborate colour printing of stipple engravings was one of the most striking innovations adopted by bookseller-publishers issuing editions of *The Seasons*. According to Joan M. Friedman, 'demand for color book illustrations' increased at the end of the eighteenth century, 'if only among a limited audience of the educated and the well-to-do'.[36] Throughout the century, plates in botanical and anatomical works, as well as in magazines featuring fashion plates, had been hand-coloured. Illustrations of literary texts were rarely issued in colour until the 1790s, but were occasionally personalised by owners through hand-colouring. Colour printing as such, on the French model, became available in Britain at the end of the century. The technologies of colour printing *à la poupée*, using a ragdoll to apply individually coloured inks to the surface of the copper plate, were still experimental at that time, however, and only a small number of texts, including Edward Jeffery's 1796 edition of Horace Walpole's *The Castle of Otranto* and a French 1793 edition of Salomon Gessner's *Death of Abel*,[37] featured colour-printed plates. Tomkins's full-page folio plates were issued in a number of states and formats, including those printed in the coloured inks sanguine and sepia. At the same time, plates were printed in colour and were usually finished with water-colours by hand. While in 1793, an advertisement stated that 'The Price of each Number will be One Guinea[,] Proofs Two Guineas, and Prints in Colours Two Guineas', once the edition was published, the prices had significantly increased, as is indicated by the

36   Joan M. Friedman, *Color-Printing in England* (New Haven: Yale Center for British Art, 1970), p. 7.

37   *Mort d'Abel, poème de Gessner, traduit par Hubert. Édition ornée d'estampes imprimées en couleur, d'après les dessins de M. Monsiau, peintre de l'Académie* (Paris: chez Defer de Maisonneuve, 1793). For another fine, French example of colour-printed stipple engravings, see Jean de Florian's quarto edition of *Gala-tée, roman pastoral. imité de Cervantès par M. de Florian, de l'académie française, &c. édition ornée de figures en couleur, d'après les dessins de M. Monsiau* (Paris: chez Defer de Maisonneuve, 1793).

price of £14 14s. for the 'proof impressions of the plates, [in] boards'.[38]
Beyond 1798, Tomkins's edition was reissued in large quarto in 1807,
1810 and 1814.[39] The quarto edition, while certainly less expensive,
was still a collectible; it was frequently issued in ornate silk bindings.[40]

The first example of colour printing appears to have been the Scottish
quarto edition of Thomson's poem published by Robert Morison, Junior,
in Perth in 1793.[41] While this edition, which included an essay on the
poem by Robert Heron, was marketed in London and conceived to rival
Archibald Hamilton's large octavo edition of the same year, its use of
colour printing was limited to a few copies only. Extensive water-colour
washes were applied to the printed designs to enhance their brilliancy.
The use of colour strikingly distinguished Morison's ornate volume from
any of the more ambitious editions issued in London; in terms of production quality, it distinguished the Perth printer's work from all other
Scottish editions, including Foulis's folio edition. In 1794, a reviewer,
as well as commending the 'excellent' quality of the paper and engravings, notes that 'the spirited publishers [. . .] have carried typography to
a conspicuous degree in Scotland, and done honour to their country'.[42]
The edition was a milestone in the Scottish publishing of belles-lettres
and no later edition published in Scotland would rival it. Morison was
the first bookseller-publisher to issue sample material to interest the
buying and subscribing public in his project; in 1792, he published the

38   *A Catalogue of Books, in every department of literature, now on sale by John White, Horace's Head, Fleet-Street* (London: printed by Davis, Wilks, and Taylor, March 1801), p. 8.
39   The 1814 edition was issued by the London booksellers Gale, Curtis and Fenner. The work was printed in London by Whittingham and Rowland, Gos-well Street.
40   See the advertisement in *The Monthly Magazine; or, British Register* 29 (1810), 486: 'Thomson's Seasons; illustrated with engravings by Bartolozzi and Tomkins, from original pictures by W. Hamilton, R.A. imperial 4to £4 4s. – with the addition of four large Engravings, by the same artist – royal folio, £8 8s. – super royal, with proof plates, £10 10s. A few copies of the imperial 4to. edition, with the plates finely coloured, £15 15s.'.
41   One of these (call number: 53 T384 730e) is held by the Lewis Walpole Library, Farmington; another is in the author's possession. A third (call number: PR3732.S4 1793) copy, which is extra-illustrated, with many of the extra illus-trations printed in colour *à la poupée*, is held by the Yale Center for British Art.
42   *Anthologia Hibernia: or Monthly Collections of Science, Belles-Lettres, and History* 3 (1794), 48.

CELADON AND AMELIA

Plate I: William Hamilton's 'Celadon and Amelia', engraved by Francesco
Bartolozzi for *The Seasons* (London: printed for P.W. Tomkins, 1797)

Plate II: Francis Chesham's 'Summer', engraved by Charles Catton for *The Seasons. A new edition. Adorned with a set of engravings, from original paintings. Together with an original life of the author, and a critical essay on the Seasons. By Robert Heron* (Perth: printed for R. Morison, 1793)

F. Thurston del.

J. Scott

Plate IIIa: 'Musidora', from *The Seasons, to which is prefixed, a life of the au-*
thor. Together with illustrative remarks on The Seasons. By the Rev. J. Evans, A.M.
Master of a seminary for a limited number of pupils, Pullin's Row, Islington (London:
printed by J. Cundee, for T. Hurst, 1802)

Plate IIIb: 'Lavinia's Mother', from *The Seasons, to which is prefixed, a life of the author. Together with illustrative remarks on The Seasons. By the Rev. J. Evans, A.M. Master of a seminary for a limited number of pupils, Pullin's Row, Islington* (London: printed by J. Cundee, for T. Hurst, 1802)

eight-page pamphlet 'The beautiful episode of Palemon and Lavinia: from The Seasons' which was 'Intended as a specimen of a superb edition of that inimitable poem, to be printed at Perth'.[43] Priced at 3s., this publication could be consumed as a chapbook of one of Thomson's most celebrated tales, while also serving as ephemeral evidence of Morison's high printing and design standards. The few colour-printed copies of Morison's edition consolidated the reputation of excellence, especially in terms of exquisite typography, for which the firm was known.

Morison's subscription edition included full-page plates 'from original paintings' by Charles Catton (1728–98) as well as unacknowledged vignettes on the portrait frontispiece of the edition that Thomas Stothard had designed for Thomas Baker's annual diary, *The Royal Engagement Pocket Atlas*, for 1793 (Fig. 4 and Plate II).[44] The engraved title page was adorned with a landscape vignette executed by James Kirkwood. The frontispiece reproduced a painted portrait that had not been used for editions of *The Seasons* before. Unlike the prints of Tomkins's edition, Catton's designs are combinatory in subject in that they offer a range of anthropocentric interpretations of scenes from *The Seasons*, including the gathering of nuts, sheep-shearing and a depiction of a ship during a storm. The visual matrix that Catton generates is selective and promotes a reading of Thomson's text that is not based on an identification of iconographic moments and tales represented visually in other editions. Rather, Catton appears to move deliberately away from earlier painterly renderings and capture a novel approach to the poem that emphasised its polyphony. In this departure from earlier models of visual interpretation, Catton's designs represented the novelty of design by which Morison's 1790 duodecimo edition of Thomson's poem had already been distinguished. The earlier volume featured the first book illustration, in the form of a frontispiece, of the Celadon and Amelia episode. It also included a small portrait vignette of Lavinia, which did not sketch the context of love that most other illustrators highlighted in their designs.

43   A copy of this sample is held at the British Library (shelfmark: RB.23.b.5092).

44   Stothard also designed a set of twenty-four vignettes for the 1797 number of *The Royal Engagement Pocket Atlas*. For Stothard's illustrative work on the annual, see Sandro Jung, 'Thomas Stothard's Illustrations for *The Royal Engagement Pocket Atlas*, 1779–1826', *The Library* 12.1 (2011), 3–22, and Nancy Finlay, 'Thomas Stothard's Illustrations of Thomson's *Seasons* for the *Royal Engagement Pocket Atlas*', *Princeton University Library Chronicle* 42 (1980–1), 165–77.

Fig. 4: Frontispiece to *The Seasons. A new edition. Adorned with a set of engrav-ings, from original paintings. Together with an original life of the author, and a critical essay on the Seasons. By Robert Heron* (Perth: printed for R. Morison, 1793)

Morison utilised the common method of issuing his subscription edition in instalments. The wrapper of the first number states that each number would be accompanied by two plates and that these 'plates are thrown off large, to accommodate those who may wish to keep them out of the Book'.[45] So, five years before Tomkins's edition finally materialised, Morison had already targeted his volume at collectors of fine printing and sophisticatedly executed plates, which could be bound into the book or framed, depending on the buyer's preference. The colour-printed plates were personalised copies but not on the scale of Bartolozzi's engravings.

Before Tomkins's edition no English edition of a belles-lettres production had featured such ambitious colour printing as used for the plates in the volume. In France, the year Tomkins's edition was first advertised, a colour-printed edition of Milton's *Le Paradis Perdu* was published. It was 'Ornée de douze Estampes imprimées en couleur d'après les Tableaux de M. Schall',[46] engraved by Jean-Frédéric Gautier, and was one of the most significant monuments of eighteenth-century colour printing in Europe.[47] Only a small number of colour-printed editions of *Le Paradis Perdu* were produced; in terms of intensity, the colours are strikingly rich and saturated and not as subtle and lucid as the ones used by Tomkins and Bartolozzi. A significantly larger number of colour-printed copies of Tomkins's edition were issued, despite the generally widespread assumption that only five or six of these copies were produced.[48] The use of colour printing in high-end media at the

45   James Thomson, *The Seasons. A new edition. Adorned with a set of engravings, from original paintings. Together with an original life of the author, and a critical essay on the Seasons. By Robert Heron* (Perth: printed for R. Morison, 1793). The four instalments in original green wrappers are held by the NLS (shelfmark: Bdg.m.90).

46   Title page.

47   See Colin and Charlotte Franklin, *A Catalogue of Early Colour Printing: From Chiaroscuro to Aquatint* (Oxford: John Roberts Press, 1977). Also, W. Furman, 'Colorizing *Paradise Lost*: Jean-Frederic Schall's Designs for *Le Paradis Perdu* (1792)', *The Huntington Library Quarterly* 59.4 (1998), 465–502.

48   See Friedman, *Color-Printing*, p. 15. Colour-printed copies traced are held by the following repositories: Yale Center for British Art, Princeton University Library (3960.2.38.16f and NE910.G7 B2 1797f), Victoria and Albert Museum (100.C.13), Library of Congress (PR3732.S4 1797), Pierpont Morgan Library (PML 145682 and PML 77810, PML 76854), University of Virginia Library, Charlottesville (PR3732.S4 1797a), National Trust, Anglesey Abbey, The

end of the eighteenth century serves as an endorsement of the status of Tomkins's edition as a high-cultural venture that repackaged Hamilton's painterly responses to *The Seasons*. It is straightforwardly explained in the context of increasing demand for colour-printed, decorative prints and print collecting, including extra-illustrating practices.[49] Such assumptions about the association of colour printing with luxury print objects are commonplace but should be reconsidered in light of a little-known colour-printed edition of *The Seasons* that was published in 1802.

Up until the turn of the century none of the small-format editions issued in octavo or duodecimo featured colour-printed engravings. In fact, it was unusual for a small-format edition to feature colour printing, even though a very few examples featuring colour-printed portraits exist.[50] The application of colour – irrespective of whether hand-colouring or colour printing was used – enhanced the book in a way that few other packaging devices did. The association of colour with elevated status, high production quality, and upper-class consumption was confirmed throughout the last two decades of the century through the large number of mezzotints that were produced by most of the prominent print-sellers.[51] The extensive use of colour-printed plates and vignettes in a small book format tested assumptions about the format and blurred the distinction between fine-printed editions like Tomkins's that were issued in variants for which colour printing had been used and more affordable editions in smaller formats. A small-format edition boasting colour-printed engravings would occupy an intermediary position between the large and expanding market for pocket editions of *The Seasons* and the more exclusive volumes for bibliophile collectors.

Before 1802 the market for exclusive editions of *The Seasons* had been limited to those produced by means of subscription ventures. At the same time, the large number of octavo and duodecimo editions, with at times extensive and impressive paratextual paraphernalia and

Johns Hopkins University Library (821 T482S 1797 FOLIO c. 1), Colorado State University Library (PR3732.S4 1797), and UCLA Libraries and Collections (ff PR3732.S41 1797).

49   See Sandro Jung, 'Print Culture, High-Cultural Consumption, and Thomson's *The Seasons*, 1780–1797', *Eighteenth-Century Studies* 44.4 (2011), 495–514.
50   Friedman, *Color-Printing*, pp. 13–15.
51   See Sheila O'Connell, *The Popular Print in England 1550–1850* (London: British Museum Press, 2000), pp. 52–5.

illustrative engravings, were sold to the middle classes. There were also a range of editions for use in schools. Among the small-format, illustrated editions produced, those that featured as part of the popular and relatively cheap series of John Bell, Charles Cooke and Joseph Wenman were embedded within larger collections of British poetry and a canon of works available for reprinting. Rather than offering accurate visual translations of Thomson's sentimental-sublime narratives, these serial editions frequently promoted diverse and often strikingly different iconotextual readings that emphasised representationally and iconographically a sense of coherence between those texts included in a specific series.[52] The editions distinguished themselves from each other primarily through their use of different illustrative material, a feature frequently highlighted in the advertisements of these serially published volumes. At the beginning of the nineteenth century, new combinatory formats for book illustrations, including the use of both full-page copper-engraved plates and wood-engraved vignettes (as well as the increasingly prominent use of the wood engraving more generally), were introduced.

One octavo edition not only adopted the combinatory format of copper-engraved plate and vignette, but also offered buyers the opportunity of purchasing a colour-printed variant of the edition. In 1802, the bookseller Thomas Hurst issued his edition of Thomson's poem. It featured 'illustrative remarks on The Seasons' by the Rev. John Evans (1767–1827), Baptist minister and master of a 'Seminary for a limited Number of Pupils, Pullin's Row, Islington'. Hurst issued two variant editions with monochrome or colour-printed intaglio plates of designs furnished by John Thurston 'and other eminent Artists'.[53] The edition

52   See Thomas F. Bonnell, *The Most Disreputable Trade: Publishing the Classics of English Poetry 1765–1810* (Oxford: Oxford University Press, 2008), pp. 97–168.

53   The statement on the title page that Thurston and 'other eminent Artists' furnished the designs for the edition is misleading in that the usual assumption would be that these other artists were recruited by Hurst and Cundee. The contrary is the case, however, since two of the designs – the head vignettes for 'Spring' and 'Summer' – had already been published two years before Hurst issued his edition. They were printed in a French edition publishing a parallel text of *The Seasons* (with the French translation on the verso page and the English original on the recto) and featuring only two of Thomson's four 'seasons'. The two head vignettes in *The Seasons, by James Thomson. A New Edition, entirely revised, corrected, and complete. The First Part* (Paris: printed by Egron,

was printed by James Cundee, who ran the Albion Press from 1805 to 1812.[54] Hurst issued the edition in two formats, in foolscap octavo and as a demy, octodecimo pocket edition, thereby anticipating the multiple format publication that James Wallis undertook when, in 1805, he published his edition in three different book formats. The colour-printed variants were priced at 10s. 6d and 4s. 6d respectively.[55] According to an advertisement, the colour-printed copy was 2s. more expensive than the one comprising monochrome engravings. The edition used the combinatory format of four full-page plates and four head vignettes at the start of each season.[56] The plates were relatively small: the full-page plates measured 8.8 × 6.4 cm, whereas the vignettes measured, on average, 7.5 × 6 cm (Plates IIIa and IIIb). The delicate colouring applied to the eight plates is finely executed and recreates some of the auratic effect that Tomkins would have sought to establish with his colour-printed versions of Hamilton's paintings; some of the designs were finished by hand through the application of water-colour washes, but the quality of the colour printing is surprisingly high. At the same time that Hurst advertised his colour-printed edition of Thomson's poem, he also announced the publication of another colour-printed title by Cundee, an

for F. Louis, 1800) included bilingual text as well but did not print the poet's introductory, summative 'Argument' underneath each image, as Hurst's illustrations would. Rather, the French illustrations were accompanied by two-line captions from the 'season' they illustrated, in both English and French. The 'Second Part' of the edition issued by Louis, which I have not seen, according to William Bate, also contained two head vignettes at the beginning of 'Autumn' and 'Winter'; all four designs were engraved by Lambert. See 'Bibliography of Thomson's "Seasons"', *Notes and Queries*, 20 May 1882, p. 395. While the illustrations that Hurst and Cundee included in 1802 and 1804 were not reprinted in Britain, the head vignettes were reused in an American edition of 1808: *The Seasons: Containing Spring, Summer, Autumn, Winter* (Philadelphia: published by Jacob Johnson, 1808). Unlike the French and English editions, this edition's plates are wood-engraved as opposed to copper-engraved.

54   Ian Maxted, *The London Book Trades, 1775–1800: A Preliminary Checklist of Members* (Folkestone: Dawson, 1977), p. 57. See also *A Directory of Printers and Others in Allied Trades: London and Vicinity, 1800–1840*, compiled by W. B. Todd (London: Printing Historical Society, 1972), p. 51.

55   *The Monthly Epitome, or, Readers their own Reviewers* 1 (1802), 508.

56   Copies of Cundee's colour-printed editions are scarce. I have in my possession a copy of the colour-printed 1802 edition and have examined a colour-printed copy of the same edition in the NLS.

edition of a translation of Goethe's *Sorrows of Werther*,[57] 'Finely printed in Foolscap octavo, and enriched with six beautiful Engravings, from original Designs, by Mr. Hopwood, price 6s. b[oar]ds. or 10s. 6d. with the Plates printed in Colours'.[58]

The edition of *The Seasons* was re-issued by Cundee's Albion Press in 1805.[59] Apart from 'notes and illustrations', the volume included a frontispiece featuring a portrait engraving of Thomson and an engraved title page with a motif – the twelve signs of the zodiac – that had not been used in any other edition of Thomson's text. It sold at 6s. and appears to have been issued with monochrome engravings only.[60] The 'Advertisement' in the second edition reveals the editor's targeting his explanatory notes at 'the young reader' – in the hope of 'drawing his notice to the beauties both of language and sentiment scattered throughout his [Thomson's] delightful work'. A newspaper advertisement characterised the edition as 'considerably improved, by the addition of Eight emblematic Wood Engravings, together with Eight elegant Plates illustrative of the Seasons'.[61] The first edition had included only one wood engraving – a tailpiece at the end of the table of contents. While Hurst does not appear on the colophon of the second edition of *The Seasons* any more, Cundee assumed responsibility for the edition as publisher, also taking the decision to replace the colour printing by means of added wood-engraved visual devices. Cundee's adoption of new visual

57   The only colour-printed copy of this edition I have been able to trace is held by the Beinecke Rare Book and Manuscript Library, Yale University (Call number: BEIN Speck Jc2 802g Copy 2).

58   J. Gordon, *History of the Rebellion in Ireland* (London: T. Hurst, 1803), unpaginated advertisement leaves.

59   Apart from serving as printer for Hurst's first edition of *The Seasons*, Cundee produced a range of editions of English classics, including, in 1804, a two-volume edition of *Paradise Lost* and, in 1806, an edition of the poetical works of Oliver Goldsmith. It is not clear whether any other titles, including Hurst's editions of William Somervile's *The Chase*, William Falconer's *The Shipwreck* and Bunyan's *The Pilgrim's Progress*, were issued in colour-printed format as well. Nor it is clear whether Cundee (and Hurst) conceived of their editions of poetry as forming part of a series, even though Cundee issued a standardised frontispiece in these editions that may indicate serial intention. Hurst's edition of *The Seasons* advertised itself as 'intended as an uniform Companion to the Farmer's Boy and Rural Tales, by Robert Bloomfield'.

60   *Jackson's Oxford Journal*, 16 November 1805.

61   *The Bury and Norwich Post*, 25 September 1805.

devices testifies to booksellers' needs to improve their own editions in the continuously changing market for paratextual packaging.

Little is known about Hurst or Cundee. In accounts of eighteenth-century colour printing, Cundee is not mentioned and his colour-printed works are rare. Cundee's use of colour printing in the 1802 edition ought to be considered as part of his intention to distinguish Hurst's edition from a major fine-printed edition published in the same year: Du Roveray's edition comprising plates designed by Hamilton and Fuseli. Hurst had commissioned plate designs of two of the well-known tales from *The Seasons* and had the edition printed by Bensley. While Musidora was conventionally rendered, the plate referring to the Palemon and Lavinia episode shifts focus and no longer represents the two lovers. Rather, Lavinia's mother is introduced, an interpretative visualisation of an iconographic moment that would be illustrated again, in another edition, in 1805.[62] The full-page plate for *Winter* adopts as its subject the ravaging wolves that had already featured in Tomkins's edition. The vignettes do not illustrate any of the specific tales in the poem but generate a sense of the seasons through the activities and landscapes depicted. Using colour printing for an octavo edition, as Edward Jeffery had done before him, Hurst demonstrated the significance not only of the visual material included but the ways in which this material was realised on the page. Going beyond the degree of tonal sophistication expected of an intaglio engraving at the beginning of the nineteenth century, Cundee's colour-printed designs are exceptional examples of a printer's experimentation with a marketing device that would ensure the sale of his edition as the most impressive product in its price–format category. One year after Hurst published his edition of *The Seasons*, Joseph Johnson issued the second edition of the two-volume *Poems of William Cowper*,[63] the first edition having been published in 1800. Thomas Stothard had contributed a series of ten full-page plate designs and Johnson had some of these plates printed in colour and finished with a series of bright water-colour washes. Johnson's colour-printed

---

62   James Wallis's edition, in three formats.
63   I have two of these colour-printed editions in my possession. Digital scans of the colour plates in my copies are available via my Database of Eighteenth-Century Book Illustration: www.decbi.com. Other copies are held by the university libraries of Durham (shelfmarks: SC 08062 and SC 08063), Oxford (shelfmark: 2799 f.226 vols. 1–2), and St. Andrews (shelfmark: s PR3380. A2E03 vols. 1–2).

plates represent another bookseller's experiment with colour for one of his best-selling titles, an experiment that he did not repeat in subsequent editions of Cowper's *Poems*.

Thomson's *The Seasons* serves as a paradigmatic example of the ways in which members of the book trade sought to capitalise on the text's print capital. Building on a new impetus to repackage the work in ways that distinguished their editions and paratexts from earlier models of the 1730s and 1770s, booksellers in the 1790s published expensive, high-end editions in quarto and folio formats with exquisite, sophisticatedly engraved plates. These editions demonstrate that there was a growing market for fine-printed editions on which three ambitious editions of the poem could successfully be sold. The most luxurious of these editions, Tomkins's edition set new standards for the printing and material packaging of an English author's works. Bartolozzi's reputation as one of the foremost engravers of his day, his skill in the stipple medium, and Tomkins's marketing skills combined to make their edition a most coveted collectible for bibliophiles. Their use of colour-printing *à la poupée* on a scale only used in France at the time served other bookseller-publishers such as Hurst and Johnson as a model for their own editions. Some highly popular eighteenth-century texts such as Gessner's poems, Goethe's *Sorrows of Werther*, Walpole's *Castle of Otranto* and, above all, Thomson's *The Seasons* were appropriated in a range of new ways for an ever-increasing reading public.[64] As the century neared its end, new paratexts, including prefaces, notes and glossaries, were added to editions of these texts to underpin their significant cultural status. Innovations in printing technology were quickly applied by publishers of the classics of English literature. With the transition, in the 1820s, from copper to steel engravings and the increasing popularity and sophistication of the wood engraving, colour printing – despite the development of chromolithography – was not widely applied to literary texts. It was not employed in editions of *The Seasons* again until Joseph Martin Kronheim, in 1866, produced colour plates using his version of the Baxter process involving oil colours. The short-lived Baxter process was the last colour-printing technology used in a nineteenth-century edition of Thomson's work. It certainly distinguished Kronheim's edition from the others available on the market for illustrated books, but Kronheim's plates no longer relied on the close interpretative relationship between text and image. The edition's plates provided glimpses of

64   See St. Clair, *Reading Nation*, p. 114.

the atmospheric canvas of nature rather than authenticating Thomson's
tales and descriptions. The packaging and paratextual shaping of *The
Seasons* throughout the eighteenth and the first half of the nineteenth
centuries reflect the dynamics of the competitive forces regulating the
market for illustrated books.

   Publishing proposals and prospectuses offer hitherto largely neglected information on the ways in which bookseller-publishers gauged interest in their projected edition. These ephemeral productions served
as samples of printing and type design, but they also functioned as media used by their publishers to respond to competitors' projects. This
responsive element is evident in Murray's attempt to outdo Tomkins's
ambitious iconotextual narrative by increasing the number of plates included in his projected venture by one.[65] Equally, Tomkins chose a new
typeface designed by Vincent Figgins for his edition, thereby claiming
the novelty and elegance of Figgins's work for his volume. Booksellers'
collaboration with other members of the book and print trade facilitated the utilisation of skills and the sharing of expertise that resulted in
editions such as Tomkins's. Artists such as William Hamilton, Thomas
Stothard and Henry Singleton derived significant income from producing designs for book illustrations or for having their paintings issued in
engraved formats. The close relationship between booksellers, printsellers and artists in the early 1790s resulted in some of the most ambitious
(and widely known) visual narratives of the poets of Britain. Due to the
wars in Europe, from the late 1790s the declining demand for exclusive
printing work such as Morison's and Tomkins's editions of *The Seasons*
necessitated the re-alignment of publishers to cater for a less affluent
market. This shift is best reflected in the fine-printed editions in octavo
that were issued by Du Roveray and Wallis in the first decade of the new
century. Hurst's edition featuring colour-printed plates demonstrates
that even at a time when booksellers decided to choose more affordable
formats, individual editions were still distinguished by unique branding
and packaging devices that clearly drew on consumers' association of
colour printing with the high-end editions of the 1790s.

65   In 1778, Murray had distinguished his edition from those of his competitors by commissioning John Aikin to produce 'an essay on the plan and character of the poem', which the bookseller continued to use for another twenty years
in his editions of Thomson's poem.

Print Illustrations and the Cultural Materialism of Scott's Waverley Novels

PETER GARSIDE

THE EXTENSIVE INFLUENCE OF SCOTT'S FICTION on art in the nineteenth century has long been a subject of commentary, while a parallel, if less developed, line of enquiry has examined the symbiosis between text and illustrative material in the production of collected sets of the Waverley novels. Until recently, however, general analysis has largely concentrated on exhibition painting, quantifiable as it is from sources such as the catalogues of the Royal Academy and British Institution. Catherine Gordon thus points to the exhibition by over three hundred painters and sculptors of more than a thousand Scott-related works between 1805 and 1870, with an increasing choice of the novels rather than poetry for subject-matter.[1] Likewise, Richard Altick locates an equivalent heyday for Scott illustration: 'The great age of Scott painting was the period 1830–50. During those two decades, well over 400 examples were exhibited, an average of more than twenty a year.'[2] Though never openly stated, in both critics one senses an underlying feeling that print illustrations were for the most part an offshoot of this 'primary' field of activity. However, there are a number of reasons for believing the opposite to have been the case, with the print market providing the chief motor force for the production of Scott imagery. In many instances paintings and drawings were commissioned for engraving first, and only exhibited subsequently. Copyright, in so far as it existed for images, was held firstly by the engraver or his employer (not the designer as such), one token of this being the common appearance of the printmaker's name with date on imprints. A number of eminent painters made more money from engraving than from the sale of their works, with even more run-of-the-

---

1   Catherine Gordon, 'The Illustration of Sir Walter Scott: Nineteenth-Century Enthusiasm and Adaptation', *Journal of the Warburg and Courtauld Institutes* 34 (1971), 297.
2   Altick, *Paintings from Books*, p. 430.

mill artists being advised to sell reproduction rights before exhibiting. The expense of reproduction, especially in the age of steel engraving, often outweighed the cost of commissioning a design or securing the rights to a painting. Indubitably, too, print illustrations played a more far-reaching role in influencing the reception of Scott's fiction than the relatively closed world of connoisseur art. Yet notwithstanding significant inroads made in recent years by Richard Hill and Ruth McAdams,[3] a full account of print illustrations of the Waverley novels still remains a desideratum both for Scott scholarship and the history of the book.

A useful preliminary tool nevertheless can be found in the online database, Illustrating Scott, 1814–1901, which contains just over fifteen hundred records of print illustrations of Scott's fiction produced in Britain during the nineteenth century.[4] The largest number (approximately 1,075) derive from collected editions of Scott's fiction, stretching from the earliest sets in the 1820s to near the end of the century. Where feasible, all the illustrations in these sets were recorded, though in the case of the copiously illustrated Abbotsford edition (1842–7), which includes nearly two thousand wood engravings, only the steel-engraved plates have been included. Some 375 further entries have been found in other books devoted to providing illustrations of Scott's fiction, spanning the period from the earliest contemporary suites to the 1880s. Finally, the database includes over fifty entries describing engravings found in early periodicals from 1819 to 1833. The print images included normally depict incidents, characters and scenery from the novels, though non-pictorial designs such as maps are excluded. Normally only the first appearance of a print illustration is recorded, though in some cases dual entries are created, for instance where the omission of a re-engraving would compromise coverage of a significant later collected edition.

In all, work by nearly 220 artists and over 180 engravers is listed, each

3   Richard J. Hill, Picturing Scotland through the Waverley Novels: Walter Scott and the Origins of the Victorian Illustrated Novel (Farnham: Ashgate, 2010); Ruth M. McAdams, 'The Posthumous British Editions of Sir Walter Scott's Waverley Novels, 1832–1871, and the Evolution of his Literary Legacy' (unpublished M.Phil. thesis, University of Edinburgh, 2008). Thanks are also due to Dr Paul Barnaby for guidance.
4   Illustrating Scott: A Database of Printed Illustrations to the Waverley Novels, 1814–1901, compiled by Peter Garside and Ruth McAdams: http://illustrating-scott.lib.ed.ac.uk/.

of whom can be searched for individually. The database also includes a comprehensive field comprising some 580 keywords, characterising significant visual components such as characters, locations, and a range of subjects and themes. Statistical analysis has already led to a number of conclusions, some interestingly at odds with previous conceptions. Compared with Gordon and Altick's optimum period of 1830–50, the database reveals an earlier surge in 1820–1 of some seventy print illustrations, this being followed by an extraordinarily large spike of over a hundred images in 1832. As in painting, the Jewess Rebecca from *Ivanhoe* (1820) proves to be one of the most-portrayed Scott heroines, with almost twice as many occurrences compared with her Anglo-Saxon counterpart Rowena (twenty-one to twelve), a pattern repeated in some other similar dark/fair juxtapositions. Ann Rigney's observation of a shift amongst artists of John Everett Millais' generation to Effie Deans as the younger 'fallen' sister in *The Heart of Mid-Lothian* (1818), in preference to the dourly virtuous Jeanie, however, is not borne out by the print record, where the latter's thirty-four occurrences (a fair proportion in the later period) outmatch Effie's tally by nearly three to one.[5] Even allowing for the flattening effects of 'compulsory' illustration in the case of collected editions, the number of images generated by individual novels also point to differences in popularity compared to painting. Whereas in Altick's count *Ivanhoe* is by far the most popular source for subjects in the database it is only sixth, well behind *Waverley* (1814), with some eighty print illustrations, as well as six other novels set in Scotland rather than the English medieval past. An interesting disparity is also found in the case of *The Monastery* (1820), which according to the database generated sixty-six print illustrations over the full period covered, compared with the fairly anaemic history outlined by Altick, tailing off with only seven paintings after 1850.[6] Likewise, while Gordon points to an early avoidance of *The Bride of Lammermoor* (1819), apparent in only three illustrations in the following decade, the database records up to fifteen instances belonging to that period. More particularly, the classic scene depicting Lucy Ashton at the Fountain, which Gordon later presents as if originating with a painting by Samuel Howell in 1830, had already been

<hr />

5 See Ann Rigney, *The Afterlives of Walter Scott: Memory on the Move* (Oxford: Oxford University Press, 2012), pp. 38–40.

6 Altick, *Paintings from Books*, pp. 433–5.

anticipated in print from designs by Thomas Stothard (1819), William Allan (1820) and Charles Robert Leslie (1823).[7]

As its compilers acknowledge, the *Illustrating Scott* database is by no means all-inclusive. Subsequent research has already revealed a number of omissions in the earlier period covered, both in periodicals and in the form of prints appearing in larger collections. The decision to include only the steel plates from the Abbotsford edition, though made partly in an effort to maintain the overall equilibrium of the database, still has the effect of obscuring an iconography widely deployed on later occasions. Investigation in the period immediately following 1901 has also revealed a surprisingly large number of late editions of Scott's fiction, some of these (aided by new processes in reproduction) more densely illustrated than many of their predecessors. More generally still, the database's policy of prioritising imagery on its first occurrence means that the large-scale recycling of Scott pictorial material, a common factor throughout the period, tends at times to be only fleetingly visible. The following survey attempts to supply some of these absences while tracking the main phases in print illustration of Scott's novels to the present day.

Early Sets and Suites

Scott's original novels in the 1810s, as mainly published from Scotland by Archibald Constable, all lacked illustrations and were undistinguishable in appearance from other three- or four-volume duodecimo novels of the period. In fact, Joseph Ogle Robinson of Hurst, Robinson & Co., Constable's new London partners from 1819, complained bitterly of their poor quality. Pressure from this quarter was one of the factors which led to the idea of including illustrations, first activated at an important turning point at the end of that year, with the first retrospective collection of Scott's fiction, *Novels and Tales of the Author of Waverley*, in twelve octavo volumes, and Scott's significant shift to medieval subject-matter in *Ivanhoe* (itself the first original title to be issued in the larger octavo format). From the start it seems to have been Constable's intention to supply the *Novels and Tales* set with vignette titles, though for the 1819 octavo issue it was only practical to include the same image (a somewhat routine view of Edinburgh Castle, drawn and engraved by the

7   Gordon, 'Illustration of Scott', pp. 311–12, 313.

Edinburgh firm of W. & D. Lizars). For the sixteen-volume set of *Novels and Tales* published in a smaller duodecimo format in 1821, however, it was possible to provide a distinct image for each title page, all of scenes and places relating to the novels contained, these being based on a list of subjects approved by Scott and sent on by Constable to the artist Alexander Nasmyth (the engraving being carried out by William Home Lizars).[8] The designs were also marketed separately by Constable as a suite in *Sixteen Engravings from Real Scenes supposed to be described in the Novels and Tales* (1821), where location titles are for the first time supplied. Nasmyth also provided similar designs for the succeeding collected sets, *Historical Romances* (1822) and *Novels and Romances* (1823/24), in their octavo and duodecimo forms, the use of the engraver William Archibald maintaining their full Scottish manufacture, though there is no evidence of these prints being marketed separately.

The next major development with regard to collected sets occurs with the 1823 *Novels and Tales*, issued in the much smaller octodecimo format, and aimed at a wider market than its predecessors. By then, Hurst, Robinson & Co., who enjoyed close links with the more diverse and technologically advanced London print trade, had effectively taken over the provision of illustrative materials. For this set not only were the Nasmyth–Lizars title page vignettes re-engraved by Charles Heath, possibly in steel, but there are also indications of re-drawing in an effort to tie the imagery more closely to the fictional narrative. Each of the twelve volumes also contained new frontispiece plates, depicting key incidents in the novels, all after drawings by the American-born artist Charles Robert Leslie, and engraved by a number of London engravers, including Heath. The first plate (Fig.1) depicts the celebrated scene from *Waverley* with Flora MacIvor in the Glen of Glennaquoich, which was also illustrated by a number of other contemporary artists, including William Allan and Louisa Sharpe, and remained durable over the period. Similar sequences of plates were produced by various artists and engravers for the octodecimo *Historical Romances* (1824) and *Novels and Romances* (1825), where the title-page vignettes are this time given as engraved by Edward Finden. Hurst, Robinson & Co.'s tightening grip on this aspect of the Waverley enterprise is also evident in their marketing of all three

8   NLS, MS 791, pp. 68–9 (1 June 1820). Thanks are due to the Trustees of the National Library of Scotland for permission to cite and quote from manuscripts in the library's care.

Fig. 1: Flora in the Glen of Glennaquoich (1823; reprinted 1832), by Charles Robert Leslie; engraved by Charles Heath

sequences of plates as independent suites, beginning with *A New Series of Illustrations to the Novels and Tales* (1823).

A parallel development occurs in a number of independent suites of illustrations, which had reached a high point of production by the mid-1820s. The single output from the Scottish side is found in William Allan's *Illustrations of the Novels and Tales of the Author of Waverley* (1820), a set of twelve plates depicting situation scenes, first commissioned in spring 1819, partly through Scott's own influence. Though the original plan appears to have been to have this available by November 1819, to sell alongside the octavo *Novels and Tales*, production dragged on through much of 1820, resulting in disappointing sales on publication at the end of that year. One major problem lay in difficulties faced in coordinating the transmission of designs and proofs between Edinburgh and London, where a variety of engravers had been engaged (Constable having previously rejected the idea of commissioning Heath alone[9]): a situation compounded by Allan's sense of himself as a leading Scottish historical artist and insistence on alterations. Production of the title-page vignette, engraved in Edinburgh by W. H. Lizars, and depicting 'Old Mortality' repairing inscriptions on Covenanting gravestones, proved relatively accident-free, though the Edinburgh trade at this point lacked the capacity to produce the whole set. In a visit to London late in 1820, Robert Cadell as Constable's junior partner faced multiple frustrations in endeavouring to bring the project to a head, resisting in the process Robinson's attempts to take over the management, and evidently just managing to secure possession of the copper plates, themselves in a much-worn state.[10]

By the time Allan's *Illustrations* came out, the London trade was already producing its own brand of illustrative suites, concentrating on individual novels, and usually titled 'Illustrations of [name of novel]' on the paper wrappers. The process here appears to have been initiated by an agreement between Constable and Hurst, Robinson & Co. to provide such as a suite to accompany *Ivanhoe*, this duly appearing early in 1820, with engravings by Charles Heath from drawings by Richard Westall.[11] The Westall–Heath combination also produced *Illustrations of*

---

9   NLS, MS 790, p. 495.
10   See NLS, MS 323, fols. 155r, 158r, 171v–2r.
11   The circumstances underlying the agreement are indicated in Cadell's letter to Constable of 26 October 1819: 'Heath the Engraver has this morning proposed to Robinson to Illustrate the three Vols of this book and to have them

Fig. 2: 'Landed—landed! . . . swimming with me' [Father Philip and the White Lady of Avenel] (1821), by Richard Westall; engraved by Charles Heath

The Monastery, in the wake of the publication of that novel in 1820, and a more retrospective *Illustrations of Guy Mannering* in 1821. (For another suite published that year, *Illustrations of Kenilworth*, the artist was Charles Robert Leslie.) All these sets were published under the imprint of Hurst, Robinson & Co., in association with Charles Heath as print-maker, Constable & Co. (who for a moment toyed with the idea of legal intervention[12]) eventually settling down to taking a silent third share. Richard Westall, a classically trained artist who had worked on the Boydell Shakespeare and had already provided the designs for equally unauthorised illustrations of Scott's poems, is in many ways the antith-esis of Allan. With little apparent concern for historical authenticity, Westall usually confines his designs to a few figures, and accentuates the dramatic rather than the everyday. Characteristic of this is the title-page vignette to *Illustrations of The Monastery* (Fig. 2), depicting the unhors-ing and ducking of Father Philip by the White Lady of Avenel, whose ethereal figure wafts aloft with book in hand. Notwithstanding the reser-vations of the reviewers about the introduction of a real (unexplained) supernatural being into the story, the White Lady proved to be one of the most commonly illustrated figures of Scott's. One plate in the sequence, depicting the more mortal Lady of Avenel holding her child Mary in her arms, is especially interesting for bearing the legend 'Engraved on Steel by Cha[rle]s Heath', making it one of earliest book illustrations to acknowledge use of this method, with its obvious advantage in generat-ing a far greater number of impressions than the softer copper. This was followed by a shorter set to accompany *The Abbot* (1820), from designs by Henry Corbould, and possibly another for *The Pirate* (1822); so that by 1825 Hurst, Robinson & Co. were marketing as many as ten sets of illustrations, only one of which (Allan's) could in any way be said to be controlled by Constable or have the approval of the author.

Another fertile source for largely unauthorised illustration is found in the case of periodicals at this period. Prominent here is *The Lady's Magazine* whose monthly numbers contained forty-six original illustra-tive plates between 1819–29, accompanied with generous extracts from the novels. Roughly, these can be divided into three phases. For the first, James Heath (Charles's father) and the veteran artist and book il-lustrator Thomas Stothard combine to provide a set of six retrospective

out ten days after the book itself . . . R says that Heath will do it on his own if we dont join' (NLS, MS 323, fol. 27r).
12   See NLS, MS 23619, fol. 34v.

illustrations for Scott's *Tales of My Landlord* series of novels, commencing in August 1819 with the Mermaiden's Fountain scene from *The Bride of Lammermoor*, arguably the first-published illustration of its kind and certainly of this scene. This is followed by a middle sequence tracking novels on their first appearance, from *Ivanhoe* to *The Pirate*, one plate usually being provided to match each of the three volumes, and where Westall, Stothard and Corbould are prominent as artists. Though James rather than Charles Heath is more often named as the engraver, there is a strong correlation here with the Hurst–Robinson suites of *Illustrations*, as if the Heath print business stood at the heart of a joint enterprise. The last stage, terminating with *Anne of Geierstein* (1829), introduces a new range of artists but without any slowing of the pace, coverage of *Woodstock* (1826) generating a fuller suite of six plates, all designed by Henry Courtney Selous and engraved by Ebenezer Stalker. The researches of Sandro Jung have also brought to light suites of illustrations relating to five Scott novels in issues of *The Royal Engagement Pocket Atlas*, between 1817 and 1824, each featuring a frontispiece and twenty-four oblong designs at the head of pages.[13] In spite of the spatial limitation inherent in the latter, Stothard still manages to anticipate some of the most frequently illustrated incidents in Scott, as in his representation of the scene in *Ivanhoe* where Rebecca flees from the advances of the Norman baron Bois-Guilbert on the ramparts of Torquilstone Castle.[14] An unauthorised portrait of Rebecca (designer Charles Robert Leslie; engraver Charles Heath), showing her alone in prison, and ostensibly accompanying an unrelated poem with that title, also featured in the first issue of *The Keepsake* (1827), whose main proprietor was Charles Heath. One of the most successful of a new species of annual in which steel engraving had become central, this on its own signalled a new phase in the history of Scott illustration.

The Magnum Opus Edition and its Offshoots

Steel engraving also played a crucial part in the launching of the Magnum Opus edition of the Waverley novels, all of whose forty-eight volumes, published at monthly intervals between 1829 and 1833, con-

13 For further information about this publication, see Jung's 'Thomas Stothard's Illustrations'.
14 At the head of August in the *Pocket Atlas* for 1821.

tained a frontispiece plate and vignette title page. After the chain of bankruptcies in 1826 precipitated by the failure of Hurst, Robinson & Co., this offered a major opportunity to recoup the situation, not only for Scott but also for Robert Cadell as the edition's main publisher. On a textual front, the addition of new authorial Introductions and Notes helped unify the Waverley novels as a complete body of work in a way not previously possible, initiating at the same time a new span of copyright stretching into the 1850s. From Cadell's vantage point especially, it also afforded a chance to acquire a new stock of imagery, existing resources having been much depleted, most notably through the sale of the 1823 octodecimo *Novels and Tales* to the London firm of Hurst, Chance & Co.[15] The copious records kept by Cadell show commitment to the illustrative side of the project right from the first calculations and a readiness to defend the cost of superior engraving in the face of any reservations expressed by Scott and the trustees governing his affairs. From an early stage, too, Cadell recognised that, in order to achieve a standard matching the annuals, the best London engravers needed to be employed.[16] To this end, he turned not to Charles Heath, but to Henry Graves of Moon, Boys & Co., successors in part to Hurst, Robinson & Co. Graves, as Scott was informed early in 1829, was to have 'the entire charge of the illustrative part of our undertaking';[17] and it was he who carried out most of the leg-work in London, engaging engravers, liaising with artists, transmitting proofs to Edinburgh, and (at least in the earlier stages) overseeing printing from the plates in London.

   For the designs, Cadell first sent out feelers to Henry Corbould, finally engaging him on 20 May 1828 to provide specimens for the earliest novels.[18] In the following months, however, Corbould's name slips from view, as Cadell (sometimes prompted by Scott) began to enlist an essentially different set of artists, less immediately connected with book illustration than those of the Stothard–Corbould circle, early recruits

---

15   For this sale, see the firm's letter to Scott of 25 January 1828 (NLS, MS 3906, fol. 47v).

16   'I do think it absolutely necessary to have all the Engraving done in London' (NLS, MS 112, p. 384). In the same proposal, made to Scott's Trustees in March 1828, Cadell estimated the cost of designs at £5 5s. od each, and the engraving of plates at £42 (vignettes £31 10s.).

17   NLS, MS 794, fol. 319r (Scott to Cadell, 16 January 1829). Cadell had originally written Graves on 6 June 1828, offering his firm at the same time 'the sale of the separate illustrations on Commission' (NLS, MS 794, fol. 295r).

18   NLS, MS 794, fol. 292.

WAVERLEY.

They found the good old careful officer, engaged in reading the Evening
Service of the Episcopal Church to the remainder of his
troop, and Saunders Saunderson in military array performing the functions of clerk.

Fig. 3. 'They found . . . functions of clerk' [Baron of Bradwardine reading the
Service before the Battle of Prestonpans] (1829), by Gilbert Stuart Newton;
engraved by Charles Rolls

including Edwin Landseer, David Wilkie and Gilbert Stuart Newton (for whom Scott had recently sat for a portrait). From the commencement of publication, starting with *Waverley* in June 1829, Cadell found himself under immense pressure to secure material on time, to the extent that at one point an appeal was made to Charles Heath for assistance. This in turn led to a proposal from Heath for a trade-off between engraving work and new copy for *The Keepsake* (whose number for 1829 had legitimately featured several shorter pieces by Scott, with illustrative plates). Heath's case in making this proposal can hardly have been aided by his somewhat tactless suggestion to Scott that, as the Magnum did not include new work, 'the Plates will be a great attraction [. . .] much of the extensiveness of the sale will depend on their *excellence* both as to design and Engraving'.[19] At this point, the relationship was effectively ended with Heath, who is credited with the engraving of just one of Magnum's ninety-six illustrations (a frontispiece to *The Abbot* in volume 20). The offending remark, however, is not too unlike views held by Cadell himself, whose own conviction that the huge sales rapidly achieved by the Magnum (ascending from a projected twelve thousand to thirty thousand in a few months) was in part attributable to its illustrations is a matter of record.

Though not his chief priority, there is evidence of Scott taking an informed interest in the illustrations as they appeared, to the extent of requiring changes to be made, and in few instances exercising his right of veto. (Reading between the lines, there is a likelihood that he also played a part in the edging out of Corbould.) Surviving remarks show in particular a concern for accuracy of historical detail and the preservation of Scottish characteristics, as opposed to the figurative and dramatic emphasis found in Westall and his successors. One early illustration that drew a measure of approval was the Canadian-born Newton's portrayal of the Baron of Bradwardine reading the Evening Service of the Episcopal Church to his troop prior to the Battle of Prestonpans, which provided the frontispiece plate for volume 2 (Fig. 3). 'If you see Newton', Scott wrote to his son-in-law J. G. Lockhart in London, 'tell him how much I admire the Baron of Bradwardine performing the service. It is a fine idea happily brought out.'[20] Details which Newton picked out include the spectacles the Baron is described as wearing

19   NLS, MS 3908, fol. 99r (Heath to Scott, 23 February 1829).
20   *The Letters of Sir Walter Scott*, ed. H. J. C. Grierson, 12 vols. (London, 1932–7), XI, p. 141 (16 February 1829).

at this point; the white cockade in the Baron's hat, and that on the ground beside the kneeling Saunders Saunderson, Bradwardine's butler in peacetime; and (in the background) the figures of Waverley and Fergus MacIvor rushing on to the scene. Less accurate, arguably, is the Hanoverian-style uniform worn by the standard-bearer, and the grenadier-guards-like appearance of the troops faintly visible behind him, though Scott was apparently prepared to allow some latitude in view of Newton's promptness and the personal connection through Lockhart. One other significant feature of the plate is its Edinburgh imprint, which reads 'Edinburgh: Published June 1 by Cadell & Co. and Simpkin & Marshall, London', leaving little doubt about Cadell's ultimate proprietorship. In line with the original agreement with Graves, the illustrations were subsequently issued separately in batches by Moon, Boys & Graves, but on a commission basis and with Cadell as the primary publisher on the imprint. The steel plates themselves, of which double copies had been made, were also retained by Cadell, along with the stereotypes used in printing the main text.

The early 1830s saw a plethora of Magnum spin-offs, aimed at cashing in on its unprecedented success. One of the more visible of these is *The Waverley Album*, first published for Charles Heath in 1832, and containing all fifty of the vignettes and frontispieces originally generated by the duodecimo and octodecimo collected sets up to the *Novels and Romances*, accompanied by short extracts keyed to the Magnum edition. According to its preface, 'the Plates having passed into other hands, the present proprietor hopes that their reappearance in a collected form, at a price unexampled even in this age of cheap publications, will not be deemed unacceptable'. One noticeable difference here is the attribution of the design of the 1823 *Novels and Tales* vignettes to Peter De Wint, opening up the possibility that he might have been responsible for variations made there to the original Nasmyth designs. Another is the replacement of some of the place names found in *Sixteen Engravings* with names from the actual novels, so that for instance Craigcrook becomes Tully-Veolan for *Waverley*. The collection was evidently reissued several times, before being recycled yet again in the form of *The Book of Waverley Gems*, first published by Henry Bohn in 1846, with the addition of ten plates leading up to *The Surgeon's Daughter* (1827), the majority by Henry Selous, at least some matching those found earlier in *The Lady's Magazine*.

Recent research has also uncovered a more concerted attempt by Heath to provide fresh suites for individual novels, to coincide with the Magnum, under the lead title *Heath's Historical Illustrations*.[21] This commenced with a suite of six plates to accompany *Guy Mannering*; and it appears to have ground to a halt with another set illustrating *Rob Roy*, later recycled, with larger slices of text, in *The Waverley Keepsake* (1837). All the plates concerned bear the imprint of Jennings & Chaplin, who also managed the sale of the plates from the original *Keepsake*. The same concern also appears as the publishers of W. H. Harrison's *Christmas Tales* (1833), a collection of four original stories, accompanied by six plates all palpably first designed to illustrate novels by Scott, a provenance cheerily acknowledged in the work's preface. A similar kind of overspill, possibly involving work originally targeted at inclusion in the Magnum, can be sensed in *The Keepsake for 1833*, where no less than four of the plates (including Louisa Sharpe's 'Flora') clearly relate to incidents in the Waverley novels, though re-assigned now to illustrate other pieces.

The Magnum edition was also instrumental in encouraging more substantial series of illustrations, keyed to passages in the novels and usually offering the option of insertion there. Two main types are distinguishable: illustrations showing locations, and sets depicting the main Scott heroines. In the first category, James Skene could claim authorial guidance for *Sketches of the Existing Locations alluded to in the Waverley Novels* (1829–31), which was intended to run concurrently with the Magnum volumes, but ran out of steam after some sixty plates when the strain of both designing and etching proved too much for Skene. The mantle was then taken on by the London publisher Charles Tilt, whose *Landscape Illustrations of the Waverley Novels* (1832), involving various artists, stretched to eighty plates (originally published serially), some of which have only a tangential relation with the novels concerned. Key instances of the other main type are *Portraits of the Principal Female Characters in the Waverley Novels*, some thirty-five illustrations brought together by Tilt in 1834, and *The Waverley Gallery*, a separate series of thirty-six plates first published as a unit by Tilt and Bogue in 1841. Both publications tie in with the larger phenomenon of depicting celebrity females in annual-like publications such as *Heath's Book of Beauty*. Notwithstanding this formulaic element, the Scott portraits are mostly designed to fit specific descriptions in the novels,

21   For further information on this and the other instances mentioned, see my article 'Illustrating the Waverley Novels: Scott, Scotland, and the London Print Trade, 1819–1836', *The Library*, 7th series 11.2 (2010), 168–96.

Rebecca

London, Published Feb. 15, 1833, by Chapman & Hall, Strand.

Fig. 4: Rebecca (1834) by Solomon Alexander Hart; engraved by John Cochran

which themselves are often given as accompanying texts. The portrait of Rebecca in *Ivanhoe* (Fig. 4) thus picks up on the yellow silk turban mentioned in Scott's narrative account, while managing to combine intimations of the orient with the absolute latest in-fashion wear. Both types of illustration re-surface in various guises in the following decades, feeding off later collected Waverley editions, one of the more tangible examples being *The New Waverley Album* (1859), a selection from Tilt's *Landscape Illustrations* with fresh commentaries.

Later Cadell Editions

After Scott's death in 1832 Robert Cadell went on to become 'sole proprietor and publisher' of the Waverley novels, a position he held until his death in 1849.[22] His first exploitation of the Magnum copyrights, however, came in the form of a release in parts managed by the London number specialists, Fisher, Son & Co. in 1836–9. One explanation for this apparent off-loading of material might lie in Cadell's preoccupation with the Magnum's immediate successors, ending with Lockhart's *Life* of Scott in 1838. Cadell had also previously toyed with the idea of a number publication with its potential for reaching new areas of the market, having approached the Glasgow firm of Blackie with this in mind as early as 1829, conscious that his own concern then lacked the infrastructure for such an exercise.[23] His proposal to Fisher, dated 11 February 1834, offers to provide text in quires from the Magnum stereotypes, with Fisher having the distribution of parts through his own canvassers, but hedges on the matter of illustration. Fisher in his reply of 15 February expressed a willingness to provide his own plates: 'If this plan were adopted, & your terms liberal, we would find our own plates [. . .] & enter heartily into the matter [. . .]'.[24] The Fisher firm already had a track record for providing plates in literary albums and travel books; its imprints also included a Paris branch, a factor which might also have attracted Cadell in view of the surge in Scott's popularity in France and existence there of a market for print

---

22   James Thin, *Reminiscences of Booksellers and Bookselling in Edinburgh in the Time of William IV* (Edinburgh, 1905), p. 25.
23   See NLS, MS 21002, fol. 84r (Blackie, Fullarton & Co. to Cadell, 7 April 1829).
24   NLS, MS 920, fols. 19v–20v.

Fig. 5: Fray at Jeanie Mac Alpine's / Fray chez Jeanne Mac Alpine (1836), by
George Cruikshank

illustrations in some ways more extensive than in Britain.

    The Fisher edition was published in 240 weekly parts, at 1s. each,
along with a monthly issue in forty-eight volumes at 5s. each (the same
as the Magnum). Illustrations were a major feature from the start, the
first part listing seventeen artists on its outer wrapper, headed by J. M.
W. Turner, the sixth announcing the additional acquisition of George
Cruikshank, also at this time on the point of providing illustrations
for Dickens's *Sketches by Boz*. As a whole, the set contains 135 plates,
thirty-six of them by Cruikshank, only one of which (an especially ver-
tiginous representation of Rebecca on the ramparts) is steel-engraved.
The remaining Cruikshank plates follow his more familiar practice of
etching, and are mainly in a comic style. Not untypical of these is his
depiction of the 'Fray at Jeanie Mac Alpine's' from *Rob Roy*, which provides a rather unusual mixture of the accurate and far-fetched (Fig. 5).
Unlike in other illustrations of this scene, Baillie Nicol Jarvie (in the
middle) appears to be handling something not unlike 'the red-hot coul-
ter of plough' (chapter 28) actually described by Scott, rather than
the more simple poker or sword that he is more commonly shown as
wielding. On the other hand, the dandy-like fencing posture adopted

Fig. 6: Edinburgh. March of the Highlanders / Edimbourgh. Marche des Montagnards (1836), by J. M. W. Turner; engraved by Charles Higham

by Frank Osbaldistone hardly fits with the earnest young narrator of the novel. As for the Highlanders, it is almost as if Scott's earlier expressed fears about what his poem *The Lady of the Lake* (1810) might suffer at the hands of Richard Westall ('I expect to see my chieftain [. . .] in the guize of a recruiting serjaint of the Black Watch') had come home to roost with a vengeance.[25]

Landscape scenes are a dominant feature of the main body of steel plates, which were provided by a number of mainly English artists, including Henry Melville (twenty-five plates); while Edward Francis Finden, who had been heavily involved in Tilt's *Landscape Illustrations*, is one of the more frequently named amongst a variety of London line engravers. J. M. W. Turner's contribution is limited to six illustrations, where scenery generally overwhelms the figures depicted. Turner's first plate, 'March of the Highlanders', illustrating *Waverley*, supposedly shows the marshalling of the Jacobite army in Edinburgh in 1814 (Fig. 6). Yet it anachronistically includes the North Bridge, a symptom

---

25   *Letters of Scott*, ed. Grierson, II, p. 321.

of its actually being derived from an earlier planned painting of George IV's visit to Edinburgh in 1822.[26] In the later stages of the issue, there are signs of a running out of steam in the importation of a number of plates from Tilt's *Landscape Illustrations* and *Portraits of the Principal Female Characters*, the former reinforcing the emphasis on topography, the latter introducing a new element in focusing on Scott heroines. The original illustrations for the set, comprising 108 plates, were also published concurrently by Fisher as *Landscape-Historical Illustrations of Scotland and the Waverley Novels* (1836–8), with prose descriptions by the Rev. George Newenham Wright. All the plates involved carry the Fisher imprint alone, with a date, and there is no indication of Cadell having any proprietary stake in this side of the project. As such, the Fisher plates continued to have a life outside the main copyright ownership of the novels. One instance of this can be found in the marketing of the plates, initially in fifty-four parts at 6d each, as an accompaniment for Cadell's own later editions in the 1840s.[27] A selection of the plates, lithographically reproduced and generally providing one Cruikshank and one landscape image per novel, also appeared as *The Waverley Garland* in 1871.

In the 1840s Cadell brought out three main editions in his own name, all directed at a different level of the market. At the cheap end, the People's edition sold originally in weekly sheets at 2d (267 in all), beginning 1 January 1842 and not ending until early in 1847, the complete set then being available in five volumes at £2 10s. Originally the double-columned part issue featured no illustrations, a factor no doubt encouraging the separate issue of the plates from the Fisher edition, already mentioned. Only on the completion of individual volumes were engraved title pages apparently made available, these each offering a collage of images relating to the titles included. Two of these are attributed to the artist William Harvey, who may have designed the whole, and all are given as engraved by Robert Edward Branston. Sales soon proved to be outstanding, Cadell raising the impression as high as sixty thousand, and his trustees after his death calculating a total sale over seven million weekly sheets. A more moderate success was achieved

26 See Gerald Finley, *Landscapes of Memory: Turner as Illustrator of Scott* (London: Scolar Press, 1980), p. 258, n. 52.

27 *Plates to Illustrate all Editions of the Waverley Novels. People's Edition*, published by Houlston & Stoneman [and others], n.d. The series continued with numbers 55–6, consisting mostly of topographical plates.

by the Cabinet edition (a name applied retrospectively), published in twenty-five volumes between 1841–3, this representing the first set to include full-length novels within single volumes, the price of 4s. significantly undercutting the two volumes of the Magnum required at 10s. Illustrations were limited to a vignette title page for each volume, supplemented by a frontispiece engraving for the final volume depicting John Greenshield's statue of a sitting Scott, which had already served as a frontispiece for Lockhart's *Life* of Scott. Eight of the title-page vignettes are re-engravings of images from Allan's *Illustrations*; while others appear to be original, Alexander Fraser the Elder, the artist of nine illustrations in the Magnum, providing the vignettes for *Ivanhoe* and *Kenilworth*. As a whole these lack the definition and detail of earlier vignettes, indicating a cheaper mode of production. The sales of the edition were commensurately unspectacular, amounting to some eleven thousand sets by Cadell's death.

The most lavish demonstration of Cadell's conviction that '[t]his is the age of graphically illustrated books' is found in the Abbotsford edition, which has attracted special attention for its centrality in the history of the Victorian illustrated book.[28] First published in 120 parts at 2s. 6d each, commencing 30 April 1842, its final issue early in 1847 advertised full sets in twelve volumes adorned by '2000 illustrations in steel and wood'. In all, some three hundred individuals were involved, 189 artists, and 113 engravers not also artists, the names regularly featuring in lists in the inside covers of parts and at the beginning of volumes. Two clear categories of illustration are found: 120 steel plates, mostly depicting places supposedly associated with the narratives, just over a quarter of which are by the English landscape artist, Clarkson Stanfield; and approaching two thousand wood engravings invasively present throughout the text, a part of the project supervised in London on Cadell's behalf by William Dickes, who also supplied many of the designs. For the latter category, the edition took full advantage of the new potential for wood engraving to be fastened up with letter type,

---

28   See Richard Maxwell, 'Walter Scott, Historical Fiction, and the Genesis of the Victorian Illustrated Book', in *The Victorian Illustrated Book*, ed. Richard Maxwell (Charlottesville and London: University Press of Virginia, 2002), pp. 1–51; also Ruth M. McAdams, 'Publishing Abbotsford: Walter Scott's Literary Legacy and the Abbotsford Edition of the Waverley Novels', *Journal of the Edinburgh Bibliographical Society* 3 (2008), 12–37. The quotation is from 'Notice to the Abbotsford Edition', dated 17 January 1842.

here ingeniously implemented in headpieces and tailpieces of various
sizes, images artfully positioned down the side of pages, or otherwise
integrated into the main text. A distinct shift in subject-matter is also
apparent in the inclusion of an array of alternative imagery depicting
or relating to extraneous historical personages, objects and events, especially as evident in Scott's own collections at Abbotsford. One early
example is the engraving of 'Sir Walter Scott's Chair' at Abbotsford,
which features in the Prospectus for the edition, then again near the
beginning of the first number; while another interesting tailpiece is
Dickes's 'Macdonell of Glengarry (after Raeburn), the Fergus Mac-Ivor
of the Tale', positioned at the end of chapter 25 in *Waverley*. Though
not an outstanding commercial success – a reflection perhaps of its premium price or even a reaction against over-embellishment of a classic
novelist – the Abbotsford edition left Cadell with a potent collection of
re-usable plates and woodblocks, a far cry from 1820 when in London
he had sought to retrieve the Allan copper plates.

A. & C. Black to the Centenary

By the completion of his main editions, Cadell was already intent on
retiring, the value of the Magnum text being significantly enhanced by
the 1842 Act extending copyright to forty-two rather than twenty-eight
years. On his death in 1849, the sale was taken on by the trustees, leading to the eventual purchase of the stock, copyrights and plant by Adam
and Charles Black in April 1851 for some £27,000. For the Blacks the
exploitation of this acquisition became a leading concern, encouraging
a move to larger premises, and ensuring manufacture in Scotland for
another generation. The firm also kept meticulous records of this side of
their business, now held as a unit in the National Library of Scotland.
The first item there is a 'Minute Book of the Proprietors of Sir Walter
Scott's Works', comprising detailed accounts of regular committee
meetings and yearly summaries of sales and new undertakings. Another
main component is a collection of three large scrapbook-type albums,
containing wood and steel engravings used in different editions, the
first and longest sequence including numbered imagery mainly from the
Abbotsford edition on a title-by-title basis (the run for *Waverley* provides more than 120 images, spread over forty pages). Most of these are
titled, apparently in Cadell's hand, and it seems reasonable to assume
that the earlier parts of this resource were acquired as part of the sale,

along with the actual physical plates and woodblocks.[29]

In spite of the wealth of this repository, the Blacks decided at an early point to include fresh imagery in their first independent set of the Waverley novels, which eventually appeared as the Library edition (1852–3). At a meeting on 18 November 1851 it was proposed to place frontispieces from the Abbotsford edition alongside 'new vignettes entirely confined to figure subjects, drawn by different artists in England and Scotland'.[30] The insistence on figures evidently marks a resolve to offset the landscape-orientation of the Abbotsford steel plates, and signals in some respects a return to an earlier convention of 'situation' scenes. Other factors that might have influenced the Blacks' decision to strike out on their own could include uncertainty about the physical condition of some of the existing woodblocks and plates and a desire to distinguish their own product from Cadell's remaining stock, then being sold at remainder prices. One pressing concern evident in the earliest minutes is the imminent expiry of copyright on the original Scott novels, beginning with *Waverley* in 1856; though, in the event, hardly any advantage was made of this by rival publishers, so great was the association of Scott's *oeuvre* with the Magnum text. By the time of the summary of operations in 30 June 1852 a clear decision had been made to provide 'new frontispieces and vignettes to the greater part of the volumes'. An agreement had also been entered into with the London print publishers Messrs Lloyd Bros & Co. 'to produce first class pictures and sell the Copyright to the Proprietors for 15% on the value of the painting, which is not to exceed £50 or £60'. The cost for 'each plate including copyright of the picture and the engraving' was estimated at an average of £40. By the sixteenth meeting on 26 September 1853, the 'painting, engraving &c' is described as 'nearly finished', and a monthly sale of about a thousand copies ongoing.[31]

As a whole, the Library edition follows the original Magnum pattern in providing a frontispiece and title-page vignette for each of the twenty-five volumes, generally with a short extract from the novel underneath. Not all the designs are original, some of the frontispieces deriving from the Abbotsford edition, mostly depicting historical figures. Amongst the new designers, a fair proportion are of Scottish origin, the brothers Thomas and John Faed being especially noticeable. The majority of the

---

29   NLS, Acc. 9765. Item 1 is the minute book; items 7–9 are the albums.
30   NLS, Acc 9765/1, p. 7.
31   Ibid., pp. 30–1, 53–4.

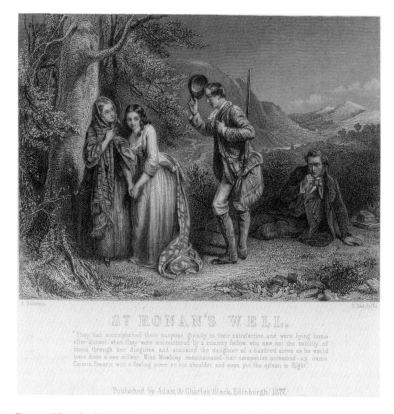

Fig. 7: 'They had accomplished . . . sylvan to flight' [Frank Tyrrel's meeting Clara Mowbray] (1853; reprinted 1877), by Abraham Solomon; engraved by Edward Radclyffe

original illustrations depict situations from the novels, with the vignettes usually restricted to a few figures, and the frontispieces offering greater detail in costumery and scenery. Amongst the engravers, Lumb Stocks and James Stephenson, both based in London, are leading contributors. The attention to detail and intricacy of engraving are typified by the frontispiece to *St. Ronan's Well*, by Abraham Solomon, depicting Frank Tyrrel rescuing Clara Mowbray and her companion, who have gone out dressed as country girls, from the unwanted attentions of a local rustic (Fig. 7). The incident is told retrospectively in the novel, which would place it about 1800, but the costumes (including Tyrrel's hunting gear) are more reminiscent of the mid-nineteenth century, while the spurned rustic has more than a touch of the Victorian stage melodrama villain. The Black records also contain a volume with extensive press cuttings, a large proportion of which point to the illustrations as the highlight of the edition. According to the *Glasgow Herald*, reviewing this particular volume: 'The figures are beautifully disposed and delineated, and the accessories of sky, hill, dale, and woodland, are delightfully sketched.'[32] At a later point some sets were apparently re-issued as a 'de luxe' edition, with additional plates from the Magnum and Abbotsford editions; while an entirely new edition was released in 1876-7.

Other Black sets belonging to the 1850s and 1860s are generally developments from the three-pronged assault on the market initiated by Cadell. Versions of the Cabinet edition can be found in an 'Eighteenpence' edition (1855-6), re-employing the Cabinet vignettes, followed by the newly set Railway edition of 1856-8, which found greater success when relaunched as a new paperback Shilling edition in 1862-3, illustrated with woodcut vignettes taken chiefly from the Magnum. A reissue of the People's edition in the 1850s, as separate novels, was eventually followed by the Sixpenny/Copyright edition of 1866-8, each of whose twenty-five pamphlet-like volumes feature a garishly-coloured image on the front cover, followed by a large title-page illustration, the latter mostly wood engravings derived from the Magnum. The volume containing *Waverley* thus features a coloured wrapper image of Scott's desk at Abbotsford, based on the original design in the Abbotsford edition, and a cruder version of the Magnum illustration showing Bradwardine before Prestonpans, in which the original standard-bearer has disappeared and the remaining troop are even more inappropriately Hanoverian in appearance. The fullest use of pre-existing materials, however, came with the first main reissue of the forty-eight-volume Magnum set, when it was discovered that some of the stereotype plates were damaged beyond use. The decision to re-set the edition allowed the incorporation of wood engravings from the Abbotsford edition, in addition to the original Magnum frontispieces and vignettes, and gives the resulting 'Pictorial' edition (1859-61) a somewhat hybrid look. This in turn was re-issued as the Roxburgh edition (1865-8), with superior bindings; then again as the Illustrated edition (1877-9), with Magnum-style cloth boards. The Black records contain a volume of the printed lists of illustrations, keyed in hand by number to the images pasted in the large albums previously mentioned,

---

32   NLS, Acc 9765/2, fol. 13 (newspaper cutting).

an indication of the extensiveness of the firm's eventual exploitation of
the stock of imagery first assembled by Cadell.[33]

The Centenary edition (twenty-five volumes, 1870–1), so titled to
coincide with the 1871 centenary celebrations of Scott's birth, represented the last chance for the Blacks to stamp their authority on the
Waverley novels before the expiry of the Magnum copyrights. To this
end, it made first use of Scott's interleaved set, inherited from Cadell,
publishing from it twenty-four of some thirty manuscript notes omit-
ted from the Magnum edition. The set also rearranged the paratextual
materials from the Magnum, while adding extra notes by David Laing.
Compared with these interventions, the illustrative part of the edition
gives the impression of being a secondary consideration, and there are no
signs of any great expense being involved. Each volume contains a wood-
engraved frontispiece and vignette, as well as two headpieces, the latter
originating from the Abbotsford edition. Four of the frontispieces are
re-engravings of Charles Robert Leslie's illustrations for the octodecimo
1823 *Novels and Tales*, which presumably were by now long out of copyright. A number of vignettes, such as that in the first volume depicting
Waverley leaving Waverley-Honour, lack any attribution. 'The Brothers
Dalziel', the most noticeable named engravers, had no other involvement in Scott illustration according to the *Illustrating Scott* database.

On the other hand, there are no signs of any diminution in the fas-
cination for illustration in the centenary celebrations as a whole. The
catalogue of the Centenary Exhibition in Edinburgh includes a sizeable
section of 'Engraved Illustrations' of Scott's works, bringing together
older collections such as those by Nasmyth and Skene, while giving
special attention to the individual engravings in the suites of illustrations issued by The Royal Association for Promotion of the Fine Arts in
Scotland (RAPFAS), whose policy was to provide subscribing members
with high-quality engravings taken from paintings purchased from bodies such as the Royal Scottish Academy.[34] By the time of the Centenary
Exhibition six suites illustrating different novels, all with Scottish
subject-matter, had been completed, totalling thirty-eight illustrations.
Eight Engravings in Illustration of Waverley (1865), the first in the ser-
ies, was based entirely on work by Scottish painters, such as Robert
Herdman and John Blake McDonald. Herdman's 'Waverley's Last
Visit to Flora Mac-Ivor', engraved by Lumb Stocks, and derived from

33   NLS, Acc 9765/12.
34   *The Scott Exhibition MDCCCLXXI* (Edinburgh, 1872), pp. 190–3.

a painting dated 1864, is notable for its concentration on a prevailing mood, rather than action, with Flora sewing her brother's shroud prior to execution, and Waverley himself an indistinct figure in the doorway (Fig. 8). As the instance of Lumb Stocks indicates, the majority of engravers in the earlier RAPFAS volumes are English; but by the time of the last in the sequence, *Six Engravings in Illustration of St. Ronan's Well* (1882), Scottish engravers such as William Forrest are more visible. In all, the Association produced twelve sets illustrating the Scottish novels, comprising seventy-four illustrations, which would go on to provide a fertile source for subsequent print illustration.

Post-Copyright Editions

The end of copyright on the Magnum text, beginning in 1871, resulted in a flood of editions by rival publishers. Collected sets with illustrations include an edition by G. Routledge & Sons (twenty-three volumes, 1875–6), with plates from the Fisher edition, and the 'Illustrated Waverley Novels', published by Marcus Ward & Co. (twenty-five volumes, 1877–9), packed with illustrations by a number of French artists, including Adolphe Lalauze and Edouard Rion. The Blacks also continued to vary the pattern of their illustrative content: the Pocket edition (twenty-five volumes, 1873–4) incorporating illustrations from the Library edition; and a reissue of the Centenary edition, in 1889–91, juxtaposing frontispieces from the Library edition with Magnum vignettes.

The 1890s saw the launch of a number of even more grandiose sets, their local-sounding names masking production on an industrial scale in an increasingly London-centred and imperial market. In both the Border and Dryburgh editions, published almost simultaneously between 1892–4, illustration plays a leading role, though the procurement methods differ significantly. The Border edition, originally published by John C. Nimmo in forty-eight volumes, contains in all 251 images (including a series vignette depicting Abbotsford and the Tweed), usually with five plates per volume, leading to ten images for a normal-sized novel. Nearly forty of its illustrations match engravings found in the RAPFAS suites, the same artist being acknowledged in each case, though the engravers differ. In the case of *Waverley*, five of the plates have this origin, the last of these being Robert Herdman's 'Waverley's Last Visit to Flora Mac-Ivor'. While the majority of images depict 'situation' scenes, a fair proportion are relatively context-less, working through association rather than by literal representation. Two other instances in *Waverley*

Fig. 8: Waverley's Last Visit to Flora Mac-Ivor (1865), by Robert Herdman;
engraved by Lumb Stocks

are Herdman's 'Prince Charles Edward in Shelter' and John Pettie's 'Disbanded' (depicting a Highland soldier in retreat after Culloden), both of which relate to events outside the main narrative of the novel. Elsewhere, the edition includes two plates from paintings belonging to the late 1870s by Millais, 'Effie and Geordie' and 'Lucy and the Master', both of which focus on the star-crossed lovers rather than narrative-specific incidents. Scottish artists are well represented for the Scottish novels, though French artists such as Lalauze provide a good proportion of the medieval materials. In some cases a single artist is responsible for a full suite, the illustrator Gordon Frederick Browne for instance producing the designs for *The Monastery* and *The Abbot*. Though no publisher records apparently survive, the overall sense is of a mixed process of procurement, with an initially heavy input of RAPFAS imagery, followed by a growing dependence on professional book illustrators.

Compared with this, the Dryburgh edition, published in twenty-five volumes by A. & C. Black from their new London headquarters, was a tightly run operation from the start, with one artist being engaged per title, and the wood engraving centralised under one individual (James Davis Cooper). As in the case of its rival, some 250 illustrations are involved, these being evenly distributed between the volumes, each of which contains one title-page vignette and nine plates. Compared with the 'academy' emphasis apparent in the Border edition, most of the artists engaged appear to have specialised in book illustration, some of the larger inputs coming from Paul Hardy, Godfrey C. Hindley and Gordon Browne. Mostly the illustrations depict incidents from the narrative, with a fairly high incidence of subjects already chosen by previous artists, begging the question of whether the illustrator was working primarily from the text or from an accumulated repertoire of artists' set-pieces. The Black records include a ledger account for the edition, where expenses are itemised according to the costs of drawing, commission and engraving.[35] Generally the cost of drawing falls within the range of 8–12 guineas for a plate, and 5–6 guineas for a vignette, though a handful of artists, such as Charles Martin Hardie, stand out as having received more. The price of engraving is steady (£12 a plate; £5 for a vignette), while commission is set at 15 per cent of the drawing. The accounts also add the cost of providing 'Electros of above' (5s. plates; 2s. 6d vignettes), referring to use of the process of electrotyping. As a whole, the total cost per volume for illustration generally falls in the

35   NLS, Acc 9765/13.

range of £225–70, significantly less than in the days of steel engraving, and very possibly one reason why the Blacks decided to commission new pieces rather than continue their previous practice of recycling. New materials of course allowed further re-packaging by the Blacks, the Dryburgh plates later providing frontispieces for both their Soho (1903–05: in colour) and School (1900–13) editions.

Illustrated sets by other publishers tend to follow either in the path of eclectically mixing old images or providing newly commissioned material. An interesting hybrid is found in the Melrose edition (1897–8), offering a combination of twenty-five original frontispieces in colour, and over two hundred full-size plates, including the Cruikshank etchings from the Fisher edition and the full body of RAPFAS engravings. The acquisition of these is proclaimed in a surviving copy of the Publisher's Sample book: 'Such a gallery of the finest illustrations to the Waverley Novels by the leading artists has never before been given in any, even the most expensive editions.'[36] Some surviving copies, however, contain only the black-and-white plates, indicating that a premium price was demanded for the coloured frontispieces. Wholesale recycling also occurs with the Bouverie edition (twenty-five volumes, 1901), printed in Edinburgh by R. & R. Clark Ltd, which combines imagery from the Abbotsford and Library editions, as well as Tilt's Landscape Illustrations. The Century Scott (twenty-five volumes, 1898), published by T. Fisher Unwin, in contrast features regular frontispiece portraits of heroines, some clearly matching those in Portraits of the Principal Female Characters (1834). The most diverse collection of all, however, is found in the Fine Art Scott (1910), published by the Educational Book Company, which incorporates some forty plates per volume/novel, some deriving from early sources such as The Keepsake and Heath's Illustrations. In all these projects, new mechanical processes facilitating the reproduction of imagery undoubtedly played a key role.

Elsewhere, the Holyrood edition (twenty-five volumes, 1903) follows the pattern of the Dryburgh edition in providing suites of six new woodblock plates per novel, each commissioned from a different artist, at least one of whom (Paul Hardy) had also worked for the Dryburgh. The illustrator for The Monastery was the Indian-born Byam Shaw, who follows in the path of a number of predecessors in selecting the duel between Sir Piercie Shafton and Halbert Glendinning as one of his subjects, though unlike most he shows Shafton still upright and clearly alive (Fig. 9). Here one

36 [Publisher's Sample Book], The Caxton Publishing Co., London, n.d. (NLS, shelfmark AB.3.209.25).

THE DUEL BETWEEN HALBERT AND SIR PIERCIE SHAFTON

Fig. 9: The Duel between Halbert and Sir Piercie Shafton (1903), by Byam Shaw

senses an element of the routine, interchangeable with other 'adventure' stories, indicative possibly of a shift to an adolescent and non-sophisticated readership. Similar characteristics are discernible in Scott volumes produced as part of Collins's Illustrated Pocket Classics and Nelson's New Century Library, marketed both singly and in larger units. In the case of the former, volumes usually provide a frontispiece plus seven plates, each set by its own named illustrator. Dating such volumes is often problematic, but the heyday of these series appears to have been around 1910. There is little sign of illustrated sets, other than those directed at children, having survived in any strength the shock of the Great War.

What was left of Scott's reputation as an adult novelist suffered further damage from the modernists, for whom text alone ruled supreme. Those who like the present writer discovered Scott in the 1960s, sensing a possible revival, had a choice between second-hand sets from the 1890s at knock-down prices and the unadorned single titles selected by the Everyman's Library. More recently, this situation has been complicated through a return by textual scholars to pre-Magnum editions, first evident in Claire Lamont's first-edition-based *Waverley* published by the Clarendon Press in 1981. The Edinburgh Edition of the Waverley Novels (1993–2013) contains large amounts of textual commentary and annotation, but no graphic illustrations, apart from reproduction of the Magnum illustrations in its final two volumes, which are there for primarily historical reasons. In an adjacent area, however, it is possible to claim a revival of illustration, sometimes unexpectedly linking with earlier examples. Colour illustrations have become an increasingly important feature on the covers of paperbacks, as they vie for attention not only in book shops but on websites such as Amazon. When first issued as a paperback in 1986, Lamont's *Waverley* carried on its cover a colour reproduction of Raeburn's 'Colonel Alexander Macdonell of Glengarry', which, as previously noted, had served as an illustration in the Abbotsford edition, though the rationale behind its selection there was undoubtedly different. Both the Everyman's and World's Classics paperback editions of *The Bride of Lammermoor* feature Millais' portrait of 'Lucy and the Master', as found earlier in the Border edition. A similarly 'associationist' kind of imagery is claimable in the use of John Pettie's 'Disbanded' for the cover of Andrew Hook's Penguin edition of *Waverley*, which for a while gave way to a picture of Charles Edward meeting his real-life protector Flora Macdonald, a step yet further away from the novel itself. The most recent Penguin *Waverley* shows a detail from a portrait of Flora Macdonald by Allan Ramsay, a choice perhaps motivated by a desire to accentuate its 'feminine' qualities and attract women readers, but also more broadly reflecting the widespread female portraiture of the 1830s and 1840s. Viewed in this light, it becomes possible to discern a continuing process in illustrating Scott's novels.

Beyond Usefulness and Ephemerality: The Discursive Almanac, 1828–60

BRIAN MAIDMENT

The Early Nineteenth-Century Almanac

The presence of the almanac in eighteenth- and nineteenth-century households from right across the social scale has long been noted by historians of print culture. Characterised as publications within the important category of 'pocket usefulness' by James Raven,[1] almanacs were a vital source of information within an agricultural society. If the almanac was not always to be found in the pocket, then it may have moved no further than the table – 'Of all books the Almanack is the most indispensable. So constant is the need for it that, unlike other books, it is not deposited on the shelf, but lies ready to hand on the table.'[2] As William St. Clair elaborates:

> Almanacs gave the dates of the monthly and annual fairs held in the larger towns, essential information for an agricultural economy. They gave much information about the tides on which all sea-borne and much river-borne trade depended. They set out the dates of church festivals, used to recommend the best times for crop planting and harvesting, as well as for the renewals of labour contracts, the collection of tithes, taxes and rents, and for scheduling religious festivals. They also set out the dates of law and university terms.[3]

One of the almanac's great apologists and entrepreneurs, Charles Knight, included a more conceptualised account of the nature and function of the almanac by way of introduction to the monthly calendar that was being introduced into the *Penny Magazine* in 1839:

---

1 Raven, *Business of Books*, p. 274.
2 Dionysius Lardner, *The Museum of Science and Art*, 12 vols. (London: Walton and Maberley, 1854–6), VII, p. 2.
3 St. Clair, *Reading Nation*, p. 58.

An Almanac, rightly considered, is a text for the most amusing and instructive comment. An Almanac directs us to the observance of periods connected with our social duties; – an Almanac has relation to all the wonderful phenomena of the heavenly bodies; – an Almanac leads us to the consideration of the changes of the Seasons and to the Natural History of the Year; an Almanac has reference to the customs of our ancestors which shed so rich a light over the whole history of their social arrangements; an Almanack directly or incidentally notices great Historical Events – or points out the areas which were rendered illustrious by the lives of those who have given enduring impulses to the course of the world's thought and actions.[4]

Knight was here pursuing his extended project of managing the cultural advance of the almanac, especially within the artisan classes, in the wake of the repeal of the almanac duty in 1834, a shift towards deregulation that he had vigorously supported.

Such descriptions of the role and function of the almanac have considered the genre as essentially forming a reference book, largely ignoring the quite different, but equally omnipresent, manifestation of almanacs as broadsheets to be found in offices, public gathering places and factories as well as in the domestic interior. Because of the ephemerality and haphazard survival of broadside almanacs, this essay too limits its interest to 'book' or pamphlet almanacs which will be considered within the broad context of rapid change within the production of print culture. Yet obviously broadsheet almanacs in a huge variety of modes continued to be produced throughout the century, ranging from exhortatory Owenite sheets through the self-consciously glamorous and sophisticated Oxford almanacs to highly coloured decorative lithographs attractive to young women in the compilation of the fashionable scrap albums which formed an important element in printed visual culture from the 1830s on (Fig. 1).

St. Clair notes that the Stationers' Company, which had been granted a perpetual corporate monopoly on the printing and selling of almanacs and prognostications in 1603, was 'for nearly two hundred years engaged in a constant struggle against the producers of unauthorised almanacs, of local piracies, and of almanacs printed abroad'.[5]

---

4   *Penny Magazine* 434, 5 January 1839, p. 1.
5   St. Clair, *Reading Nation*, p. 58.

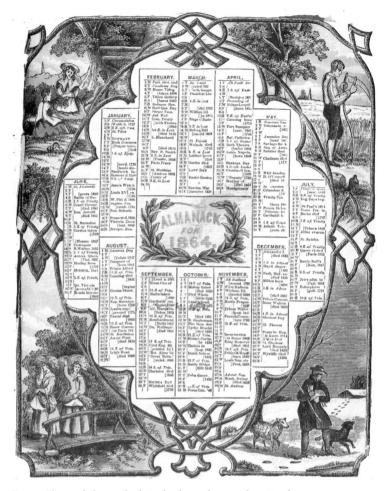

Fig. 1: Chromolithographed single-sheet almanac for 1864 from an anonymous scrap album

There are a number of available accounts of these 'struggles' over the manufacture and distribution of almanacs in the eighteenth and early nineteenth centuries which emphasise that conflict over the almanac form was both economic and cultural.[6] The economic battles largely con-

6   See Bernard Capp, *Astrology and the Popular Press: English Almanacs 1500–*

cerned commercial hostility to the lucrative monopoly enjoyed by the Stationers' Company – as St. Clair puts it, 'the main collective institution of the book industry was thus granted the right to take a rent every year in perpetuity from all of the wide range of economic activities and religious and cultural practices which depended on participants having access, each year, to the printed information which almanacs contained'.[7]

However, cultural conflicts over the almanac were more complex and diffuse, and focused largely on the popularity of the predictive and prognosticating elements of the almanacs.[8] As Louis James observes, 'It is [. . .] too simple to see almanacs as only 'prophetic'. Yet prophetic almanacs remained the most interesting, and probably the most widely circulated, of the many genres well on into the century.'[9] The 'preliminary observations' offered as a preface to the first volume of the Society for Diffusion of Useful Knowledge's *British Almanac* in 1828 give a clear summary of the position:

> The Almanacs most in demand are remarkable for the mixture of ignorance and imposture which they contain, with much useful matter; and it is not very creditable either to those who prepare, or to those that buy them, that their circulation should be so extensive, and that the worst by far are those chiefly used by the people.[10]

The often wildly improbable prognostications of almanacs deeply

---

1800 (London: Faber and Faber, 1979); Maureen Perkins, *Visions of the Future: Almanacs, Time and Cultural Change* (Oxford: Clarendon Press, 1996); Jill Allaway, ' "Paper Ghosts": The Almanack and Year Book 1790–1860' (unpublished doctoral thesis, University of Huddersfield, 2003); and Brian Maidment, 'Re-Arranging the Year: The Almanac, the Day Book and the Year Book as Popular Literary Forms, 1789–1860', in *Rethinking Victorian Culture*, ed. Juliet John and Alice Jenkins (Basingstoke: Macmillan, 2000), pp. 91–111.

7   St. Clair, *Reading Nation*, p. 58.

8   For prognostication, popular superstition and the almanac, see Keith Thomas, *Religion and the Decline of Magic* (London: Weidenfeld and Nicolson, 1971); Ronald Hutton, *Stations of the Sun: A History of the Ritual Year in Britain* (Oxford: Oxford University Press, 1996); and Louis James, *Print and the People, 1819–1851* (London: Alan Lane, 1976).

9   James, *Print and the People*, p. 54. But see Allaway, ' "Paper Ghosts" ', for a broad overview of the sub-genres used by almanacs in the first half of the nineteenth century.

10   *The British Almanac for 1828* (London: Baldwin and Cradock, 1828), p. 3.

offended those entrepreneurs of print culture, both individual and institutional, who sought to develop rational information as the central
element in the mass of books, magazines, pamphlets and tracts aimed at
the enhancement of artisan progress.

Anxiety about the need to represent the almanac as a rational, or
even scientific, genre led to the production of a considerable body of
secondary literature in the first half of the nineteenth century analysing
the origins and mechanics of the calendar and its redeployment through
the almanac form. The SPCK's multi-volume *Instructor*, a small-format
serialised encyclopaedia aimed at the artisan reader and frequently re-
published through the 1840s, offered as its fourth volume *The Book of the
Calendar, the Months, and the Seasons* which contained a careful description of the contents of the standard almanac, relating them carefully to a
scientific understanding of the calendar year.[11] *The Original*, a serial-cum-
journal written by Thomas Walker and launched in 1835, devoted a long
section to the almanac.[12] Dionysius Lardner's twelve-volume *Museum
of Science and Art* (1854–6) included an extensive account of the history of the almanac in its seventh volume *Common Things Explained*.[13]
To such explanatory and justificatory accounts in the informative literature aimed at artisan readers should be added the prefaces offered by
the almanacs themselves and already alluded to in the case of the *British
Almanac* and its supplementary volumes. It is evident, then, that the almanac form was subject to considerable scrutiny, elucidation and justifi-
cation during the period in the first half of the nineteenth century, when
many publishers and entrepreneurs of print culture were seeking to shrug
off its populist interest in prediction and to insist on its utilitarian value.

This essay is centrally concerned with the consequences of the almanac's engagement with Victorian print culture and with changing defini-
tions of the genre within mass-circulation literature between 1828 and
1860. The main focus, therefore, is not the battles between the cham-
pions and entrepreneurs of the widespread distribution of utilitarian
and, as they saw it, socially progressive information and the defenders of
the hugely popular prognosticating and superstitious almanacs that had
brought in huge profits over the previous half-century. Rather, the aim is

---

11   Anon., *The Book of the Calendar, the Months, and the Seasons* (London: J.
W. Parker for the SPCK, 1840).

12   Thomas Walker, *The Original* (London: H.Renshaw,1836), pp. 126–35.

13   Dionysius Lardner, *Common Things Explained* (London: Walton and Maberley, 1855).

to study some of the ways in which almanacs published in this period developed into new hybrid genres, either through the use of supplements or through the incorporation of various forms of secondary material, both textual and visual, within the traditional almanac form and function.[14] Such developments were complex, and, at risk of simplification, this essay will engage in a range of detailed readings of almanacs in order to clarify the developmental process through which the early Victorian almanac engaged with a mass readership. The first element of this discussion will be a consideration of the innovations brought about by Charles Knight and the Society for the Diffusion of Useful Knowledge (SDUK) in their *British Almanac* first published in 1828. The second group of readings will focus on two almanacs from 1836, early in the almanac's process of re-definition, to suggest the ways in which supplementary and hybrid elements in the almanac were used to differentiate between various kinds of implied readers and to broaden the content of the genre in significant ways. The third group of readings will consider the development of the almanac as a mechanism through which publishers in the 1830s, 1840s and 1850s sought to extend their brand image and capitalise on the emergence of a mass readership among the lower middle and artisan classes. As a contributor to *George Cruikshank's Table Book* noted in 1845, 'now there is no excuse for the most penurious person being without one. [. . .] Almanacks are the cheap philanthropy, the conventional generosity of the age [. . .] every periodical gives one away in the course of the year.'[15] Such almanacs were largely published on the back of, or perhaps as supplements to, successful periodicals, yet they began to suggest a number of distinctive new generic features in the early Victorian period. The fourth area of interest will concern comic almanacs from the 1830s and 1840s. While the two most celebrated and long-lived comic almanacs, the *Comic Almanack* (1835 to 1853) and the *Punch Almanack* (1841 on), will inevitably dominate this discussion, there will also be some consideration of other travesty almanacs, most obviously Gilbert Abbott à Beckett's *The Almanack of the Month*. This essay is thus shaped by discussion of a series of representative instances in the development

14   While focused on an American almanac, Teresa A. Goddu's 'The Antislavery Almanac and the Discourse of Numeracy', *Book History* 12 (2009), 129–55, has many useful things to say about the ways in which illustrations render the almanac text more complex.
15   *George Cruikshank's Table Book*, ed. Gilbert Abbott à Beckett (London: Bell and Daldy, 1869), pp. 5–6.

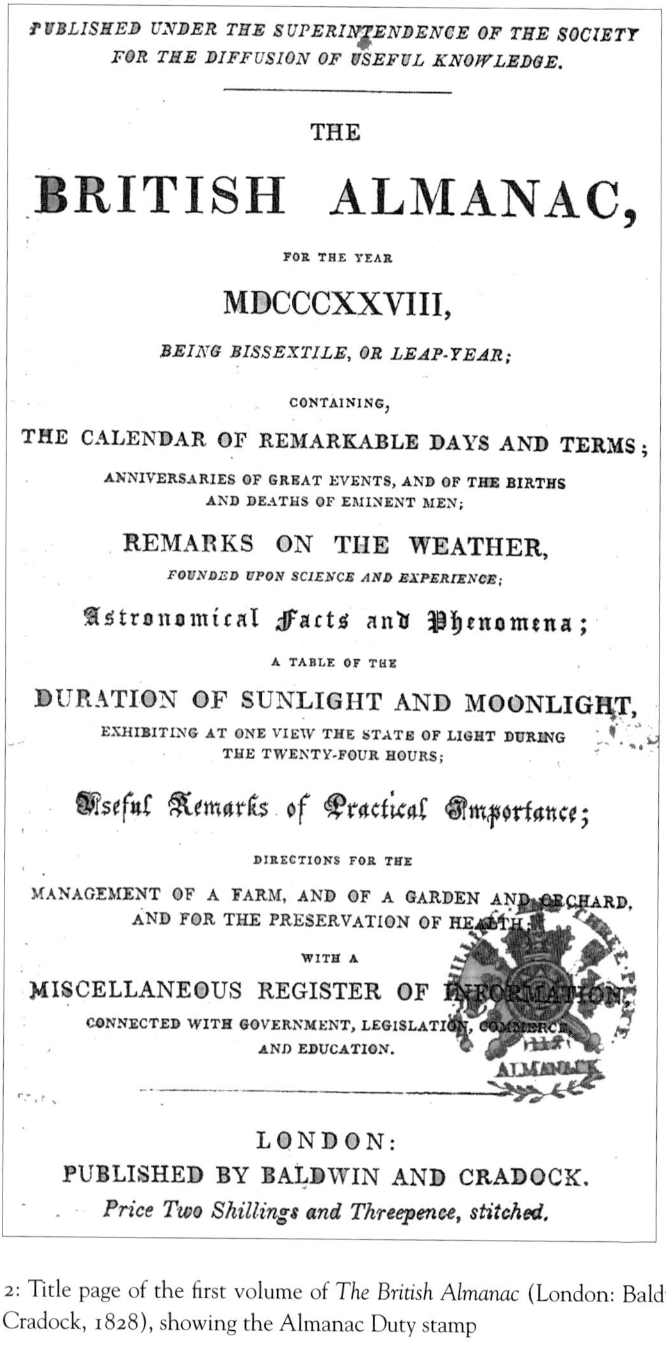

PUBLISHED UNDER THE SUPERINTENDENCE OF THE SOCIETY
FOR THE DIFFUSION OF USEFUL KNOWLEDGE.

THE

BRITISH ALMANAC,

FOR THE YEAR

MDCCCXXVIII,

BEING BISSEXTILE, OR LEAP-YEAR;

CONTAINING,

THE CALENDAR OF REMARKABLE DAYS AND TERMS;

ANNIVERSARIES OF GREAT EVENTS, AND OF THE BIRTHS
AND DEATHS OF EMINENT MEN;

REMARKS ON THE WEATHER,

FOUNDED UPON SCIENCE AND EXPERIENCE;

Astronomical Facts and Phenomena;

A TABLE OF THE

DURATION OF SUNLIGHT AND MOONLIGHT,

EXHIBITING AT ONE VIEW THE STATE OF LIGHT DURING
THE TWENTY-FOUR HOURS;

Useful Remarks of Practical Importance;

DIRECTIONS FOR THE

MANAGEMENT OF A FARM, AND OF A GARDEN AND ORCHARD,
AND FOR THE PRESERVATION OF HEALTH;

WITH A

MISCELLANEOUS REGISTER OF INFORMATION,

CONNECTED WITH GOVERNMENT, LEGISLATION, COMMERCE,
AND EDUCATION.

LONDON:

PUBLISHED BY BALDWIN AND CRADOCK.

Price Two Shillings and Threepence, stitched.

Fig. 2: Title page of the first volume of *The British Almanac* (London: Baldwin and Cradock, 1828), showing the Almanac Duty stamp

of the almanac form. Such a method of approach risks simplification and atypicality, but nonetheless begins to offer an account of complexities of an omnipresent form of Victorian print culture.

1828 *and the* British Almanac

As already suggested, the launch of the *British Almanac* in 1828 represents a key moment of development for the almanac form (Fig. 2). It became an immediate best-seller. In her biography of the SDUK's publisher, Charles Knight, Valerie Gray notes that the first issue of the *British Almanac*, despite being 'late in the field and expensive' sold 10,000 copies in its first week.[16] Gray further cites William Clowes's optimistic claim that the first issue sold 20,000 copies in all, and that the circulation rose to 37,000 in 1829 and 42,000 in 1830.[17] Such figures are even more impressive given that the *British Almanac* was never cheap, initially priced at 1s., with an additional 1s. 3d of almanac tax bringing the overall cost up to 2s. 3d. Although the basic price of 1s. was retained, in 1850 the price of the *British Almanac* together with the annual *Companion to the Almanac* (another Knight 'brainwave', according to Gray, containing 'supplementary articles on issues of the day'),[18] still cost the considerable amount of 4s. in a cloth-bound volume even after the abolition of the almanac tax. Despite the high cost, both Knight himself and Gray regarded the *British Almanac* as a publication that 'reached a very broad spectrum of the reading public',[19] forming 'a class of publications which are more than any other species of book in the hands of persons of every degree'.[20] Gray attributes the cross-class appeal of such publications to Knight's 'common touch' and refusal to underestimate his readers, providing only, to use Knight's own words, 'whatever is best and most permanent in literature' with 'a character of universality'[21] – rather ambitious claims to make about a literary genre previously characterised by its impermanence and ephemerality.

16   Valerie Gray, *Charles Knight: Educator, Publisher, Writer* (Aldershot: Ashgate, 2006), p. 47.

17   Ibid., pp. 153–4.

18   Ibid., p. 47.

19   Ibid., p. 47.

20   The quotation is from an article probably by Knight in the *Athenaeum*, 2 January 1828, p. 4.

21   Gray, *Charles Knight*, p. 154.

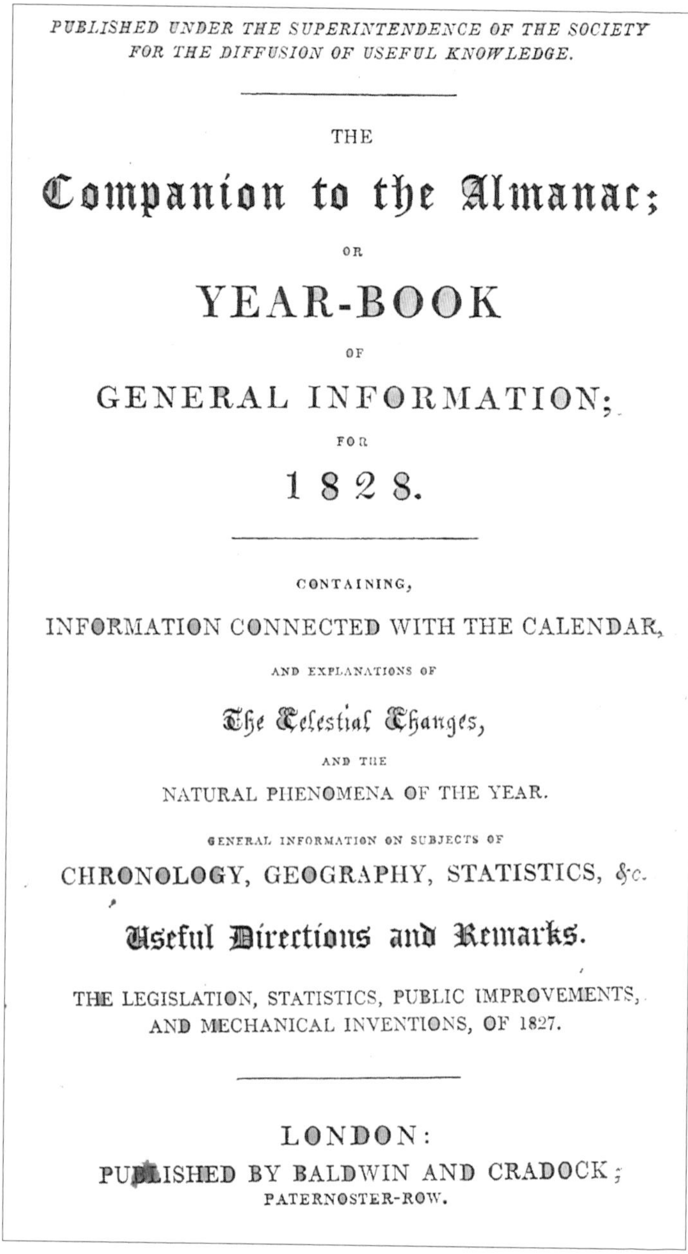

PUBLISHED UNDER THE SUPERINTENDENCE OF THE SOCIETY
FOR THE DIFFUSION OF USEFUL KNOWLEDGE.

THE

Companion to the Almanac;

OR

YEAR-BOOK

OF

GENERAL INFORMATION;

FOR

1 8 2 8.

CONTAINING,

INFORMATION CONNECTED WITH THE CALENDAR,

AND EXPLANATIONS OF

The Celestial Changes,

AND THE

NATURAL PHENOMENA OF THE YEAR.

GENERAL INFORMATION ON SUBJECTS OF

CHRONOLOGY, GEOGRAPHY, STATISTICS, &c.

Useful Directions and Remarks.

THE LEGISLATION, STATISTICS, PUBLIC IMPROVEMENTS,
AND MECHANICAL INVENTIONS, OF 1827.

LONDON:

PUBLISHED BY BALDWIN AND CRADOCK;
PATERNOSTER-ROW.

Fig. 3: Title page of *The Companion to the Almanac* (London: Baldwin and Cradock, 1828)

But with Knight the notion of permanence became central to the almanac. The 'Preliminary Observations' to the 1828 *Companion to the Almanac* made Knight's intentions for the publication quite clear. He startlingly envisioned the almanac, previously conceived as forming only a useful guide to a single year and thus becoming immediately anachronistic once the following New Year was reached, as something close to the part-issue works of information that were soon to form the central platform of the SDUK's address to the artisan classes through serial publications like the *Penny Magazine*[22] and the *Penny Cyclopaedia*.

[. . .] by annually varying the contents of this little work, a body of most important information may be gradually collected; – and a record preserved of the most important features of the passing year. The conductors, therefore, beg to impress upon the purchasers of the almanac, that it is not a merely temporary work; and they entreat them to preserve it as the first of a Series, to be annually published, with such improvements as will naturally arise out of a diligent and systematic collection of the various facts that appear of the most consequence to be generally diffused, as auxiliary to the great object of increasing the ability to acquire *Useful Knowledge*.[23]

Such a reconceptualisation of the almanac genre as a permanent source of knowledge and understanding to its readers sought to harness the ubiquity and traditional utility of the almanac form to the broader approaches to cheap, improving mass-circulation literature aimed at newly literate artisan and working-men readers that characterised print culture in the 1830s and 1840s.

The radicalism of the *British Almanac*, however, lay not so much in its studied utilitarian approach to the role and content of the almanac but in its associated 'brainwave', *The Companion to the Almanac; or Year-book of General Information* (Fig. 3).[24] The *Companion* was edited and

22   Knight, in his quest to assimilate the almanac into respectable artisan culture, introduced a half-page *monthly* almanac into the *Penny Magazine* in January 1839, subsequently moving it to the monthly 'Supplements' of the magazine. In introducing this innovation, Knight stated that the repeal of the almanac duty in 1834 had resulted in a trebling of the consumption of almanacs, and that a monthly 'calendar' would not reduce the usefulness of the SDUK's *British Almanac*. *Penny Magazine* 434, 5 January 1839, p. 1.

23   *Companion to the British Almanac* (London: Charles Knight, 1828), p. iv.

24   Mark Turner has recently published an essay that discusses in detail the

substantially written by Augustus De Morgan. De Morgan was an important figure in the history of the almanac, and the author of *The Book of Almanacs* (1851), a publication that explained the ways in which the key dates within any year could be calculated.[25] His various prefaces to the *Companion* also contained much information about the technical details and formulaic layout of the almanac. The use of 'year book' supplements opened up a range of possibilities for the almanac. Cleansed of its ludicrous prognostications, impenetrable hieroglyphs and improbable long-range weather forecasts, the utilitarian almanac was able, by its use of supplementary year books, to begin to direct itself to niche markets, and to offer substantial amounts of information and even opinion that extended the role of the almanac in important ways.

Informative 'supplements' or 'year books', in imitation of their successful use in almanacs, became a relatively common element in early Victorian serials and magazines. A *Companion to the Newspaper* was launched as a monthly publication to accompany the *Penny Magazine* on 1 March 1833, a few months after the launch of its host periodical. The *Companion*, at 2d for each close-printed sixteen-page issue, was a considerable further outlay for subscribers to the *Penny Magazine*, but it brought the reader into much closer contact with current events, and, indeed, was something of a subterfuge for circumventing the Stamp Duty on topical publications.[26] Dickens's *Household Words* from its first issue in March 1850 offered a similar monthly 2d supplement which formed a *Household Narrative of Current Events*. Again, the information offered here both rendered the host journal more topically political and

---

SDUK and Knight's *Companion to the Newspaper* ('Companions, Supplements, and the Proliferation of Print in the 1830s', *Victorian Periodicals Review* 43.2 (2010), 119–32). He gives an account of the *Companion to the Almanac* on pp. 123–4 of this essay, stressing the *Companion's* role as a 'lasting work of reference'. Turner's essay, in its broader consideration of the supplement to journals of rational information, gives an important context for this essay, as indeed does this entire issue of *Victorian Periodicals Review* which focuses on supplements and the periodical press.

25   Augustus De Morgan, *The Book of Almanacs* (London: Taylor, Walton and Maberley, 1851).

26   The title *Companion to the Newspaper*, used in preference to 'Companion to the *Penny Magazine*', emphasises that the information to be found there was both topical and permanent. The *Companion* formed both a commentary on contemporary events and an encyclopaedia of 'useful' information. See Turner, 'Companions, Supplements', pp. 125–7.

formed a serialised encyclopaedia of enduringly useful information. The *British Almanac*'s innovations of the late 1820s, in bringing together the traditional content of the ephemeral almanac with more topical 'supplementary' information, had opened the way for the almanac to transmute into genres previously the preserve of the encyclopaedia, the newspaper or the current affairs magazine.

Hybrid Almanacs of the 1830s and 1840s

The hybridisation of the almanac form in the 1830s was an inevitable consequence of Knight's drive to give permanence and broad topical utility to its content. Knight saw the almanac, to use the 1828 *Companion to the British Almanac*'s phrases, as 'not merely a temporary work', but rather interested in 'the most permanent features of the passing year'.[27] If almanacs were to develop their content to meet the interests and needs of an emergent mass readership, then the nature of the discursive elements situated within, around and supplementary to the formulaic calendar elements of the text needed to be entirely reconsidered. Obviously, superstitious and fancifully predictive elements would have to be eliminated, as they had been in the severe pages of the *British Almanac*. But, more radically, if Knight's particular vision of the ideal almanac was to be fulfilled, it would become both a permanent reference work more like an encyclopaedia than a diary and, more significant still, a record of current events that would include, among much else, contentious political decisions, accounts of popular unrest and discontent, and details of the economy. In short, in such a genre the topical was inevitably coeval with the political, and, while Knight and the SDUK were committed to a concept of information as an ideologically neutral and entirely secular commodity, Knight was well aware that the publishing activities of the Society had been ridiculed both by radicals (for its definition of 'useful knowledge' as entirely apolitical) and by sectarian conservatives (for its insistence on the secularity of useful knowledge).

Driven by understandings like these, and with Knight's influential views in mind, early and mid-Victorian almanacs became literary and visual *hybrids*. Such hybridity involved the incorporation of both textual and graphic elements belonging to a broad variety of print genres

27   *Companion to the British Almanac*, p. iv.

PUBLISHED UNDER THE SUPERINTENDENCE OF THE SOCIETY FOR THE DIFFUSION OF USEFUL KNOWLEDGE.

THE

BRITISH

WORKING-MAN'S ALMANAC

FOR THE YEAR

1836.

CONTENTS.

	Page
Explanatory Notices	2
Preliminary Notes for the Year	2
Eclipses in 1836 — The Four Quarters—Halley's Comet	2
High Water at Outports	3
CALENDAR FOR THE YEAR	4 to 27
Weights and Measures: 1. Length — 2. Surface — 3. Solidity and Capacity—4. Weight—5. Angular—6. Time	28-30
Regulation of Weights and Measures	30
Taxes on Windows	31
Stamps on Receipts	32
Savings' Bank Interest Table	32
Rule for calculating Interest	32

	Page
Table to calculate Wages and other Payments	32
General Post Office, London	33
Twopenny Post	33
Right of Voting: Counties, Cities, and Boroughs	34
Registration	35
Municipal Reform Bill	36-37
Circuits of Judges	38
Quarter Sessions in England and Wales	39
The Royal Family	41
Ministry of England	42
Law: England, Scotland, Ireland	42
Law Officers	43
The Kitchen Garden	44

LONDON:

CHARLES KNIGHT, 22, LUDGATE-STREET.

Price Three-pence sewed,

Or Sixteen-pence bound in cloth with the 'Working-Man's Year-Book.'

WM. CLOWES AND SONS, PRINTERS, DUKE-STREET, LAMBETH.

Fig. 4: Title page of *The British Working-Man's Almanac* for 1836 (London: Charles Knight, 1836)

ranging from graphic caricature to popular history, and brought the almanac into close alignment with a whole range of texts being produced
largely to satisfy the hunger for print culture among the respectable artisan and urban lower middle classes. Accordingly, almanacs began to
construct an 'artisan year', which had already been prefigured in the
illustrated year books of William Hone and William Howitt. This 'artisan year' has been described as 'an agricultural calendar rewritten by a
combination of Blake and Smollett. It constructs an Albion of festivals,
customs and remembrances, which is independent both of conventional history and of the obligations, reminders and orthodoxies of the "useful" almanac'.[28] In the new mass-circulation almanacs of the Victorian
period, often hosted by established periodicals addressed to artisan readers, Hone and Howitt's year of customs, traditions and rural continuities
was increasingly replaced by a year of historical celebrations and urban
events that together constructed a British national identity appropriate
to the new industrial labouring classes. It is the nature of that identity
which forms a central focus for discussion.

1836: The SDUK and The British Working-Man's Almanac

If the claims cited above that the utilitarian and informative *British
Almanac* reached across social classes and offered even modest readers
something to meet their needs are true, it is worth considering why
Knight and the SDUK felt the need, in the 1830s, to develop another
clearly related almanac publication called *The British Working-Man's
Almanac* (Fig. 4), very similar in construction and layout to the *British
Almanac* if with a much reduced page size, and also to publish an associated *Working-Man's Yearbook*. One obvious reason must have been cost.
The *British Working-Man's Almanac* was available on its own in 1836
as a sewn forty-eight-page pamphlet for 3d, with the accompanying
Yearbook at 9d. The two together in a cloth binding cost 1s. 4d, a considerable difference to the *British* combined volume at 4s. However, the
implication is that the *British Working-Man's Almanac* was targeted at a
different readership to the *British Almanac*, thus acknowledging that the
parent almanac had not in fact reached down to artisan or labouring-
class readers. Beyond the large price difference linked to a smaller format, how did the two almanacs differ in terms of content and address?

28   Maidment, 'Re-Arranging the Year', p. 106.

As with the *British Almanac*, the central focus of the *British Working-Man's Almanac* was less on the traditional almanac content, which comprised a slimmed-down version of the utilitarian information to be found widely in many other almanacs, as on the supplementary *Yearbook*. Despite the title, the *Yearbook* was hardly topical at all, perhaps in deference to the SDUK's pursuit of a studied 'neutrality' in its publications, but instead comprised a series of quite lengthy essays, published anonymously, and clearly directed at supporting the cultural, economic and intellectual progress of thoughtful artisans. The essays were carefully written to offer information without commentary; it is largely left to the reader to relate the assembled facts to their socio-political context. Even where the topic was potentially deeply controversial, as in successive essays on the Poor Law Amendment Act in the 1835 and 1836 volumes, the *Working-Man's Yearbook* was eager to appear even-handed. Essentially a closely evidenced celebration of the effectiveness of the Act in eradicating old abuses, the author nonetheless considered the nature and extent of the opposition to the Act.

Such elaborate and studied even-handedness in the *Yearbook* was an essential element in its optimistic overall view of progress both within the socio-political lives of artisans and in the wider economy of the nation. Thus an alarmingly full and detailed list of the particular occupational diseases suffered by tradesmen was offset against a wide-ranging account of 'The Condition of Working Men in Europe' which was clearly meant to cheer up British working men and women, despite leaving out the 'more striking contrasts' that might have been made with the 'misery to which tyranny has reduced the cultivators of the soil in Turkey'.[29] More practical advice was offered in essays on the benefits of Provident Societies, and more industrial encouragement in an article on 'Value of an Acquaintance with the Fine Arts to a Working-Man' that underlined the increasing importance of taste and good design in the expansion of a commodity manufacturing economy. Again, here broad evidence from European countries was used to structure the main arguments, although in this instance Europe provided evidence of progressive good practice. Overall, the *Yearbook* deployed its information in ways that encouraged the economic and social engagement of its assumed artisan readers in a collective and progressive national economic and social project.

The *Working-Man's Yearbook*, despite its dependence on a relatively

29   *British Working-Man's Almanac for 1836*, p. 5.

traditional host almanac, presupposed a very particular, class-based readership among male urban artisans with a very carefully defined set of interests. It managed to construct a rather flattering assumed reader – a thoughtful workman keen to be better informed both about his own circumstances and the wider development of labour across industrialising Europe, and keen to make up his own mind about the implications of rapid legislative, economic and social change. Although the *Yearbook* assumed in its readers an unwavering commitment to an optimistic and progressivist reading of British industrial society, it did manage to make an engagement with that society sound valuable and within the reach of even modestly situated artisans. In doing this, the *Yearbook* made the essay a key way of addressing artisans, a generic assumption that was central to the development of artisan periodicals like Cassell's *Working Man's Friend* or *Howitt's Journal*. More important for the development of the almanac form, the *Working-Man's Yearbook* began to link the apparently neutral information held within the almanac with the formation of opinion. The polemical almanac, here largely disguised by the restraint of the *Yearbook*'s opinions, its appeal to the artisan reader to think things through, and the separating out of various forms of information into the main almanac and a supplementary year book, nonetheless begins to become visible at this point.

The Political Almanack for 1836

The *Political Almanack for 1836* is a different kind of literary hybrid than the *British Working-Man's Almanac* (Figs. 5 and 6). The hybridity of the *BWMA* was largely the outcome of its importation into the almanac of material usually found outside the traditional almanac, in particular essays addressed very deliberately at the perceived intellectual and cultural interests of respectable working men. Such essays were more frequently found in discursive forms like periodicals or the small-format cloth-bound cheap publications of the SPCK (Society for Promoting Christian Knowledge), William and Robert Chambers or the SDUK.[30] The discursive almanac was thus superimposed on the utilitarian almanac, tying down socially unaligned information to a more particular

---

30   The serialised *Chambers's Papers for the People* and the essays submitted by readers to *Douglas Jerrolds' Shilling Magazine* provide obvious examples of these kinds of publications.

THE

POLITICAL

A L M A N A C K

FOR

1836,

BEING BISSEXTILE OR LEAP-YEAR;

COMPRISING

THE NATURAL PHENOMENA, FESTIVALS, HOLIDAYS, ETC.;

WITH A LARGE QUANTITY

OF

POLITICAL AND COMMERCIAL

INFORMATION;

AND

THIRTEEN HUMOROUS ENGRAVINGS,

FROM DESIGNS BY

ROBERT SEYMOUR;

WITH

𝕻𝔬𝔢𝔱𝔦𝔠𝔞𝔩 𝕮𝔬𝔫𝔱𝔯𝔦𝔟𝔲𝔱𝔦𝔬𝔫𝔰 𝔣𝔯𝔬𝔪 𝕻𝔬𝔭𝔲𝔩𝔞𝔯 𝕻𝔢𝔫𝔰.

LONDON:

EFFINGHAM WILSON, ROYAL EXCHANGE.

Price One Shilling and Sixpence.

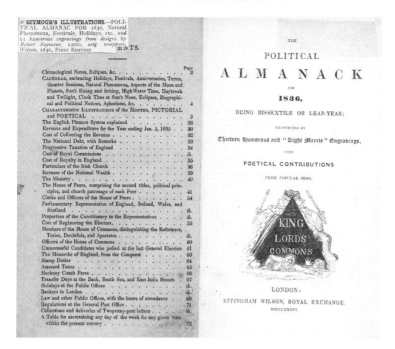

SEYMOUR'S ILLUSTRATIONS.—POLI-
TICAL ALMANAC FOR 1836, Natural
Phenomena, Festivals, Holidays, etc., *and*
13 *humorous engravings from designs by
Robert Seymour*, 12mo, *orig. wrappers,
Wilson, 1836*, FIRST EDITION

CONTENTS.

Page
Chronological Notes, Eclipses, &c.   3
CALENDAR, embracing Holidays, Festivals, Anniversaries, Terms,
    Quarter Sessions, Natural Phenomena, Aspects of the Moon and
    Planets, Sun's Rising and Setting, High Water Time, Daybreak
    and Twilight, Clock Time at Sun's Noon, Eclipses, Biographi-
    cal and Political Notices, Aphorisms, &c.   4
CHARACTERISTIC ILLUSTRATIONS of the MONTHS, PICTORIAL
    and POETICAL   5
The English Finance System explained 28
Revenue and Expenditure for the Year ending Jan. 5, 1835 . . 30
Cost of Collecting the Revenue 32
The National Debt, with Remarks 33
Progressive Taxation of England 34
Cost of Royal Commissions . . . . *ib.*
Cost of Royalty in England 35
Particulars of the Irish Church 36
Increase of the National Wealth 39
The Ministry 40
The House of Peers, comprising the second titles, political prin-
    ciples, and church patronage of each Peer 41
Clerks and Officers of the House of Peers 54
Parliamentary Representation of England, Ireland, Wales, and
    Scotland . . . . *ib.*
Proportion of the Constituency to the Representatives . . . *ib.*
Cost of Registering the Electors 55
Members of the House of Commons, distinguishing the Reformers,
    Tories, Doubtfuls, and Apostates . . . . *ib.*
Officers of the House of Commons 60
Unsuccessful Candidates who polled at the last General Election 61
The Monarchs of England, from the Conquest 63
Stamp Duties 64
Assessed Taxes 65
Hackney Coach Fares 66
Transfer Days at the Bank, South Sea, and East India Houses 67
Holidays at the Public Offices . . . . *ib.*
Bankers in London . . . . *ib.*
Law and other Public Offices, with the hours of attendance . 68
Regulations at the General Post Office 71
Collections and deliveries of Twopenny-post letters . . . . *ib.*
A Table for ascertaining any day of the week for any given time
    within the present century 72

THE

POLITICAL

A L M A N A C K

FOR

1836,

BEING BISSEXTILE OR LEAP-YEAR;

ILLUSTRATED BY

Thirteen Humorous and "Right Merrie" Engravings,

WITH

POETICAL CONTRIBUTIONS

FROM POPULAR PENS.

KING
LORDS
COMMONS

LONDON:

EFFINGHAM WILSON, ROYAL EXCHANGE.

MDCCCXXXVI.

Fig. 5 (left): Cover page for *The Political Almanack for 1836* (London: Effingham Wilson, 1836)

Fig. 6 (above): Title page opening for *The Political Almanack for 1836*

class-based category of readers, but, of course, also introducing a mode of potential cultural condescension in which the interests, tastes and beliefs of artisan readers are presumed or even pre-empted by the editors and writers of the almanac's more discursive elements. The *Political Almanack* works in different, and perhaps unexpected, ways to superimpose the 'political' on the informational elements of the almanac. Most of the content of the *Political Almanack* is at first glance traditionally apolitical, especially given that its publisher, Effingham Wilson, was well known for bringing out controversial, liberal or even radical works.[31] The monthly calendar, for instance, was filled out with trite

31   The firm published, for example, many pamphlets inveighing against various forms of taxation as well as such controversial volumes as William

AUGUST.

GLEANING FOR THE PEOPLE.

COMES Lammas Day—brown Autumn now matures
Its August harvest—by a patient people
In sorrow sown—that august personages
At will may reap the product of their labours.
Now jocund to the field the Manor's Lord
Brings the State waggon, for the golden store.
Proud in its front the flaunting dame, his wife,
Her top-knot crown'd with many a sparkling gem,
Sits, whip in hand, eager to urge it onwards.
The courtly Farmer, by the Corn Laws shielded,
Has brought his servants to help house the spoil ;
The *females* of his household come with *rakes*,
And there's a knave, his face o'ergrown with hair,
In soldier's jacket dress'd, who lends a hand—
One who can turn his hand to anything ;
Nor does the Church neglect to take its tithe—
The Parson's there.   All with stout pitchforks arm'd.
Alas the day ! they'll soon lay bare the fields,
Sheaf after sheaf they gather, till all 's got,
And what, poor labourer, is left for thee?
From Dan to Beersheba all is not barren,
DAN yet some gleanings can procure for thee.
See from Hibernia wends a sturdy band,
In 'kerchiefs green, with shamrock on their brows,
To glean the leavings for the starving poor :
Prosper their efforts, 'tis the cause of good,
And grant, oh gracious Heaven ! in thy mercy,
The Farmer's agents do not, in their zeal,
So overload the waggon of the State,
That it o'erturn and bury all in ruin !

and unexceptional moral exhortations – 'folly is a fatal enemy', the 12 December entry informs the reader, while 'glory follows action' according to the entry for 19 March. Also to be found is the range of factual information traditional to the almanac.

But, of course, the editors of almanacs were well aware that the choice of what information to offer their readers was a highly political one. Thus, among the detail of stamp duty and the commercial year, a list of the House of Peers included not just names and titles but also numbers of livings held by each lord and the pensions they received. It was through such an accumulation of detailed information rather than any outspoken editorial intervention or political commentary that the *Political Almanack* managed to construct a model of the British nation built out of taxes, privileges and petty oppressions. But, while such selection of cumulative information provided one way in which almanacs politicised themselves and positioned their readers, the *Political Almanack*'s more inventive and spectacular appropriation of the political was through the introduction of a new type of almanac page opposite the monthly chart comprising a poem acting as an extended caption to a wood-engraved caricature (Fig. 7). In effect this was a kind of page borrowed from the circumambient mass of visual culture, more specifically the comic annuals, *jeux d'esprit* and miscellanies illustrated by vignette wood engravings by the likes of Robert Cruikshank, which were a rapidly increasing popular element in the print marketplace. But in commissioning Robert Seymour to draw these explicitly political satires in the busy, detailed, emblematic manner of single-plate etched and engraved caricature inherited from the eighteenth century, the *Political Almanack* broke new ground. Normally the use of the vignette wood engraving for political commentary had led artists, and C. J. Grant and Seymour in particular, to simplify their images into single joke, linear images using the thick black line of the woodcut to make emphatic and easily read-off commentary on events of the day, as Seymour had famously done in his illustrations for Gilbert

Howitt's *Popular History of Priestcraft* (1833) and many reprints in the 1830s of John Wade's *Extraordinary Black Book* that listed 'places, pensions and sinecures' as well as biographies, topographical and literary works, including the George Cruikshank-illustrated *Sunday in London*.

Fig. 7 (left): 'August' page from *The Political Almanack for 1836* showing Robert Seymour's wood-engraved vignette

Abbott à Beckett's periodical *Figaro in London*. But in *The Political Almanack*, Seymour attempted something far more difficult: he tried to bring the complexity, allusiveness, verbalness and graphic codes of the eighteenth-century etched and engraved caricature tradition into the tiny compass of the vignette wood engraving, and to combine these vignettes with an extended satirical verbal commentary.

Seymour's image for August provides a clear example of such complexity and allusiveness (Fig. 7). In the foreground, the well-fed and well-padded wife of the 'Manor's Lord' (representing here both the affluent farmer and the greedy Government) sweeps out of the picture bearing off for her own purposes a rich swathe of ironically labelled 'GLEANINGS FOR THE PEOPLE'. The harvesting scene in the background, where an emblematically dressed peer and clergyman pitchfork hay off a wagon, shows through attached labels how the labour and productivity of the mass of population is siphoned off through unjust taxes – thus the sheaf of corn in the middle distance represents the 'taxes on knowledge' through which topical printed matter was rendered too expensive ever to reach the hands of those who had most to gain from reading it. More complex still is the caption attached to the load of hay: 'AUGUST MEASURES FOR AUGUST PERSONAGES'. There are two interdependent puns here, the first on 'measure' (at once both a bushel of corn and an Act of Parliament) and the second on 'August' (the month of plentiful harvesting that delivers profits only to those 'august' members of society who can control the 'measures' through which wealth is managed). This kind of visual and verbal density is clearly underpinned by the delicacy of the drawing and the tonal variety through which the image is rendered, and by the crowded graphics of the image. Both are underlined by the outspoken poem that re-renders the image through a verbal equivalent.

'Hybridity' here, then, means the discovery of forms and modes through which the genteel discourse of eighteenth-century visual satire, political in focus and outspoken in its critique of the ruling establishment of 'the old corruption', could be brought together with the new information culture of the 1830s to form something at once traditional and radically new. A traditional but nonetheless radical political denunciation of a privileged and corrupt social elite is given a startling new form in the wood-engraved vignette, a form which had been increasingly prominent in humorous print culture since the early 1820s. While the basis of the graphic satire contained in the vignette acknowledges its formal and methodological origins in etched and engraved single-plate caricature, the miniaturisation of the image, its technical accomplishment, its accompanying poem and its startling juxtaposition against the traditional almanac chart of the month all point the almanac in a new direction. The incorporation of complex visual elements into the predominantly typographic construction of the distinctive almanac form is a major development. If in this case the address of the image remained essentially genteel, the liberation of the almanac from textuality represented by such experiments suggested that more demotic forms of visuality could be adduced to the traditional almanac form. Later publishers and entrepreneurs of print culture were not slow to understand such developments.

The 1850s: The Almanac, National Identity, Publishing Policy and Class

Cassell's *Illustrated Family Almanack* (Fig. 8) is characteristic of the ways in which the almanac might be used to further the brand identity of a publisher or a particular publication, and it is a useful publication in offering a paradigm of the relationship between a host publication and its almanac appendage. First, the almanac is conceived on a different scale to its host periodical – the massive, multi-columned page of *Cassell's Illustrated Family Paper* is perforce scaled down to accommodate the traditional monthly layout of the almanac. Second, the usual almanac information is encased in, even overwhelmed by, wood-engraved illustration. Each monthly table of lunar movements and daily events is held in a ruled page beneath a crudely drawn image of appropriate rural activities (Fig. 9), thus evoking the kinds of celebration of the rural year offered in year books by the likes of William Howitt and Thomas Miller, which had been specifically aimed at reinforcing the class identity and upholding the social worth of the artisan classes. Opposite each tabular page is a much more highly finished if rather clumsily drawn and printed full-page wood engraving of a dramatic scene from British history. The somewhat histrionic version of the English national past evoked by this sequence of images is less melodramatically stated by the daily entries in the tabular pages, which comprise a list of apparently random events which, on closer inspection, offer a generally positive account of the British experience: the birthdays of reformers and statesmen, the founding of the Ashmolean Museum, the opening of the Great Exhibition. The memorialising impulse here, despite acknowledging the horrors of the Crimean War in 1854, constructs a nation of liberal, democratic achievement, a nation, for example, that voted on 21 May 1811 against restricting the rights of Dissenters, and on 1 October 1828 celebrated

Fig. 8: Title page for the *Illustrated Family Almanack* (London: John Cassell, 1855)

Fig. 9 (right): Double-page spread for 'September' from the 1855 *Illustrated Family Almanack*. The running head for the page refers to the volume as *Cassell's Family Almanack*, reinforcing the publication's close identification with Cassell's brand.

THE GREAT FIRE OF LONDON, Which began September 2, 1666, and continued for three days, destroying 13,000 houses and 89 churches.

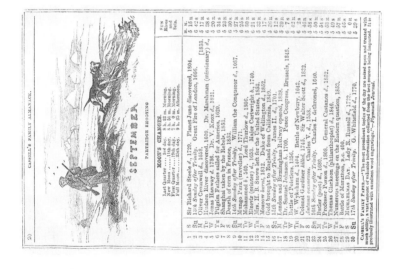

Fig. 10: Title page for the first volume of the *Illustrated London Almanack* for 1845 (London: Office of the *Illustrated London News*, 1845)

the opening of London University. It is also a year that acknowledges the experience of the artisans at whom Cassell has directed his many publications; accordingly, the labour disputes in Preston in 1853, where 'upwards of 20,000 people' were 'thrown out of employ' were duly noted against 15 October.

In this almanac, then, a number of characteristic elements can be detected: a deliberate difference in scale and format from the host publication; the retention of traditional almanac elements in terms of the information offered and the graphic conventions used to deploy it; the extensive, even overwhelming, use of wood-engraved illustration in a variety of modes; and the construction of a very particular memorialised national year out of carefully chosen information and graphic historical narratives, a year aimed at confirming the identity and values of a precisely delineated social class – in this case the respectable, socially ambitious, but perhaps progressive and liberal artisan classes.

Such a model of characteristics also holds true for the *Illustrated London Almanack* (*ILA*), first published in 1845 (Fig. 10), and reaching, if its own publicity is to be believed, a circulation of 80,000 copies in 1848. In this case, however, there is some ambiguity between an artisan and a middle-class address (if I can use such shorthand terms here), between rural and urban interests, and over the extent to which the scientific apparatus of the almanac (the solar charts, astronomical observations and heavenly movements), is retained as a central element. Using a smaller double-columned page than the massive multi-columned broadsheet of the periodical, the *ILA* extends the monthly structure to four quite elaborate pages. The first and second pages contain date charts for the ecclesiastical year, information about time and tides, and, on the second page (or the third in later years) a detailed analysis of planetary topography during the relevant month. Half the first page is given over to an illustration that varied in content and mode from year to year, shifting between allegorical or symbolic images that evoked the method, if not the opacity, of the traditional hieroglyph and more evidently decorative naturalistic images of the kind to be found in any issue of the *Illustrated London News* (*ILN*). The additional two pages that push the *ILA* into another mode altogether largely comprise the kind of content that had made the *Penny Magazine* such an exemplary periodical: a combination of relatively naturalistic and often large-scale illustrations of events, eminent people, trades and commercial activities and aspects of the rural scenes combined with themed sequences of prose articles chronicling the rural year, offering information about natural history or describing

THE ILLUSTRATED LONDON ALMANACK FOR 1852.

DECEMBER.

THE EARL OF DERWENTWATER EXECUTED FOR HIGH TREASON, DECEMBER 8, 1746.

THE fortunes of the ill-fated Earl of Derwentwater, who devoted himself to a fallen cause, urged by a principle, and paid the penalty upon the scaffold, on Tower-hill, have scarcely at this day ceased to be deplored in Northumberland; whilst the melancholy event is kept in memory by the desolated Hall of Dilston, the seat of the unfortunate nobleman. It is situated about two miles distant from Hexham, in Northumberland, on an eminence at the entrance to a deep woody dell, near the confluence of the Devil-water and the river Tyne. The Hall was rebuilt in 1768, but has fallen to ruin, with the exception of the chapel belonging to it, which is kept in repair, and whose vault contains the remains of the Radcliffe family. Strange tales have mixed themselves with the superstitions of the simple inhabitants of the Devil-water, and the neighbourhood of Corbridge, relating to the portents which accompanied the death of the unfortunate nobleman, and the downfall of an ancient family; and the aurora borealis, which made an extraordinarily vivid appearance in Northumberland on the night of the execution, is still called by the old people *Lord Derwentwater's corpse lights.* The Earl was denied his last request, to be laid with his ancestors; embodied in a ballad well known in the north country as "Derwentwater's Farewell:"—

> "Albeit that here in London town
>   It is my fate to die,
> Oh, carry me to Northumberland,
>   In my father's grave to lie.
> There chant my holy requiem
>   In Hexham's holy towers,
> And let six maids of fair Tynedale
>   Scatter my grave with flowers."

And his remains were ostensibly interred in the churchyard of St. Giles's-in-the-Fields, where there is a stone to his memory, on the north side of the churchyard, not far from the tomb of the Pendrells, celebrated for their devotion to an earlier member of the Stuart family, in whose cause the Earl fell a sacrifice. (See *Sketches of Northumbrian Castles, &c.,* by W. F. S. Gibson, Esq., F.S.A., Second Series.)

REMAINS OF DILSTON HALL, THE SEAT OF THE LAST EARL OF DERWENTWATER, NORTHUMBERLAND.

SIR ISAAC NEWTON BORN DECEMBER 25, O.S., 1642.

IN the stone-built manor-house of Woolsthorpe, eight miles south of Grantham, Lincoln, was born the illustrious Newton, whose fame will last as long as the earth shall endure. At his birth he was so little that he might have been put into a quart mug. When Dr. Stukeley visited the house in 1727, he was shown Sir Isaac's study, the book-shelves in which were his own making, being pieces of deal boxes. The premises were repaired in 1798 by Mr. Turner, then the proprietor, by whom also a marble tablet was placed over the mantelpiece of the room in which Newton was born,—on the first floor, left of the staircase. It bears the inscription—"Sir Isaac Newton, son of Isaac Newton, lord of the manor of Woolsthorpe, was born in this room, on the 25th of December, 1642." At the foot are the lines from Pope :—

> "Nature and Nature's laws lay hid in night;
>   God said, 'Let Newton be,' and all was light."

In a room on the same floor is preserved the oaken study; two dials are engraved upon the southern wall, but the styles are wanting. The celebrated apple-tree, the fall of one of the apples of which is said to have turned the thoughts of Newton to the subject of gravitation, was blown down by the wind about 16 years since; but another tree was grafted on its stock.

VIRGIN AND CHILD, (BYZANTINE SCHOOL.)

THE NATIVITY.

THE Nativity has been variously commemorated by the early Christian artists. The specimen here engraved is from the Byzantine class, which comprises productions of Eastern art, between the tenth and thirteenth centuries. The present picture is in the Wallerstein Gallery; the master is, of course, unknown: it represents a Virgin and Child, of a peculiar treatment, the drapery consisting entirely of black, edged with red, and heightened with gold. The usual monogrammatic contractions are introduced in the back of the picture, and both figures have *nimbi.* The painting is round and soft, and deeply-toned in the flesh-tints.

BIRTH-PLACE OF SIR ISAAC NEWTON, WOOLSTHORPE MANOR-HOUSE LINCOLNSHIRE.

51

Fig. 11: Page 51 of the *Illustrated London Almanack* for 1852

historic events (Fig. 11). Such material is curiously at odds with the more sophisticated, better informed and better educated readership traditionally addressed by the *ILN*.

The *ILA* usefully provided a gloss on its own assumptions, voiced by the almanac itself as an introduction to the tenth year of its publication in 1854. This gloss confirms as deliberate policy a number of features already suggested. First, the *ILA* acknowledged that it had deliberately tried to make the almanac a more entertaining genre; on first publication, the *ILA* claims, 'I was then looked upon with surprise, not unmixed with suspicion: it seemed that I had lost the gravity of exterior which long generations of my predecessors had perpetuated and made their own'. I take 'gravity of exterior' to refer to the ponderous scientific and pseudo-scientific apparatus that many almanacs had propagated as well as their dependence on a mass of tabular information. But the *ILA* wanted to be sure its readers recognised that a serious scientific content had been included. James Glaiser, FRS, had been retained to supervise the 'care of my vital parts', as the voice of the almanac put it, but the almanac had also 'permitted a little trifling with that most inviolate portion of myself – the Calendar'. Furthermore, the voice of the almanac recognised the shift that was taking place between the rural and the urban interests of almanac readers, acknowledging that for many readers 'the memory of hours spent amid scenes such as I then depicted [i.e. the rural year and its activities] [. . .] are among those the memory of which scarcely sleeps amid the din of city life, the pursuits of labour, or the cultivation of intellect'. This, then, is a publication deliberately encouraging the urban reader to fantasise a rural otherness. Rather preeningly, the *ILA* also lets its readers know that it is expensive to produce, so that the 'pleasure of pleasing was my chief remuneration'.

The editorial is equally keen to remind the reader of the *Almanac's* visual pleasures, listing the admittedly impressive array of talented artists who had drawn for its pages, Meadows, Gilbert, Harvey, Doyle and Gavarni among them. It is worth noting when thinking about the *ILA's* quest for popularity and its attack on stuffiness that Meadows, Doyle and Gavarni were all best known as comic artists. But most telling of all is the fully understood recognition that the *ILA* was deliberately compiled to outlast any topical or passing purpose dependent on the particular calendar year. The *Almanack* concludes by describing itself as a 'cheerful and discursive companion' secured by its proprietors from 'the fate of ephemeral productions' thus 'adding another volume to the floating capital of literature, at once good and easily accessible to the general public'. Thus the *ILA* becomes a 'volume' rather than a pamphlet, a source of continuing pleasure and information for an implied readership recently dislocated from a rural past, and perhaps as recently introduced to the pleasures and educative drive of the mass-circulation print culture aimed at fulfilling their interests and aspirations.

Comic Almanacs, 1830–60

The satirical opportunities offered by both the prognosticating and the rationalist almanacs had been quickly recognised by the irreverent new breed of metropolitan journalists and graphic satirists of the 1830s like Gilbert Abbott à Beckett, Henry Mayhew and George Cruikshank, who pooled their satirical experience to produce the long-running *Comic Almanack* (1835–53).[32] The *Comic Almanack* used a small page structured as a parody of the traditional almanac page and combined full-page etchings by Cruikshank with many small wood-engraved images dropped into the text; and it was still popular enough twenty years later to justify reprinting in cheap two-volume format.[33] Several contributors later worked for *Punch*, although Cruikshank, almost alone among gifted comic artists of the 1840s, never contributed to the magazine. But even before 1835 the almanac had already been subject to the caricaturist's scorn. Charles Jameson Grant's complex single-sheet, lithographed print 'The Almanack for 1833' was one of a number of related withering graphic satires of the emergence of mass-circulation magazines, conduct guides and self-help manuals produced by Grant, Newman and Phillips in a few years in the mid-1830s.[34] As ever in pursuit of elusive purchasers, Grant's print re-emerged with just the date altered in the plate for several subsequent years, his satire

---

32   For the *Comic Almanack*, see Richard A. Vogler, *Graphic Works of George Cruikshank* (New York: Dover Books, 1979); Robert L. Patten, *George Cruikshank's Life, Times and Art*, 2 vols. (Cambridge: Lutterworth Press, 1996), II, pp. 8–10, 79–80, 189–90, 198–200.

33   *The Comic Almanack 1835–1853*, 2 vols. (London: John Camden Hotten, 1871). *Punch* published several volumes devoted solely to reprints of its almanac. One volume covered the twenty years between the launch of the magazine in 1842 and 1861, while a second volume covered the years between 1852 and 1890.

34   There were nineteen of these prints. See B. E. Maidment, 'Subversive Supplements: Satirical Title Pages of the Periodical Press in the 1830s', *Victorian Periodicals Review* 43.2 (2010), 133–46.

comprising a broad critique of the genre rather than any of its local yearly manifestations.

To some extent, the popularity of the travesty almanac can be explained as simply one aspect of the increasingly inventive market for humorous visual culture in the 1820s and 1830s, a market moving beyond single-plate etched and engraved caricature as its staple product and instead driven by a commercial instinct for passing crazes and fashions, an increasing awareness of seriality as a mode of production and consumption within print culture, and a recognition of the need to extend and democratise the consumer base for visual comedy. The opportunities for graphic experimentation offered by the tabular layout and visual self-consciousness of the almanac must have also attracted the interest of publishers, entrepreneurs and authors.

But there are more substantial reasons for the success of the comic almanac connected to the battles over the ownership of the genre outlined above, battles waged between the commercial exploiters of popular credulity and those entrepreneurs of print culture who sought to use the printed word as an educative and utilitarian force within a progressive and increasingly literate society. The basis for humour in the travestied almanac was twofold. First, comic almanacs delighted in the preposterousness and portentousness of almanacs, especially in relation to their devotion to prediction. As an article called 'Something About Almanacks' (itself a satirical critique of many elements of the almanac form) in *George Cruikshank's Table Book* put it, 'It is lucky they only come once a year, or the number of errors they would be continually perpetrating would effectively poison "the soul of business".'[35] The sustained comic mockery in the humorous travesties of almanacs was in the first instance an attack on the newly, if barely, literate lower classes, with their cultural and educational shortcomings and ignorance posited as a humorous spectacle. Such humorous dismissal of the cultural claims of the artisan and labouring classes was comparable to the continuing caricature commentary on the 'March of Intellect' which formed a major theme of single-plate graphic satire in the 1820s and 1830s. The smaller size, textual density and seriality of the travesty almanacs gave them a considerable advantage over expensive single-plate caricature in sustaining and broadening a disdainful, if not entirely dismissive, critique of the cultural interests and achievements of the lower classes.

But such a traditional dismissal of lower-class aspirations was overlaid

35   *George Cruikshank's Table Book* (London: George Bell & Sons, 1878), p. 5.

THE
ALMANACK OF THE MONTH.

SOME ACCOUNT OF JANUARY.

T would be extremely easy for us to go off into a quantity of antiquarian enthusiasm about the origin of this month : we might set up a shout of, " Hail, old Januarius!" and indulge in wild-goose speculations on the origin of the

Fig. 12: Title page from the January 1846 issue of *The Almanack of the Month* (London: Punch Office, 1846)

in the comic almanacs with something more challenging: an attack on the discourses and, especially, the language used to construct social order, especially what might be called 'officialese'. Both the authority of language and the language of authority had been essential to the construction of the almanac. The tabular layout of almanac information gave it an undeniable stature and significance. As already suggested, one development of the almanac in the mid-nineteenth century was the importation of scientific authority, embodied by the likes of Augustus De Morgan, into accounts of solar activity. But the comic almanacs, largely written and illustrated by bohemian/radical metropolitan journalists and jobbing authors, disrespectfully saw the language of power as a hugely comic phenomenon, and never failed to be amused by the stuffy, po-faced qualities of regulatory language.

Given the success of the *Comic Almanack*, coupled with the emergence in the 1830s of the small-format illustrated comic gift book tied in to Christmas and family occasions, it is hardly surprising that *Punch*, with its brilliant early recognition of the importance of brand identity to a long-running publication, quickly recognised the commercial opportunity offered by publishing its own yearly almanac. Among the most visually inventive print projects of the nineteenth century, *Punch's* almanacs were a huge success, and their re-publication in volume form in 1862 suggests their sustained popularity which evidently outlived any immediate 'usefulness' they might have had in delineating the coming year. Another mark of the success of the *Punch Almanack* was the willingness of the Punch Office to launch a potentially competing venture in Gilbert Abbott à Beckett's *The Almanack of the Month*, launched in January 1846 and running throughout that year in twelve monthly issues (Fig. 12). *The Almanack of the Month* clearly subverted the temporal structure (how can you have a monthly almanac when the whole point of the genre is to have the year as the defining unit of scrutiny?) and uses only a single calendar page at the end of each monthly issue from the standard formal graphic structures of the traditional almanac. Indeed, the use of 'Almanack' in the title seems rather to refer more to a diary or journal format than anything else; here the 'almanac' becomes a genre of passing observation and occasional satire rather than anything more formally constituted by temporal measures.

Perhaps the oddest comic almanack, which only lasted for a single issue, was that published late in 1848 as *The Puppet-Show Almanack – 1849*. Its sister publication *The Puppet-Show* was published by George Vickers, one of the leading entrepreneurs of penny fiction in the 1840s, and edited by James Hannay, but owned and underpinned by

the experience and know-how of the Vizetelly brothers. Characterised
by J. Don Vann as one of several magazines that sought to capitalise
on *Punch's* combination of laughter and social purpose, *The Puppet-
Show*, despite carrying a number of Gavarni's powerful illustrations,
failed to last much beyond eighteen months.[36] The single appearance
of *The Puppet-Show Almanack* offered a number of eccentricities. First
of all, its six pages devoted to a month-by-month review of the year
described not the forthcoming year but the year just past, thus becoming more an annal than an almanac. The entry for March even memorialised the magazine's own founding – 'A NEW COMET is anxiously
expected, and the PUPPET-SHOW appears' – a retrospective observation rendered even odder by the pretence that 1848 was here being
predicted rather than recorded. Second, while retaining something
of the traditional almanac layout for the monthly pages (or, rather
in copying a layout directly from the *Punch Almanack*), the other elements that might be found in an almanac were disassembled and
presented as brief, sardonic elements, complete with tiny vignettes, on
pages 2 and 3 of the twelve-page supplement. Thus such staples of the
informational almanac as Law Terms, University Terms and Phases
of the Moon, as well as such perennials of the comic almanac as a
satirical list of cab fares, were all bundled together in a double-page
spread. Finally, in a bravura illustration on the final page, a gentleman
is found perusing a street advertisement for the magazine in the form
of an onomatopoeic list of attributes of the magazines, a moment of
visual self-referentiality to be widely found in Victorian periodicals,
but seldom in almanacs. It is difficult to know whether *The Puppet-
Show* is inventive and ground-breaking or merely eccentric.

A number of contributors to *Punch*, like Gilbert Abbott à Beckett
and Henry Mayhew, had also worked for the *Comic Almanack* and,
while contributors to *The Puppet-Show* like Shirley Brooks and Angus
Bethune Reach came from a slightly younger generation,[37] I think it is
fair to say that the generation of comic authors emerging in the 1840s
from bohemian/radical metropolitan circles into careers as professional
journalists, playwrights and jobbing writers had a particular and sus-

---

36   J. Don Vann, 'Comic Periodicals', in *Victorian Periodicals and Victorian Society*, ed. J. Don Vann and Rosemary VanArsdel (Aldershot and Toronto: Scolar
Press, 1994), p. 280. See also H. Vizetelly, *Glances Back Through Seventy Years*, 2
vols. (London: Kegan Paul, Trench, Trubner, 1893), 1, pp. 330–1.
37   Vizetelly, *Glances Back*, I, pp. 330–1, gives a detailed list.

tained interest in comic and satirical versions of the almanac form. It is important to ask why the form attracted so much satirical attention at this time.

By the time *Punch* began to produce its own highly subversive almanac in 1842, the almanac had become available for satire in two different ways (Fig. 13). On the one hand, as this 1842 page demonstrates, *Punch* satirised the ignorant and misleading advice and apocalyptic if generalised predictions offered in the down-market popular almanacs – the burlesque 'Prophetic' paragraph at the bottom of the right-hand column offers an immediate example of the delight *Punch* took in irrationality and mumbo-jumbo, rounded off in true Regency style with a visual–verbal pun. In the tiny accompanying silhouette the cosmic pseudo-insights of the predictive almanac are bathetically translated into early Victorian street culture: a milkmaid on her street rounds is tripped by a frantic pig that is being chased by a tiny dog and is thus, punningly, 'in the milky way'. On the other hand, this *Almanack* offers a varied satirical commentary on 'officialese' – that is, the linguistic modes of instruction and regulation through which normative social order is constructed and managed. Thus at the bottom of the page the supposedly regulated activities of London cabmen as laid out in their official scale of charges are deconstructed by an account of their actual practices which depend on highly subjective criteria derived from the willingness of their customers to be swindled through naivety, drunkenness or the urgency of their journey. In the right-hand column under 'Domestic' the conventions of the recipe are applied satirically to human rather than comestible subjects. Thus we learn how to make 'a disagreeable young man' out of a menu of grotesque physical characteristics and absurd clothes. Further up the right-hand column, 'Directions to Medical Students' offers the students not the expected rules for how to behave in the dissecting room but rather advice on how to carry out seasonal practical jokes on their fellows and teachers, thus confirming the popular view of medical students as riotous, time-wasting ne'er-do-wells. This whole page of the *Punch Almanack* pokes fun at a range of 'official' print culture in great detail. Such boisterous disrespect for the dominant culture and its use of print to maintain social order and respectability was central to *Punch*'s popularity. Worst of all, in *Punch*'s view, was the widespread attempt to regulate and repress 'fun', whether such fun was to be derived from mocking the ignorance and tastes of the labouring classes or from satirising the pretensions and anxieties of the middling classes in their quest for respectability. The visual and verbal profusion of this *Almanack* page, barely contained within the rules,

BRIAN MAIDMENT

Fig. 13: 'February' from the *Punch Almanack* for 1842

typographical structures and generic conventions of the almanac form, represents precisely the yearning for a disorderly 'other' to middle-class respectability that is central to *Punch's* conceptualisation of the function of humour. *Punch* humour was largely the product of the bohemian/radical, unaffiliated and socially indeterminate class occupied by the jobbing journalists and artists who became its inner circle of contributors. The magazine encouraged its essentially respectable readers to fantasise out an alternative society based on whimsy, travesty and satire and thus construct a carnivalesque mental world in which conformity was equated with dullness, and where civil public discourse entered the realms of the absurd and the ridiculous.

Conclusion

I have here merely nibbled at the edge of a massive subject, and have not even reached the 'radical' almanac. My conclusion is an obvious one. In the mid-Victorian period the functional and predictive almanac is augmented by a number of re-inventions of the almanac form addressing newly identified audiences within a massively expanding print culture, and replacing utility and superstition with instruction and amusement. Sold off the back of successful periodicals, some almanacs offered both utility and the kinds of visual pleasures and interpretations of the world that characterised their parent publication. Aimed predominantly at culturally ambitious readers, including artisans, serials like the *Illustrated Family Almanack* and the *ILA* combined traditional almanac information with a memorialising year constructed out of rural nostalgia and nationalistic myths. They also brought to the almanac the kinds of highly finished wood engravings, both naturalistic and emblematic in mode, which had made illustrated magazines so popular with the mass reading public. Other almanacs sought to offer a radically oppositional calendar built out of a politicised year. Still other almanacs offered a sophisticated travesty of the almanac form itself, ridiculing both its portentousness as an official document and its absurd engagement with prediction, and bringing to the form a lively visual delight drawn from adapting the caricature tradition to the new medium of the wood-engraved vignette.

In all these instances, meeting the needs, tastes and expectations of the mass reading public meant developing the almanac from something flimsy and ephemeral into something with all the added cultural weight of the bound volume destined for the library shelf or the cottage inglenook. The almanac's traditional concern with the agricultural and devotional year began to give way in the 1830s to experimental versions of an urban and secular year predicated on the assumed political, social and cultural interests of working people. By the 1850s, some almanacs had become more purposive and commercially driven, combining ways of developing the brand identity of their publishers with a structured version of a year that was at one and the same time nationalistic, moralistic and nostalgic. Such educative and ideologically self-conscious almanacs transcended the temporary or ephemeral nature of the traditional almanac, and used the widespread familiarity with the form among the poorer classes as a means of developing new kinds of almanacs that brought the genre within the reach of a widespread, cheap print culture aimed at both satisfying and educating the artisan classes. At the same time as almanacs for artisans were bringing the genre into permanence and providing it with a reformed visual and graphic identity, almanacs aimed at a more sophisticated and wealthier audience shifted towards satire and the comic as a mechanism for examining the exaggerations, shortcomings and generic structures of the almanac while simultaneously offering visual and intellectual pleasure.

The Last Years of a Victorian Monument: The Athenaeum *after Maccoll*

MARYSA DEMOOR

Question: how did a nineteenth-century dinosaur publication like the *Athenaeum* (1828–1921) prepare for the twentieth century? Answer: it appointed a new editor. This essay aims to look at the print legacy of this new editor, Vernon Horace Rendall (1869–1960), who in spite of the enormity of the task loaded onto his shoulders, has remained an unknown entity in print-culture history.[1] As was often the case it was through the columns of the *Athenaeum* that the change of captain was announced:

> Mr Maccoll, who will on the 1st of next January have been the chief editor of the *Athenaeum* for over thirty-one years, i.e. since December, 1869, retires with the New Year from this position, and will be succeeded by his assistant editor, who will give up other work to assume the post of principal editor.[2]

This sudden resignation of Norman Maccoll (1843–1904)[3] as editor-in-chief of the weekly was to signal a new but unexciting path for this major Victorian periodical. His assistant editor, Vernon Rendall, had already carried out the editorial duties for several years before being entrusted with the sole management of the prestigious publication. The result of his reign as an editor was not really something he could boast about but he did try hard to make sure the *Athenaeum* continued to be the cultural flagship it had been up to then. In short, Rendall continued the publication policy he and Maccoll had followed in the previous years.

---

1 S. D. Sharma in *Victorian Fiction: Some New Approaches* (New Delhi: Sarup, 2002) identifies him as the editor of *Notes and Queries*.
2 *Athenaeum*, 20 October 1900, p. 514.
3 *The Times*, 16 December 1904, p. 11.

The Ideal Editor: Norman Maccoll, 1871–1900

Norman Maccoll's regime as editor of the *Athenaeum* has generally been
assessed as a progressive and a liberal one.[4] He had been appointed
to the editor's chair by his friend and fellow-student at Cambridge, Sir
Charles Wentworth Dilke, when the latter inherited the journal upon
the death of his father in 1869. Sir Charles had been groomed by his
grandfather from an early age so as to cherish this heirloom and ensure its continuation. The young Dilke, displeased with current editorial policy, dismissed the then editor, William Hepworth Dixon, and a
year later Dr John Doran, a friend of Dixon's and a contributor to the
Athenaeum, who had hoped to be established as the new editor. Doran
was, by way of compensation, appointed editor of *Notes and Queries: a
Medium of Inter-Communication for Literary Men, Artists, Antiquaries,
Genealogists, etc.*, also owned by Dilke.[5] He was to be the editor of
Notes and Queries from 1872 to his death in 1878.

   Once Maccoll had accepted the position of editor at the *Athenaeum*,
Dilke left him in charge, since he himself was bent on making a career
as a politician. The face of the *Athenaeum*, however, remained that of
the owner rather than that of the editor. This was, so Rendall wrote
many years later, a deliberate policy on the part of the management
of the *Athenaeum*: 'Its editor was never photographed, so could not be
included when notable editors were figured in the press, his place being
taken by Dilke, the owner of both papers.'[6] Sir Charles, the second
baronet, regularly reviewed books for the weekly and kept a hand in
those aspects of the journal which he thought a welcome diversion in
his life, such as the overviews of foreign literatures or finding contributors for the letters from foreign correspondents. One of the most strik-

4   Leslie Marchand, *The 'Athenaeum': A Mirror of Victorian Culture* (Chapel
Hill: University of North Caroline Press, 1941), p. 338.
5   *Notes and Queries* was a spin-off of the *Athenaeum*, which had grown out
of W. T. Thoms's folklore column for the weekly. It started small with only a few
hundred readers but it quickly grew in popularity and acted as a social medium
avant la lettre among scholars hosting heated discussion and controversies. Unlike its parent journal, *Notes and Queries* has survived to the present day. For
more information on *Notes and Queries*, see *Dictionary of Nineteenth-Century
Journalism (DNCJ)*, ed. Laurel Brake and Marysa Demoor (London: British Library Publishing, 2009).
6   Vernon Rendall, ' "Athenaeum" and other Memories', *Library Review*
16.5 (1993), 303.

ing policies of the new editor and the new proprietor was the deliberate recruitment of several new specialised contributors among whom
many were high-profile intellectual women.[7] The 'marked file'[8] of the
Athenaeum for the 1870s, 1880s and 1890s reveals the names of such
ambitious writers and researchers as Vernon Lee, Charlotte Stopes,
Augusta Webster, Millicent Garrett Fawcett and Jane Ellen Harrison.
Equally, the poetry columns were to a large extent in the hands of a
series of women poets, and the proprietor's wife, Emilia Strong Dilke,
fairly frequently provided her well-informed views on current art exhi-
bitions and the artistic scene abroad.[9]

The end of Maccoll's long and fruitful editorship was suitably feted
on 15 February 1901 by a dinner at the Criterion restaurant, an event
announced first in the *Athenaeum* and afterwards discussed at length in
the *Bookman* of March 1901. Eighty men and (only) two women contributors attended the dinner.

But Norman Maccoll continued to contribute to the *Athenaeum* after his retirement in December 1900; in fact, it was he who took on
editorial responsibilities during the holidays. Then, in December 1904,
all of a sudden he died. It was an ideal opportunity for Vernon Rendall
to write about his predecessor's achievement. Rendall co-wrote the
obituary with Mrs Lucy Clifford (1846–1929)[10] and A. J. Butler (1844–
1910). Rendall, however, wrote most of it and it was he who stressed
Maccoll's skilful selection of the right contributors, his independence
from cliques and trade influences, and his anxiousness for 'perfection
of form': 'he warred ceaselessly against superfluities and introductions
to articles'. And he informs us more particularly about Maccoll's views
on women:

7   For more information on the women contributors, see Marysa Demoor,
*Their Fair Share: Women, Power and Criticism in the 'Athenaeum', from Millicent
Garrett Fawcett to Katherine Mansfield, 1870–1920* (Aldershot: Ashgate, 2000).
8   The 'marked file' is the label generally used to refer to the consecutive
editors' copy in which those editors marked the names of the authors of each
anonymous review, possibly with a view to payment. After 1906, the name was
followed by a number (probably referring to a ledger) and the sum which was to
be paid out to the reviewer.
9   The importance of the contributions by women was revealed for the first
time in Demoor, *Their Fair Share*. Since then, several scholars have elaborated
on the work of some of those reviewers.
10   For both the novelist 'Mrs W. K. Clifford' and the Italian scholar Arthur
John Butler one may find entries in the *Oxford Dictionary of National Biography*.

It may be noted that he was one of the young men who offered themselves as tutors for the first English women students at Hitchin in
1869, before Girton was built; and on the occasion of the famous
division at Cambridge concerning the admission of women to de-
grees, he went down, at some inconvenience, to record his vote in
their favour.[11]

Curiously enough, there is no mention of this overtly feminist attitude
in Leslie Marchand's history of the *Athenaeum*.[12] In fact, none of the
women reviewers recruited under Maccoll are mentioned by Marchand.
Thus, in a way, all of these women were erased from literary history.
Nearly every scholar writing about the *Athenaeum* is bound to follow
Marchand in writing that Theodore Watts-Dunton was responsible for
the poetry columns whereas, in fact, from Maccoll's editorship onwards
those reviews were mostly written by women who were often poets
themselves: Mathilde Blind, Augusta Webster, Edith Nesbit, Rosamund
Marriott Watson.[13]

Vernon Rendall's Editorship: 1900–16

Following in the shoes of a 'perfect' editor cannot have been easy for
Rendall. On top of that, Maccoll was one of Charles Dilke's friends.
But Dilke never interfered with any of Maccoll's editorial decisions
and that continued to be one of his guiding principles when Rendall
became the editor. In a 1917 assessment of the role of the Dilke family, the then editor of the *Athenaeum*, Arthur Greenwood, wrote that
Dilke 'was naturally sympathetic towards the views of his last manager
– the grandson of his first – who urged many changes, but he never departed from his rule of giving perfect freedom to his editor whose tastes
were strongly literary'.[14] 'Many changes' was surely an exaggeration,
but one fairly fundamental 'change' after Maccoll was the dismissal
of F. G. Stephens, the art critic and erstwhile Pre-Raphaelite brother,

11   *Athenaeum*, 24 December 1904, p. 874.
12   Marchand, *The 'Athenaeum'*.
13   See Demoor, *Their Fair Share*, especially chapter 6. For a comparison between the frequency of contributions by Watts-Dunton and, for example, Augusta Webster, see also Ibid., p. 114.
14   *Athenaeum*, November 1917, p. 577.

and the recruitment instead of Roger Fry – thus clearly indicating a new direction in the art criticism section. Indeed, Fry was joined as the regular art reviewer by Clive Bell, Virginia Woolf's brother-in-law, in 1909.

Revealing in respect of the editor–owner relationship is a letter from Rendall to Dilke, dated 27 April 1908, from which it appears that eight years into his editorship, Rendall saw the need to raise what he felt were serious problems related to the running of the paper and the remuneration of its editor. At that time, the relationship between the owner and his editor was less than smooth and the editor clearly felt the need to defend himself. The details of what happened or what occasioned the letter can only be gleaned from this one source, which is here reproduced in its entirety. There are no other data. The letter was written a year after the death of Joseph Knight, who had been the editor of *Notes and Queries* up until his death. It shows Rendall, now the editor of both the *Athenaeum* and *Notes and Queries* at his wits' end: how can he cope with the workload, earn enough money for all the work done, and please his employer?

Dear Sir Chas Dilke,
    I now write on the proposals made to me through J.E. Francis,[15] & I fear I shall have to bother you with a long letter, as I regard the matter as very serious. I understand that you are gravely dissatisfied, & am surprised that, if so, you did not write to me directly. I have been sounded as to 'retrospective' proposals, which I gather to mean that you expect me to pay back money already received for N & Q. This is after a definite settlement by Hudson (representing you), J.E. Francis, and myself that my offer of reduction of my own pay for Randall was not at present to be accepted. To go back on such a settlement seems to me amazing. I regard it as quite impossible, & I am so indignant that a repetition of the suggestion will lead at once to my looking for work elsewhere. I can only hope that there is some misunderstanding on the point. As regards assistance to me I cannot act until I know how much you are prepared to give up – a matter which may also invoke my disappearance. I do not, it appears, know exactly how the papers stand, for I understood that there was

15   More information on J. Edward Francis and his part in the publication of the *Athenaeum* may be gleaned from the *Oxford Dictionary of National Biography* entry on his uncle John Francis.

a profit last year. I had in view an assistant R.G. Pickthall (who has the advantage of being a friend of mine & would, therefore, come to help me for less) but he has deteriorated in energy, and is a slow worker, & I have now decided that he would not do. I have not been encouraged to make arrangements by last year's experience which was a great disappointment to me. I certainly understood that Ll. Sanders[16] would read such proofs as were necessary while I was away at <illegible word>, & thought the experiment wd be very useful as indicating a possible means of running the paper in my absence. As a matter of fact, this was not tried at all. Later, a month of your editing was expected. In consideration (very rightly) of your health & arrangements this came to be about ⅓ of the period for me, & I had proofs etc sent to me all the time, which ought, I think to have been avoided. I might reasonably have expected to be paid for proofreading in holiday-time, but I made no claim, as no one seemed even to think of such a thing. Besides pay – I think that your severe criticism would frighten any assistant who did not know the work when he began.

I think myself that a few mistakes (one to a scheme such as that of Ll. Sanders just mentioned) would be much less important than the securing of a month's proper holiday for the editor. However, I have no confidence that you share that view.

As to John Randall, we agree concerning his great merits of accuracy & care. But I doubt if you have realized (1) how slowly he works (2) what his inability to write a review of any kind implies. He had, so far as I am aware, no powers of initiative as to cutting out & modifying doubtful things, & I doubt if he cd acquire such powers. Nor can he see matters involving any subtlety. There was recently in N & Q a decidedly indecent suggestion in the first article. It was not brought to me in MS as doubtful, not queried in proof. I did nothing abt it on purpose to see if it would be noticed, & it came to me in the final page without a word of query, as I expected. The entry of (1) firm (2) conciliatory letters is necessary in N & Q: I have no proof that Randall can write more than a formal letter. I have been annoyed at receiving from him in holiday time things of no importance[,] which can all wait.

I have no objection to giving up N & Q altogether, but I really do

16   There is a Lloyd Charles Sanders (1857–?) who did some work on biographies.

not think that it is worth my while to do far more than my predecessor with a less competent assistant than he had for less than 100£. There should be an addition on the profit side in the sale of books – which Knight kept & I do not.

I am willing, as I told J. E. Francis last week, to give up the 50£ on N & Q on condition that I have freedom to write occasionally in other papers & make a little money. I am not likely to write about things of which I do not know, & do not propose to set up as a purveyor of words without thoughts – which is the lucrative side of the profession. My main object, indeed, would be to search a little recognition for myself, since I am deprived of the time to write books of my own.

It has been a great discouragement to me that you have apparently taken as a matter of course a great amount of my gratis work for the paper, which though anonymous, has been repeatedly praised by others. On the strength of one article on Dickens I was asked to edit the millionaire's edition at 300£ or 400£ a year – I forget which. There is hardly ever a special number which secures an increase of advertisements which does not contain work done by me at high pressure which there is no time for anyone else to do. I am not aware that you know this. I resented & still resent, the ignorance or misjudgment that kept me idling away much of my time as subeditor when you might have had an opinion worth 2 guineas to a publisher on any amount of novels. I have nothing of moment since to set against that ignorance or mistrust, which happens to have spoilt the brightest hopes of my life for ever. The amount of my contributions is now gathered in [the ledger], but I do not know if you have ever examined the record or Hudson.

My room is always untidy for the simple reason that I am always attempting to squeeze in a few more notices of books which would not be noticed at all, unless I did them. If, after all this work, you are greatly dissatisfied, it becomes a question with me whether I should not go elsewhere, where recognition is assured, & where I might, perhaps, hope to be a moderate success. I should, perhaps, add that Austin is no longer, I believe, to work for me: this will expedite matters. I have frequently preferred to tackle myself than see blundered & delayed. I really think that no one else would do half so much as I do in some ways, though they might be far more competent in others. But in the present state of affairs I do not know where I am, and am rapidly losing all confidence in being able to do anything. There are several things here I might criticize, but I have never made difficulties. Now, I am obliged to ask for a clearing up of a position which I have hardly realized, it seems, as I should have.

I must ask to be excused dining on Thursday. I have to be away on Wednesday, as one of my brothers is being married. I have written with a margin, as you generally prefer annotation to writing a fresh letter.[17]

Since Rendall stayed on as editor of the *Athenaeum* until well after Dilke's death in 1911, it seems a solution was found. From the letter we learn that Rendall thought his wages did not cover the amount of work he invested in the *Athenaeum*. He also picked up on the criticism, it seems, that his office gave an untidy impression. Finally, he feels confident enough to refuse an invitation to join his employer for dinner. All in all, we have to deduce that Rendall knew he was in a strong position as an editor and Dilke was bound to give in to his remonstrations in spite of the latter's alleged dissatisfaction.

When comparing the journal under Maccoll to its set-up under Rendall we find there is hardly any difference. The 'marked file' reveals that the new editor did not want to change too much: many of the old contributors were kept on after 1900 – old hands such as Andrew Lang, Charlotte Stopes, the Marriott Watsons – and the views on literature expressed in its pages were very rarely encouraging towards the new and the daring. Under Rendall's editorship, however, the recruitment policies did become more conservative with regard to women. Rendall's editorial article on the state of journalism of 7 May 1910 pronounces women to be 'hopeless slaves to the cliché', in other words, they are not original, innovative or creative like men are.[18] Therefore, although quite a number of *Athenaeum* reviews were still being written by women up to and including the first two years of the war, the subjects they now tackled seldom fell outside the range of the so-called 'soft' subjects. Also unchanged was the weekly's layout. Thus with the journal's masthead remaining the same one, and each page still containing three columns,

---

17   British Library Add. Ms 43 920, ff.77–86. Cited by permission of the British Library.

18   His letters also reveal a strong reactionary stance towards Jews. In a letter of 22 November 1924, he observed: 'It would be a terrible prospect if the world did away with nationalism & decided to be ruled by the Jews instead' (British Library Add. MS 59669). Cited by permission of the British Library.

THE ATHENÆUM

Journal of English and Foreign Literature, Science, the Fine Arts, Music and the Drama.

No. 3749.	SATURDAY, SEPTEMBER 2, 1899.	PRICE THREEPENCE REGISTERED AS A NEWSPAPER

NEWSVENDORS' BENEVOLENT and PROVIDENT INSTITUTION.

BOOKSELLERS' SEASIDE HOLIDAY HOME, 40, ROYAL PARADE, EASTBOURNE.

A WELL-KNOWN ADVERTISING AGENCY

COACHING in SCIENCE—CHEMISTRY.

TO AUTHORS, EDITORS, PUBLISHERS.

COLLABORATION.—A DRAMATIST,

A PUPIL-GOVERNESS WANTED

SCHOLASTIC SCIENCE MASTER WANTED

UNIVERSITY COLLEGE of WALES, ABERYSTWYTH.

CENTRAL TECHNICAL SCHOOLS for CORNWALL at TRURO.

CASSEL, NORTH GERMANY. KLOSTERZENSTR. 18.

UNIVERSITY of DURHAM.

HINDHEAD SCHOOL for GIRLS.

UNIVERSITY COLLEGE, LONDON.

VICTORIA UNIVERSITY. THE YORKSHIRE COLLEGE, LEEDS.

UNIVERSITY COLLEGE of WALES, ABERYSTWYTH.

UNIVERSITY COLLEGE of NORTH WALES, BANGOR.

GUY'S HOSPITAL — PRELIM. SCIENTIFIC

KING'S COLLEGE, LONDON.

FRANCE.—The ATHENÆUM can be obtained at the following Railway Stations in France:—

NOTICE.

CHANGE of NAME.

TO BE SOLD by TENDER, the old-established

UNIVERSITY OF LONDON. SPECIAL CLASSES.

LONDON HOSPITAL MEDICAL COLLEGE.

ST. BARTHOLOMEW'S HOSPITAL and COLLEGE.

ST. BARTHOLOMEW'S HOSPITAL and COLLEGE. OPEN SCHOLARSHIPS.

MADAME AUBERT introduces English and French GOVERNESSES

EDUCATION.—Thoroughly RELIABLE ADVICE

ADVICE as to SCHOLASTIC ASSOCIATION

Fig. 1: *Athenaeum* issue, 2 September 1899 (under Maccoll)

the early-twentieth-century reader would continue to see and recognise the very Victorian face and voice of the weekly.

More interesting perhaps, certainly in view of the fact that modernist 'little magazines' were cropping up like mushrooms in those first years of the new century, was Rendall's wish, after having been the *Athenaeum*'s editor for nearly ten years, to become visible in the pages of the journal and, especially, to show that the *Athenaeum*'s first concern was with literature. Perhaps, he had felt prompted to take a stand as a result of the tongue-in-cheek criticism levelled at the journal's literary criticism in some of the modernist papers. *The New Age* in particular aimed its sharp barbs at this venerable institution. Most of its criticism has to be read as suffused with irony:

> The 'Athenaeum' is my joy. Its reviews of fiction are not so good as those of 'Punch,' but its humour is superior. In last week's issue it 'noticed with deep regret' the death of W. G. Headlam, Fellow of King's College, Cambridge. It 'noticed' (simply) the death of Mary Elizabeth Hawker (author of 'Mademoiselle Ixe'). And it did not 'notice' the death of Allen Raine; it was content to impart its knowledge of the fact that in the case of Allen Raine death had occurred. In some respects the 'Athenaeum' is exasperating.
>
> The writing of it is atrocious. The leading literary journal has the effrontery to print such sentences as: 'A work of this kind may, and perhaps ought to, be judged,' etc. On the same page is a reference to Mr. Kipling's 'Paget, M.P.' But, then, even Sir Charles Dilke cannot, or will not, write grammatically. The most exasperating thing about the 'Athenaeum' is that one cannot ascertain both the price and the publisher of a book from any single issue in which the book is mentioned.[19]

A few months later the weekly is again the subject of critique when the same contributor, Jacob Tonson (pseudonym of Arnold Bennett), returns to his favourite subject:

> The 'Athenaeum' is a serious journal, genuinely devoted to learning. The mischief is that it will persist in talking about literature. [. . .] I do not wish to be accused of breaking a butterfly on a wheel, but the 'Athenaeum's' review of Mr. Joseph Conrad's new book, 'A

Set of Six,' in its four thousand two hundred and eighteenth issue, really calls for protest. At that age the 'Athenaeum' ought, at any rate, to know better than to make itself ridiculous. It owes an apology to Mr. Conrad. Here we have a Pole who has taken the trouble to come from the ends of the earth to England to learn to speak the English language and to write it like a genius; and he is received in this grotesque fashion by the leading literary journal! Truly, the 'Athenaeum's' review resembles nothing so much as the antics of a provincial mayor round a foreign monarch sojourning in his town. For, of course, the 'Athenaeum,' is obsequious. In common with every paper in this country, it has learnt that the proper thing is to praise Mr. Conrad's work. Not to appreciate Mr. Conrad's work at this time of day would amount to bad form. There is a cliché in nearly every line of the 'Athenaeum's' discriminating notice. 'Mr. Conrad is not the kind of author whose work one is content to meet only in fugitive form.'[20]

There was no direct reaction to these attacks but a couple of years later Rendall explicitly announces his intention, in a manifesto-like editorial of 1 January 1910, to devote, from time to time, 'our first article to themes of literary interest' and expressed the need for the occasional in-depth analysis of what he calls 'the practical politics of the literary commonwealth' (p. 5). But those editorials remained fairly lifeless and so unremarkable that no study of print culture was ever to refer to them.

It is ironic that in spite of Rendall's endeavour to become as notable an editor as Maccoll and more of an identifiable voice in the pages of the *Athenaeum*, he has no entry in the *Oxford Dictionary of National Biography*, and in the collected letters of Katherine Mansfield, the editors identify the name Vernon Rendall merely as 'a copy reader with the *Athenaeum*'.[21] If I observed earlier that *Athenaeum* editors wrote about each other and indeed about their contributors when they came to die, partly in order to enhance the importance of their own position, none ever wrote about Rendall, simply because he lived too long, dying at the ripe old age of ninety-one in 1960 (the subsequent editors all died before him). The influential monograph on the *Athenaeum* written by Leslie Marchand and published in 1941 refers to Rendall as

20   *The New Age*, 19 September 1908, p. 412.
21   *Collected Letters of Katherine Mansfield*, 5 vols., ed. Vincent O'Sullivan and Margaret Scott (London: Clarendon Press, 1993), III, p. 149.

THE ATHENÆUM

A JOURNAL OF POLITICS, LITERATURE, SCIENCE AND THE ARTS

No. 4624   DECEMBER 1917   1s. Net

International Economic Relations :

III. Economic Militarism

A World safe for Democracy

The Sword of the Spirit

Adventures in Books

Gift - Book   Supplement

Published at
THE ATHENÆUM OFFICE
Bream's Buildings : Chancery Lane
London : E.C.

Fig. 2: the masthead of the Athenaeum under Arthur Greenwood, during the war

a correspondent of the author, but it says nothing about his role as an editor. In truth, however, there is also the fact that he failed to leave a mark as the editor of an important cultural weekly. Indeed, Rendall's resignation or dismissal two years into the war happened unnoticed. There were, at the time, more world-shocking things going on.

The War Years

In the early years of the war period, the *Athenaeum* tried to stick to business as usual. But soon it was confronted with an acute scarcity of paper, a labour shortage and a need for capital which made the management decide first to establish a co-operative scheme (*Athenaeum*, 13 March 1915) and later to opt for a monthly publication instead of a weekly one. Edmund Gosse was given the honour of introducing the new format and frequency in a signed, semi-autobiographical leader in January 1916:

> [F]or this innovation, or rather renovation courage is needed. I know *The Athenaeum* has never lacked courage. [. . .] The change now proposed by its proprietors is certainly a proof of courage in that they prefer to forego their weekly number in favour of a monthly publication which shall be more in accordance with these ideals, and also a return to a greater consideration of the interest of the reader and buyer.

Then at the end of 1916, a more thorough change was introduced, which may or may not have been unconnected with the death of its owner, John Collins Francis, in December of that year. The editorial of December 1916 promised that the *Athenaeum* was henceforth to be 'an organ for the expression and criticism of ideas of Reconstruction'. Its subtitle changed from 'Journal of Literature, Science; the Fine Arts, Music, and the Drama' to 'Journal of Politics, Literature, Science and the Arts'. The new editor was Arthur Greenwood (1880–1954), a young and promising Labour politician who combined the responsibilities of his editorship with a job as a civil servant at the Ministry of Reconstruction. Henceforth, the war became even more of a prominent theme. The masthead changed and the classical temple on the cover page was replaced by a cameo portrait featuring a classical profile of a young male warrior (Figs. 1 and 2).

Many of the reviews published during the Greenwood era were left unidentified in the 'marked file.' From those columns that were marked, it appears that not one of the former reviewers was kept on. Greenwood surrounded himself with a new generation of writers who shared his progressive attitude towards the future, post-war period. Remarkably, during those two last years of the war several of the reviews are marked in the 'marked file' as 'gratis'. Under his editorship the journal also came with a series of supplements, little booklets on one or another aspect of the war.

Summing up: Rendall's Legacy

In the last years of the nineteenth century the weekly, mainstream periodical *Athenaeum* was associated with the names of two men: the editor Norman Maccoll and the owner Charles Dilke. From 1896 onwards, however, much of the behind-the-scenes work was dealt with by a much younger man who was to be rewarded for all the hard but invisible work by being named as the dauphin editor upon Maccoll's unannounced retirement in 1900. Vernon Rendall, [22] the man who led the *Athenaeum* from 1900 to 1916 is an almost unknown entity because so little has been written about him. There was no one left to write about his merits after his death. Unless of course there were no merits to write about? There are, however, some material clues that tell us more. There is, to start with, the 'marked file' listing all the contributions by Rendall during and before his editorship and there are, scattered across a range of archives, the letters written to Rendall. Also, his name turns up in Google books especially as a man to be thanked for his help in checking the proofs of one of his colleagues' books. Andrew Lang, for instance, thanks Gosse and Rendall for having read the proofs of his Tennyson biography. Similarly Frank Carr Nicholson professes indebtedness to Rendall for having read his manuscript of *Old German Love Songs* in 1907. Rendall was, if not a very imaginative person, certainly a very hard-working one. The long letter to Charles Dilke which I quoted above attests to Rendall's way of working and the problems he experienced in his work environment. Upon his death in 1960, *The Times* published two short obituaries of Rendall. The first one was published on 16 May after being announced briefly on the front page. The title was 'Mr Vernon Rendall. Sometime editor of the *Athenaeum*'. It is this

---

22   Rendall, ' "Athenaeum" and other Memories', 302–305

obituary that tells us for certain that Rendall became assistant editor in 1896, then succeeded Maccoll as editor in 1900 and remained in that position until 1916. From 1907 to 1912, he combined the responsibilities of the *Athenaeum* editorship with those of *Notes and Queries* and returned to the editor's chair when from 1926 to 1931 he became literary editor of the *English Review*.[23] He left that position when the editor of the *English Review*, Ernest Remnant, was succeeded by Douglas Jerrold. The other obituary is interesting because of its description of the man Rendall. The description was authored by Frank Swinnerton, a journalist, contributor to the *Athenaeum* and *Rhythm* and one who must have known Rendall quite well. Swinnerton tells us that he was a very tall man who became very short-sighted toward the end of his life. As a result he had become accident-prone, especially when he went down a staircase. He had been a keen cricketer in his youth and he had made his mark as an excellent classical scholar.[24] This more personal recollection has to be read next to Rendall's complaining letter so as to achieve a more rounded picture of the man. Even so, in spite of all the positive characteristics and the appreciative comments on the man and editor, Rendall's achievement has been fragmented and as a result his contribution to press history has not been given appropriate notice.

Ironically, Rendall's disappearance from the *Athenaeum* at the end of 1916 coincided with the publication of a short editorial entitled 'The Future of "The Athenaeum"' as if Rendall's disappearance meant that the magazine finally had a future again. The future of the new editor, however, was to be disappointingly short. After the thirty-year stint given to Maccoll and the twenty-year stint that Rendall had had, Greenwood was to be given only two years (and those mainly war years) to leave his stamp on the paper, and then it was John Middleton Murry's turn. Middleton Murry was a harbinger of a modern age, and under his editorship the *Athenaeum* became the flagship of a modernist generation with authors like Eliot, Pound, Mansfield and Woolf now writing for the *Athenaeum*. Murry's *Athenaeum* years, however, have been dealt with elsewhere,[25] so I would like to close this brief account by paying some attention to the transitional figure of Arthur Greenwood.

23   *The Times*, 16 May 1960.
24   *The Times*, 24 May 1960.
25   See Marysa Demoor, 'John Middleton Murry's Editorial Apprenticeships: Getting Modernist "Rhythm" into the *Athenaeum*, 1919–1921', *English Literature in Transition* 52.2 (2009), 123–43, and Oscar Wellens's 'The Brief and

From an Amateur Editor to an Experienced One: Arthur Greenwood to Middleton Murry

John Collins Francis, the owner of the *Athenaeum*, died on 27 December 1916; therefore, the changes implemented by the management from 1 January 1917 must have been prepared and condoned by the late owner. The editorial (December 1916) referred to above promised that the *Athenaeum* was henceforth to be 'an organ for the expression and criticism of ideas of Reconstruction'. Arthur Greenwood, whose main innovation consisted in the supplements mentioned earlier, announced the series of supplements in December 1916, when he wrote that the group of men and women who had promised their cooperation would continue to record and review the intellectual life of the country while also expressing and criticising the ideas of reconstruction. The publication of the supplements had started already in September 1916. Subjects included: 'War and Education' (September 1916), 'War and Women' (October 1916), 'War and Wages' (November 1916). The editor clearly had a purpose with those papers. They sought to move readers to think about those specific aspects of life covered in the pages of the *Athenaeum*. In the April 1917 issue, Greenwood urged his readers to form circles, small think tanks:

> We, therefore, suggest the formation of Athenaeum 'circles'. A few friends or a handful of members of any society or organisation – religious, political, industrial, social – might arrange to meet weekly or fortnightly, but preferably the former, for the discussion of the articles in the current *Athenaeum*, or of some special aspect of Reconstruction. [. . .] As the 'circles' proceeded, interest in the vital problems of the future would be deepened, and the enthusiasm of the members would extend that interest beyond the immediate 'circle'. (p. 163)

Greenwood's motives were excellent. He clearly wanted the *Athenaeum* supplement publications to lead to an inclusive discussion policy. There are no records, however, of possible outcomes of the *Athenaeum* circles. More striking perhaps is the move after Greenwood's editorship to a much more exclusive group of writers and thinkers, with Murry opting for his close friends and former and current colleagues when allocating

Brilliant Life of the *Athenaeum* under Mr Middleton Murry', *Neophilologus* 85.1 (2001), 137–52.

books for review. Murry was to be *Athenaeum* editor from April 1919 up to and including 11 February 1921, after which date the *Athenaeum* amalgamated with the *Nation*. There was only a brief apologetic editorial to precede that very last publication in which the editor argues:

> To those of our readers who may, not unnaturally, hesitate about the expediency of uniting the *Athenaeum*, which has no politics, with the *Nation*, which is primarily a political organ, the reply is simple. Pure literary criticism is independent of political philosophies; while in the case of the criticism of works having a political import, it will be found that the ideal background of the writers in *The Athenaeum* is akin to, if not identical with, that of *The Nation*. (p. 145)

He does suggest that the reason for the disappearance of the *Athenaeum* as an independent paper is to be explained by the general public's lack of interest in literature: 'It is useless to lament the fact that the general public is more interested in the news that the wife of a newly created peer has "gone in for" bobsleighing or fortune-telling than in a careful criticism of Mr. Wells' "History of the World". There may come a time when this surfeit of sensationalism will produce nausea. But in the interval it is doubly necessary that the tradition of honest criticism should be maintained' (p. 145).

Last Words

The last editor to have the privilege to comment on the *Athenaeum* was the longest living one. Vernon Rendall was interviewed for the *Library Review* before his death and the text was published many years later, in 1993, under the title '*Athenaeum* and Other Memories'. It is an article in which he dwells on his memories of William Morris, Watts Dunton, Samuel Butler and Edmund Gosse with a candidness which one would expect in men who expect to die soon and who want to leave their honest impressions to posterity. In it he speaks kindly and with great admiration of Sir Charles Dilke but he remains silent on his own work for the *Athenaeum*. The article is unstructured and ends abruptly as if the speaker suddenly thought he had said enough.

Index

À Beckett, Gilbert Abbott, 163, 178, 186, 189, 190
  Almanack of the Month, The, 163, 189
  Comic Almanack, 163, 186–93
  Figaro in London, 178
Achinstein, Sharon, 41, 47, 52–5
Aeneid, 99
Aikin, John, 100, 124
Alarcon, Daniel Cooper, 10
Allan, William, 128, 129, 131, 133, 145, 146
  Illustrations of the Novels and Tales of the Author of Waverley, 131
Altick, Richard, 105, 107, 129, 131
Amore, Adelaide P., 6, 25, 30
Anderson, Benedict, 99
Appleton-Century-Crofts, 23
Archibald, William, 129
Athenaeum, The, 195–211
Athey, Stephanie, 10
Austen, Jane, 6, 66–8, 75

Baker, Ernest (*Novels of Mrs. Aphra Behn, The*), 18, 19, 20, 22, 28, 30
Baker, Thomas (*Royal Engagement Pocket Atlas, The*), 115
Barber, Mary, 65
Bartolozzi, Francesco, 101, 103, 104, 105, 107, 112, 117, 118, 123
Baxter printing process, 123
Baxter, Richard, 41, 56
Bayley, Eliza, 82
Behn, Aphra, 2, 5–32
  All the Histories and Novels, 11, 13, 14, 15, 16, 17, 18, 20, 22, 23, 24, 27
  All the Histories and Novels Written by the Late Ingenious Mrs. Behn,

  Entire in one Volume, 13, 28
Oroonoko
  Bedford Cultural Edition, 6, 26, 27
  Methuen edition, 6 n.6, 24
  Norton Critical Edition, 24, 27
  Norton Library edition, 21, 23
  Oxford World's Classics edition, 6 n.6
  Penguin Classics edition, 6 n.6, 25, 26
  paperbacks, 7
  podcasts, 7
  smartphone apps, 7
  Three Histories, 12, 22, 26
Bell, Clive, 199
Bell, John, 119
Bennett, Arnold (writing as Jacob Tonson), 204
Bensley, Thomas, 100, 122
Bentley, Gerald Eades, Junior, 51, 52
Berg, Maxine, 112
Bernbaum, Ernest, 22
bibliographic studies, 1, 8, 9, 11, 25, 79
Black, Adam and Charles, 146, 147, 149, 150, 151, 153, 154
Blackie, John, 141
Blacklock, Thomas, 69, 70, 71, 72, 75
Blackwell's *British Literature 1640–1789*, 6, 26
Blair, Hugh, 99
Blake, William, 35, 171
Blind, Mathilde, 198
Blom, Benjamin, 20
Boase, Thomas Sherrer Ross, 107
Bodleian Library, 13, 26
Bodoni, Giambattista, 101
Bohn, Henry (*The Book of Waverley Gems*), 138

Bookman, 197
Book of the Calendar, the Months, and the Seasons, 162
Boswell, James, 72, 73, 75
  Life of Johnson, 72
Boydell, John, 102, 105
Boydell Shakespeare Gallery, 103, 133
Branston, Robert Edward, 144
Brewer, John, 60, 61, 64
Briscoe, Sam, 11, 13
British Almanac, 161, 162, 163, 165–9, 171, 172
British Institution, The, 125
British Working-Man's Almanac, 171–3
Broadview Anthology of English Literature, The, 7
Bromley, William, 107
Brooke, Henry, 77
Brooks, Shirley, 190
Brown, John, of Carlisle, 69
Brown, Laura, 9, 10
Brown, Richard, 103
Brown, William, 94
Browne, Gordon Frederick, 153
Buchan, eleventh Earl of (David Steuart), 101, 104
Bucolics (Virgil), 99
Bugg, Francis, 75
Bunyan, John, 2, 33–57
Burney, Frances, 65
Burns Chronicle, 84, 85, 91
Burns Monument Museum, 83
Burns, Robert, 3, 72, 78–96
  Commonplace Book, 82
  'Geddes Burns', 79, 80
  'Glenriddell Manuscripts', 79 n.5, 83
  'Highland Lassie' note, 86, 88 n.29, 89, 92–95
  intention to emigrate to the West Indies, 84
  poems and songs
    'Auld Lang Syne', 86
    'Bob o' Dumblane', 85
    'Clout the Cauldron', 85
    'Dainty Davie', 97 n.27
    'Fy, gar rub her o'er wi' strae', 85
    'Highland Laddie', 85, 86

    'Jackie's Gray Breeks', 85
    'Kirk wad lat me be', 85
    'Low down in the Broom', 88, 89
    'Maggie Lauder', 86, 87
    'Mill, Mill, O', 85, 87 n.27
    'My Mary, dear departed shade', 88 n.29
    'Oh ono chrio', 88
    'Saw ye nae my Peggy?', 85, 87 n.27
    'The Bonie Lass made the Bed to me', 86
    'The Highland Lassie O', 84, 91
    'The Lass o' Liviston', 87 n.27
    'The Lucubrations of Henry D–nd–ss in 1792', 88, 89
    'The Moudiewart', 86
    'The Posie', 85
    'Tweedside', 85, 87 n.27
    'Waukin o' the Fauld', 85
  Poems, Chiefly in the Scottish Dialect ('Edinburgh' edition), 79
  Scots Musical Museum, The, 78–96
Butler, Arthur John, 197
Butler, Samuel, 211
Byron, Lord George, 76

Cadell, Robert, 131, 135, 137, 138, 141–6, 147, 149, 150
  Waverley Garland, The, 144
Campbell, 'Highland' Mary, 84, 90
Canning, William, 9, 12, 23, 28
Cassell, John, 183
  Cassell's Illustrated Family Paper, 179
  Illustrated Family Almanack, 179
  Working Man's Friend, 173
Catton, Charles, 115
Chadwyck-Healey English Prose Full-Text Database, 7
Chambers, Robert, 173
Chambers, William, 173
Clarendon Press, 40, 156
Clifford, Lucy, 197
Clowes, William, 165
colour printing, 112–24
Collins's Illustrated Pocket Classics, 156
Comic Almanack, 163, 186–93

Companion to the [British] Almanac, 165, 167, 168, 169
Companion to the Newspaper, 168
see also *Penny Magazine*
compositors, 3, 12, 14
Conrad, Joseph, 112, 204, 205
Constable & Co., 133
Constable, Archibald, 128, 129, 131, 133
Cook, Davidson, 85, 86
Cooke, Charles, 119
Cooper, James Davis, 153
copper engraving, 2, 44, 45, 119
Copyright Act, 59, 60, 61, 64
Corbould, Henry, 133, 134, 135, 137
Cowper, William (*Poems*), 122, 123
Crawford, Robert, 90
Criterion restaurant, 197
Cromek, Robert Hartley, 81–91, 94, 95
   and Allan Cunningham, 84
   Reliques of Robert Burns, 81–2, 84, 85
   Scottish Songs, 84, 85
   Select Scotish Songs, 86 n.25
   'Strictures on Scottish Songs and Ballads, Ancient and Modern with Anecdotes of their Authors', 82, 84, 85, 89
Cruikshank, George, 142, 144, 154, 186
   George Cruikshank's Table Book, 163, 187
Cruikshank, Robert, 177
Cundee, James, 120–2
Cunningham, Allan, 85
Currie, James, 81, 82, 90, 95
   Works of Robert Burns, The, 81
Cuthbertson, David, 85

Damrosch, David, 27
Davys, Mary, 65
De Morgan, Augustus, 168, 189
   Book of Almanacs, The, 168
De Wint, Peter, 138
Defoe, Daniel, 64
DeMaria, Robert, Junior, 26, 27
Dickens, Charles, 142, 168, 201
   Household Narrative of Current Events, 168

Household Worlds, 168
   Sketches by Boz, 142
Dickes, William, 145, 146
Dissenting tradition, 33–57
Dodsley, Robert, 69, 70, 71, 72
Don Vann, Jerry, 190
Dick, James Chalmers, 83, 84, 85, 86, 87, 94, 95
   Notes on Scottish Song by Robert Burns, 84, 94
Dictionary of Literary Biography, 9
Dilke, Emilia Strong, 197
Dilke, Sir Charles Wentworth, 196, 198, 199, 202, 204, 208, 211
Dixon, William Hepworth, 196
Doran, Dr John, 196
Dryden, John, 41
Du Roveray, Francis J., 107, 122, 124
Duchovnay, Gerald, 5, 11, 12, 13, 14, 20, 25
Duesbury, William, 112
Duffy, Maureen, 9, 24
Dunan-Page, Anne, 41
Dundas, Henry, 89
Dunton, John, 75

ebooks, 7, 10
Educational Book Company, 154
Egerton, Thomas, 67, 68
English Review, 209
Essick, Robert, 109
ESTC (English Short Title Catalogue), 73, 75, 76, 77
Evans, Reverend John, 119
Everyman's Library, 156

Faed, Thomas and John, 147
Fawcett, Millicent Garrett, 197
Figgins, Vincent, 124
Finden, Edward Francis, 129, 143
Fisher, Son & Co., 141, 142, 144, 151, 154
   Landscape-Historical Illustrations of Scotland and the Waverley Novels, 144
Flaxman, John, 35, 51
Forrest, William, 151

Foulis, Andrew, 99, 114
Foxe, John, 47, 50
　　Actes and Monuments, or Book of
　　　Martyrs, 47
Foxon, David, 63, 64
Francis, J. Edward, 199, 201
Francis, John Collins, 207, 210
Fraser, Alexander, the Elder, 145
Friedman, Joan M., 113
frontispiece, 17, 34, 37, 40, 41, 43, 44,
　　45, 47, 107, 112, 115, 121, 129,
　　134, 135, 137, 138, 145, 147, 148,
　　149, 150, 151, 154, 156
Fry, Roger, 199
Fuseli, Henry, 103, 107, 109, 122

George Routledge & Sons, 151
Gainsborough, Thomas, 105
Gallagher, Catherine, 6, 26
Garside, Peter, 3, 77
Gautier, Jean-Frédéric, 117
Gavarni, Paul, 185, 190
Gay, John, 33, 34, 57
Geddes, Alexander, 89
Geddes, John, bishop, 80
George IV, king of England, 99, 144
George, Prince of Wales see George IV
Georgics (Virgil), 99
Gessner, Salomon, 113, 123
Gildon, Charles, 13, 14, 15, 16, 17, 28
Girton College, Cambridge, 198
Glasgow Herald, 149
Goethe, Johann Wolfgang von
　　(Sorrows of Young Werther, The),
　　121, 123
Gordon, Catherine, 125, 127
Gosse, Edmund, 207, 208, 211
Grangerising, 112
Grant, Charles Jameson, 177, 186
Graves, Henry, 135, 138
Gray, Valerie, 165
Greenshield, John, 145
Greenwood, Arthur, 198, 207, 208,
　　209, 210
Greenwood Press, 19
Greer, Germaine, 13
Griffith, Elizabeth, 15, 18, 22, 28

Collection of Novels, A, 15
English Nights Entertainments: The
　　History of Oroonoko, 15

Habermas, Jürgen, 58
Hamilton, Archibald, 104, 105, 114
Hamilton, William, 103, 104, 105, 107,
　　109, 113, 118, 120, 122, 124
Hanmer, Thomas, 100
Hannay, James, 189
Hardie, Charles Martin, 153
Hardy, Paul, 153, 154
Harrison, Jane Ellen, 197
Harrison, William Henry (Christmas
　　Tales), 139
Harvard Library, 22
Harvey, William, 144
Hawker, Mary Elizabeth, 204
Headlam, W. G., 204
Heath, Charles, 129, 131, 133, 134,
　　135, 137, 138, 154
　　Waverley Album, The, 138
Heath, James, 133
　　Heath's Book of Beauty, 139
　　Heath's Historical Illustrations, 139
Henderson, Philip (Shorter Novels:
　　Jacobean and Restoration), 21
Herdman, Robert, 150, 151, 153
Heron, Robert, 100, 114
Hill, Richard, 126
Hindley, Godfrey C., 153
Hogg, James, 75 n.58
Hone, William, 171
Howell, Samuel, 127
Howitt, William, 171, 179
　　Howitt's Journal, 173
Hughes, Derek, 6 n.6
Hume, David, 70, 71
Hurst, Chance & Co., 135
Hurst, Robinson & Co., 128, 129, 131,
　　133, 135
Hurst, Thomas, 119–24
hymn writing and singing, 52–5

iconography, 2, 34, 35, 41, 45, 47, 52,
　　55, 56, 102, 104, 107, 112, 115,
　　119, 122, 128

Illustrating Scott: A Database of Printed Illustrations to the Waverley Novels, 1814–1901, 126, 128, 150
Illustrated London Almanack (ILA), 183
Illustrated London News (ILN), 183

James, Louis, 161
Jeffery, Edward, 113, 122
Jennings & Chaplin, 139
Jerrold, Douglas, 209
Johns, Adrian, 50
Johnson, James, 79, 81, 82, 92, 93, 94
Johnson, Joseph, 122, 123
Johnson, Samuel (*Lives of the English Poets*), 101
Jung, Sandro, 134

Kauffmann, Angellica, 112
Keats, John, 76
Keeble, Neil H., 43
Kent, William, 99, 102
Kilmarnock Standard, The (14 May 1921), 85
King, John N., 47, 50
Kinsley, James, 91
Kipling, Rudyard, 204
Kirkwood, James, 115
Knight, Charles, 158, 159, 163, 165, 167, 169, 171
Knight, Joseph, 199, 201
Knox, Vicesimus, 64
Kronheim, Joseph Martin, 123

Ladies Magazine, The, 15
Lady's Magazine, The, 133, 138
Laing Collection (Edinburgh University), 85, 86, 87, 95
Laing, David, 150
Lalauze, Adolphe, 151, 153
Lamont, Claire (*Waverley*), 156
Landseer, Edwin, 137
Lane, William, 77
Lang, Andrew, 202, 208
Langton, Bennet, 72
Lardner, Dionysius (*Museum of Science and Art*), 162
Lee, Vernon, 197

Legat, Francis, 107
Leslie, Charles Robert, 128, 129, 133, 134, 150
  Illustrations of Kenilworth, 133
Library Review, 211
Lipking, Joanna, 6, 18, 24, 25, 27, 28
'little magazines', 204
Lizars, Daniel, 129
Lizars, William Home, 129, 131
Lloyd Bros & Co., 147
Lockhart, John Gibson, 137, 138, 141, 145
  Life of Scott, 141, 145
Lockwood, Thomas, 65
Longman Anthology of British Literature, The, 27
Longman Anthology of Women's Literature, The, 7

Maccoll, Norman, 195, 196–8, 202, 203, 205, 208, 209
Mackay, James, 83
Macklin, Thomas, 100, 101, 102, 107
  Poets' Gallery, 101, 105
Maitland, Lord Richard, 8, 12, 13, 21, 24, 26, 28,
Malone, Edmund, 73
Mandal, Anthony, 66
Mansfield, Katherine, 205, 209
Marchand, Leslie, 198, 205
Marcus Ward & Co., 151
martyrological tradition, 47
Marvell, Andrew, 37, 41
Maslen, Keith, 62
Mayhew, Henry, 186, 190
McAdams, Ruth, 126
McCarthy, William, 24, 25
McDonald, John Blake, 150
McGuirk, Carol, 80
McNaught, Duncan, 84, 85
  'Cromek Convicted', 84
Melville, Henry, 143
Meridian Anthology of Early Women Writers, 24, 25
metatext, 51
Metz, Conrad Martin, 112
Metzger, Lore, 9, 25

Millais, John Everett, 127, 153, 156
Millar, Andrew, 98, 99, 102
Miller, Thomas, 179
Milton Gallery (Fuseli), 103
Minerva Press, 67, 77
Mollineux, Mary, 41
Moon, Boys & Co., *see* Graves, Henry
Moore, Cecil A., 21, 23, 24, 28
    *Restoration Literature: Poetry and
        Prose 1660–1700*, 23
Morison, Robert, Junior, 114, 115, 117,
    124
Morris, William, 211
Murray, John, 103, 104, 105, 109, 111,
    112, 124
Murry, John Middleton, 209, 210, 211

Nasmyth, Alexander, 129, 138, 150
Nelson and Sons (Thomas Nelson and
    Sons), 22
    Nelson's English Series (*Malory to
        Mrs. Behn: Specimens of Early
        Prose Fiction*), 22
    Nelson's New Century Library, 156
Nesbit, Edith, 198
New Age, The, 204
Newton, Gilbert Stuart, 137, 138
Nichols, A. F., 83
Nicholson, Frank Carr, 208
Nimmo, John C., 151
Nonconformist poetics and worship,
    41
*Norton Anthology of Literature by
    Women, The*, 7
*Norton Anthology of English Literature,
    The*, 7
Notes and Queries, 196, 199, 209

O'Donnell, Mary Ann, 5, 6, 11, 12,
    13, 25
    *Aphra Behn: An Annotated
        Bibliography of Primary and
        Secondary Sources*, 12, 13, 15,
        16, 17, 18, 19, 20, 21, 22, 23,
        24, 25, 26, 27
Oakshott, Miss, 83
Opie, John, 105, 107

Owen, John, 37
Oxford Magazine, The, 15

paratext, 2, 3, 40, 99, 103, 109, 118,
    122, 123, 124, 150
patronage, 58, 66, 98, 99
Pearson, John, 14, 17, 18, 19, 20, 22, 28
    *Plays, Histories, and Novels of the
        Ingenious Mrs. Aphra Behn with
        Life and Memoirs, The*, 18
Penny Cyclopaedia, 167
Penny Magazine, 158, 167, 168, 183
Pettie, John, 153, 156
Pettit, Alexander, 8, 9, 26
Phaeton Press, 20
photolithography, 23
Pickering and Chatto (*The Works of
    Aphra Behn*), 26
Pickthall, R. G., 200
Pilgrim's Progress, The, 2, 33–57
Pitt, William, 89
Plummer, C., 15
podcasts, 7
Poets' Gallery, 101, 105
Political Almanack for 1836, 173–9
Ponder, Nathaniel, 34, 37, 38, 45, 47,
    50, 52, 54
Pooley, Roger, 51
Pope, Alexander, 63, 65, 99
printing for the author, 3, 58–77
Printing or Licensing Act, 59, 61
printing press, 2, 55
Prynne, William, 47
publishing 'on commission', 66–8
Punch Almanack, 163, 186, 189, 190,
    191, 193, 204
Puppet-Show Almanack, The, 189, 190

Quaritch, Mr, 83

R. & R. Clark Ltd, 154
Rabinowitz Library, 83
Raeburn, Henry, 146, 156
Raine, Allen, 204
Ralph, James, 64
Ramsay, Allan, 156
Randall, John, 199, 200

Raven, James, 64, 66, 97, 158
Reach, Angus Bethune, 190
religious dissent, 35–57
Remnant, Ernest, 209
Rendall, Vernon Horace, 195, 196, 197, 198–207
Reynolds, Sir Joshua, 105
Rhythm, 209
Richardson, Samuel, 77
Riddell, Elinor, 83
Riddell, Maria, 82, 83
Riddell, Robert, captain, 78, 79, 80, 81, 83, 84, 87, 88, 90, 91
Rigney, Ann, 127
Rion, Edouard, 151
Robinson, George, 73
Robinson, Joseph Ogle, 128, 131
Rogers, Katharine M., 24, 25
Routledge and Dutton, 19
Routledge & Sons, 151
Rowe, Elizabeth Singer, 41
Royal Academy, The, 107, 109, 125
Royal Association for Promotion of the Fine Arts in Scotland (RAPFAS), The, 150, 151, 153, 154

St. Clair, William, 75, 76, 158, 159, 161
Salkeld, John, 83
Salzman, Paul (*Oroonoko and Other Writings*), 25, 26
Sanders, Lloyd Charles, 200
Schall, Jean-Frederic, 117
Scott, Sir Walter, 3, 125–57
    Centenary Exhibition (1871), 150
    works
        Abbot, The, 133, 137, 153
        Anne of Geierstein, 134
        Bride of Lammermoor, The, 127, 134, 156
        Guy Mannering, 139
        Heart of Mid-Lothian, The, 127
        Historical Romances, 129
        Ivanhoe, 127, 128, 131, 134, 141, 145
        Keepsake, The, 134, 137, 139, 154

        Kenilworth, 145
        Lady of the Lake, The, 143
        Monastery, The, 127, 133, 153, 154
        Novels and Romances, 129, 138
        Novels and Tales of the Author of Waverley, 128, 129, 131, 135, 138, 150
        Pirate, The, 133, 134
        Rob Roy, 139, 142
        Tales of My Landlord, 134
        Waverley, 127, 129, 137, 138, 143, 146, 147, 149, 151, 156
        Waverley Keepsake, The, 139
        Woodstock, 134
Scroop, Sir Simon, 13, 15, 16
Selous, Henry Courtney, 134, 138
    Surgeon's Daughter, The, 138
Settle, Elkanah, 75
Seymour, Robert, 177, 178
Shakespeare Gallery (Boydell), 103, 105, 133
Shakespeare, William, 6, 100, 104
Sharp, William, 104
Sharpe, Louisa, 129, 139
Sharrock, Roger, 33 n.1
Shaw, Byam, 154
Shelley, Percy Bysshe, 76
Sher, Richard B., 62, 70, 72
Simpkin & Marshall, 138
Singleton, Henry, 104, 105, 107, 124
Skene, James, 139, 150
    Sketches of the Existing Locations alluded to in the Waverley Novels, 139
smartphone apps, 7
Smirke, Robert, 103
Smollett, Tobias, 77, 171
Soare, Thomas, 112
Society for Diffusion of Useful Knowledge (SDUK), The, 161, 163, 165, 167, 169, 171–3
Society for Promoting Christian Knowledge (SPCK), The, 162, 173
Solomon, Abraham (*St Ronan's Well*), 148
Spence, Joseph, 71

Spencer, Jane (*Aphra Behn's Afterlife*), 6 n.2
Stalker, Ebenezer, 134
Stanfield, Clarkson, 145
Stationers' Company, 37, 50, 59, 159, 161
Staves, Susan, 65
steel engraving, 35, 123, 126, 134, 142, 146, 154
Stephens, Frederic George, 198
Stephenson, James, 148
Stern, Simon, 26
Sterne, Laurence, 69
Steuart, David, eleventh Earl of Buchan, 101, 104
    Essays on the Lives and Writings of Fletcher of Saltoun and the Poet Thomson, 101
Stockdale, Percival, 100, 104
Stocks, Lumb, 148, 150, 151
Stopes, Charlotte, 197, 202
Stothard, Thomas, 35, 104, 105, 112, 115, 122, 124, 128, 133, 134, 135
Sturt, John, 41, 43
subscription editions, 98, 99, 100, 101, 102, 103, 104, 107, 115, 117
subscription publishing, 3, 65, 70, 71, 77, 97, 98, 118
Summers, Montague, 9, 17, 19, 20, 25, 26, 28
    Works of Aphra Behn, 10, 13, 20, 25
Suttaby, Evans and Fox, 107
Swift, Jonathan, 65
Swinnerton, Frank, 209

Taylor, Charles, 102
Temple Company, The, 19, 22, 28
Thomas, George C., of Philadelphia, 83
Thomas Nelson and Sons, 22
Thoms, W. T., 196 n.5
Thomson, Samuel, 89
    'To the Rose Bud', 89
Thomson, James, 3, 4, 97–124
    Seasons, The, 3, 4, 97–124
        'Magnificent Edition', 102
Thurston, John, 119

Tilt, Charles, 139, 141, 143, 144, 154
    Landscape Illustrations of the Waverley Novels, 139, 141, 143, 144, 154
    New Waverley Album, The, 141
    Portraits of the Principal Female Characters in the Waverley Novels, 139, 144, 154
    Waverley Gallery, The (Tilt and Bogue), 139
Times, The, 208
Todd, Janet, 25, 26, 27, 28
    Oroonoko, or, The History of the Royal Slave, 6 n.6
    Oroonoko, The Rover and Other Works, 25
Tomkins, Peltro William, 100–5, 107, 109, 112–5, 117, 118, 120, 122–4
    'Description of Pictures Illustrative of Thomson's Seasons, now exhibiting at Tomkins and Co.'s, No.49, New Bond Street', 103
Tonson, Jacob (Arnold Bennett), 204
Turner, Albert Morton, 22, 23, 28
Turner, Joseph Mallord William, 142, 143
Turner, Percie Hopkins, 22, 23, 28
Tytler, James, 'Balloon', 89

Unwin, T. Fisher, 154

Vickers, George, 189
    Puppet-Show, The, 189, 190
Virgil, 99
Vizetelly, Henry, 190
Vizetelly, James Thomas, 190

Wallis, James, 120, 124
Waverley novels, 125–57
    editions
        Abbotsford, 126, 128, 145, 146, 147, 149, 150, 151, 154, 156
        Border, 151, 153, 156
        Bouverie, 154
        Cabinet, 145, 149
        Centenary, 146, 150, 151
        Century Scott, The, 154
        Dryburgh, 151, 153, 154

Edinburgh Edition of the Waverley
     Novels, 156
*Eight Engravings in Illustration of
     Waverley*, 150
'Eighteenpence', 149
Fine Art Scott, 154
Holyrood, 154
Illustrated, 149
Library, 147, 151, 154
Magnum Opus, 134–41
Melrose, 154
Oxford World's Classics, 156
Penguin, 156
People's, 144, 149
'Pictorial', 149
Pocket, 151
Railway, 149
Roxburgh, 149
School, 154
Shilling, 149
Sixpenny/Copyright, 149
Soho, 154
suites
     Heath's Historical Illustrations, 139,
          154
     *New Series of Illustrations to the
          Novels and Tales, A*, 131
     *Six Engravings in Illustration of St.
          Ronan's Well*, 151
     *Sixteen Engravings from Real Scenes
          supposed to be described in the
          Novels and Tales*, 129

Walpole, Horace (*The Castle of
     Otranto*), 113, 123
Watson, Rosamund Marriott, 198, 202
Watts, Isaac, 41
Watts-Dunton, Theodore, 198, 211
Webster, Augusta, 197, 198
Wellington, Richard, 11, 13, 15
Wenman, Joseph, 119
Westall, Richard, 131, 133, 134, 137,
     143
     and Charles Heath, 131
     Illustrations of Guy Mannering, 133
     Illustrations of The Monastery, 133
Wharey, James Blanton, 40
Whatman, James, 100
Wheatley, Francis, 109
White, Robert, 37, 40
     'Sleeping Portrait', 37–44
Wilkie, David, 137
Wilson, Effingham, 175
Wilson, Richard, 102, 109
Wittgenstein, Ludwig, 62, 66
*Women's Writing of the Early Modern
     Period, 1588–1688: An Anthology*, 7
wood engraving, 119, 121, 123, 126, 145,
     149, 153, 177, 178, 179, 183, 193
Woolf, Virginia, 199, 209
Woollett, William, 101, 102
Working-Man's Yearbook, 172
World Burns Club, The, 93
Wright, Reverend George Newenham,
     144